SPIRIT
ETHICS

PAUL JERSILD

SPIRIT

ETHICS

SCRIPTURE
AND THE MORAL LIFE

FORTRESS PRESS
MINNEAPOLIS

For Marilyn,
fellow sojourner along the way

SPIRIT ETHICS
Scripture and the Moral Life

Library of Congress Cataloging-in-Publication Data
Jersild, Paul T., 1931–
    Spirit ethics: scripture and the moral life/Paul Jersild.
      p. cm.
    Includes bibliographical references and indexes.
    ISBN 0-8006-3232-X
    1. Christian ethics—Lutheran authors. 2. Social ethics. I. Title.

BJ1251.J376 1999
241'.0441—dc21
                                             99-050224

Manufactured in the U.S.A.   AF 1-3232
04   03   02   01   00   1   2   3   4   5   6   7   8   9   10

CONTENTS

ACKNOWLEDGMENTS

This book began to take shape during the 1995–96 school year, after my exodus from the dean's office at Lutheran Theological Southern Seminary and the consequent freedom I was given as a full-time teaching member of the faculty to carry out research and to write. I am grateful to the Seminary's Board of Trustees, administration, the library staff, students, and particularly my faculty colleagues for providing over the years a stimulating and congenial environment in which to work. In particular I want to acknowledge those individuals—faculty colleagues and others—who were kind enough to read various chapters and offer helpful comments: Agneta Enermalm, Carl Evans, Matthew Henning, Austin Jersild, Darrell Jodock, Wayne Kannaday, George Khushf, Edward Madden, John Rollefson, Charles Sigel, and S. Robert Young. They have contributed to the strengthening of this book but cannot be blamed for the weaknesses that remain.

A word of appreciation is due Marshall D. Johnson, former director of publishing at Fortress Press, who gave me the needed incentive to proceed with this work. I am also indebted to J. Michael West, senior editor at Fortress Press, for his able assistance and encouragement. And finally, I am grateful to my wife, Marilyn, for her patience during the long hours when this project dominated too much of my life.

INTRODUCTION

As a professor of theology and ethics who over the past three to four decades has been teaching in church-related colleges and seminaries, I have been long absorbed with the role of Scripture in Christian ethics. It is a controversial subject, involving issues of authority for the church as well as the issues of access and meaning that an ancient text will inevitably raise for people living in our times—an era we choose to call "postmodernity." Running throughout this book is the postmodern assumption that our historical and cultural location is decisive for our understanding and appropriation of the past; thus it has been necessary to take seriously the cultural mentality of our times, which brings its indelible character to the imagination and thinking of each one of us. Our cultural context affects the conclusions and the decisions at which we arrive; this is particularly apparent in the realms of ethical reflection and the moral life. Our cultural context also raises the questions we address to Scripture and provides the parameters for understanding its message. This does not mean that we are totally removed from the biblical past, but it does mean that any effort to recapture that past in terms of the ethical material it conveys has become much more complicated, demanding a heightened awareness of our historicity and the implications it bears for appropriating the biblical message. This in turn has considerable bearing on our understanding of the Bible's authority for the moral life.

These assumptions and the impact they have exerted throughout the church comprise one reason among several that Christian ethicists today are stressing the centrality of the church for Christian ethics. No matter how important the Bible is as the Word of God, and regardless of its preeminent status as the norm for the Christian life, the discipline of Christian ethics today is stressing the ecclesial community as the indispensable factor in creating the distinctive possibility of the Christian moral life. Thus there are three major focal points that ground my discussion here: the Bible, the church, and postmodern society. Since the Reformation there has been a continuing debate within Christianity—expressed in the opposing traditions of Catholicism and Protestantism—on the relation of church and Bible as competing authorities in understanding the theological and moral teachings of the church. Those tensions have abated considerably in the past century as the two traditions have converged, with Catholic scholars increasingly recognizing the importance of Scripture and Protestants recognizing the indispensable role of the contemporary church as scriptural interpreter. These developments within the churches, together with the emergence of postmodern thinking, are influencing the way in which many Christians are making use of Scripture in reference to the moral life. They are not as inclined to "return" to the Bible for moral direction, as though it were an ancient quarry in which nuggets of moral direction could be mined. With increasing sophistication concerning our use of Scripture, Christians generally are more ready to recognize the inevitably contemporary character of every reference to Scripture and every interpretation of its ethical message. The overwhelming variety and frequent conflict among readings of "what the Bible says"about the moral life certainly encourages that conclusion.

One implication of these developments is that we are not as ready to treat the Bible as a "sacred text" that provides the definitive answers for our moral dilemmas. Its character as the Word of God does not place it above history, as though it could communicate eternal and immutable directives that are directly applicable to every time and place. The church in every age must struggle with the Bible, seeking a viable interpretation of its message for its own time and place. This reality means that the church has never been a simply passive receptacle into which the biblical content could be poured. It is more accurately seen as an active respondent to the contents of Scripture, appropriating its message by engaging it in a process of interpretation. This act of assimilation and digestion of the biblical content is an interactive encounter between the church and its scriptural tradition, with changing insights and perspectives emerging from a process that is inherently creative. It involves the church identifying itself with the narrative of Scripture, taking seriously its call to discipleship, and then trying to discern what this means for disciplined, responsible living in this particular time.

This emphasis on the creative role of the church in discovering the meaning of Christian discipleship for its own time does not diminish the authority of Scripture for the moral life. On the contrary, it challenges a false notion of scriptural authority that has been detrimental to the life of the church. It is an authority divorced from the church's engagement, supported by formal criteria that confer perfection on the Bible and sanction its absolute status, placing it beyond question or even beyond any meaningful dialogue with the church. This kind of authority imposed "from above" becomes authoritarian in its effect. Today, as James Barr remarks, we have learned to live with "criteria which are less clear, to leave the nature of authority to emerge at the end of the theological process rather than to be there in defined form at the beginning."[1] We are willing to become more inductive rather than deductive in our understanding of biblical authority, particularly as it relates to the ethics of the Christian life. Given these developments, we are better able to recognize the authoritarian use of the Bible for what it is: a misuse of Scripture that has led to gross instances of coercion and even oppression on both theological and ethical grounds, abuses that the biblical message itself would repudiate.

There are dangers at the opposite pole as well, where instead of a questionable exalting of the Bible's authority we encounter attempts to substitute the authority of experience, usually the experience of a particular group that becomes definitive in understanding the Christian message. One sees this among certain liberation theology advocates who are willing to converse with Scripture but would make the experience of their group the ultimate authority.[2] Although each of us is undoubtedly subject to that accusation, my concern in this book is to understand the dialectic between the reader and text—between the believing community and its Scripture—as one that is defined and controlled by the authoritative message of Scripture. That message as it relates to the moral life can be captured in a variety of terms, whether it be the kingdom of God in the message and ministry of Jesus, or the crucified and risen Christ in the message of Paul and others, all of which create the new possibility of repentance, forgiveness, and new life in the Spirit. Out of this matrix a response is generated that creates new possibilities of love and justice in human relationships. While this view may differ from that of liberation theologians in its insistence on Scripture defining the meaning of liberation in terms of new life "in Christ," it also recognizes that the interpretation of that new life can and will be taken in a variety of directions and applied in a variety of ways in differing social and cultural contexts. The message of new life in Christ can bring liberation from the demons one faces in any group or in any setting.

The open-endedness implicit in our understanding of the Bible's authority for the Christian life fits well also with the nature of the life of faith. The biblical story places believers *in via*, on the way to the future as a pilgrim community that looks forward in anticipation to a divine culmination of the human story. The very notion of disciple fits this understanding of one who is "in process," a learner whose task is never complete. This future orientation of Christian life resists both the conservative temptation to idealize the past and the liberal temptation to idealize the present, as it seeks to chart the faithful course of the church. The Christian life cannot be defined without reference to God's future, which means that the church can never bring closure to the question of what God requires of it. The church's faith itself inspires a fundamental openness to the future and a willingness to live by hope and not by sight, a truth this book would emphasize in relation to the moral life and responsible Christian discipleship. This future orientation symbolized by the kingdom of God is essential to the self-understanding and witness of the church.

As a way of expressing this peculiar, Christian grasp of the moral life, the language of "spirit ethics" serves us well. It expresses the confidence of Christians that life is lived in the presence of God who empowers and strengthens the faithful life. The Spirit in Christian theology expresses both the intimacy and mystery of the divine presence, both the immediacy and the transcendence of God. These terms are defined for Christians by the story of Jesus Christ, which provides the content for our understanding of the Spirit. The faith generated by this story leads to a moral life that trusts in the presence of God as the one who strengthens and guides the believer in living one's discipleship. Life in the Spirit by definition is also life in community. The Spirit of God brings people together as a believing community, establishing relationships of support and encouragement and generating a vision of the faithful life. The richness inherent to this language of the Spirit, touching all dimensions of the faithful life, makes it indispensable for any consideration of biblical and Christian ethics.

The major role of the church in defining the Christian life and in providing for its continuing nurture and direction brings extraordinary responsibility. It must take quite seriously its obligation to cultivate a lively sense of its identity as the people of God, marked by the sign of the cross. This means particular attention being given to worship in the life of the congregation, lifting up the symbols distinctive to the Christian story that define the community and invoke God's presence. It also means that the life of Christian discipleship must be given intense and continuing attention through classes and discussion groups, with high expectations for the attendance and involvement of each church member. These activities should focus on both Scripture and the moral responsibilities of the congregation, including its relation to the immediate community as well as to the larger society. Attention should be given to the responsibilities of the church as a national and international community in the world, and to the moral life of each member in his or her vocation as an expression of one's Christian discipleship. We acknowledge the gap—oftentimes painful—between the level of committed discipleship we expect from the church and the level actually demonstrated. The distinction made by Robin Gill in addressing this disparity is helpful: the church is more of a "harbinger" than an "exemplar" of Christian values. Yet we should not discount the full impact of its witness, also as a worshiping community, with its "Scriptures, lections, liturgies, hymns and accumulated sources of long-refined wisdom" that continue to infiltrate and influence the larger society.[3]

The realm of Christian ethics and biblical authority embraces both the personal life of the Christian and the corporate life of the church in society. The latter subject of church and society, or Christian social ethics, has inspired considerable debate within the church. In recent decades there has been a disdainful repudiation of the idea broached in the 1960s that the world with its social issues should "set the agenda" for the church. In one sense this can be seen as a legitimate rejection of the liberal concern to be relevant at all costs, often at the expense of losing the distinctive identity of the church. On the other hand, however, it is good to remind ourselves that there is a sense in which the world does indeed provide the agenda for the church. Our theology and ethics are generated not in a vacuum but in response to the questions and issues raised by our culture. The issues of life and meaning that absorb our society call for an honest response on the part of the church, both in its proclamation and teaching and in its concrete ministry of service in the public world. An honest response requires careful attention to the nature of our times, seeking to meet people where they are and bringing a critical discernment to the issues of the day.

The point also must be made, however, that the interpretation of the church's message is not a one-way street from the present back to the past, with new and compelling experiences from contemporary society, or new insights from the social sciences, for example, necessitating changes in the way the church has understood its tradition. While this kind of flow is always occurring, there is also the movement from past to present in which critical theological insights, rooted in the tradition, enable the church to respond with discrimination to the changing cultural scene. We are called to a responsible engagement with our culture, not simply an optimistic endorsement of every new enthusiasm that we encounter.[4] Critical engagement, then, rather than simply a drive to be relevant, is the continuing task and responsibility of the church in relation to its cultural environment. This subject raises a host of questions and issues that are argued among Christians in every generation. Since Christian ethics and biblical authority speak also to these issues of church and society, they will be addressed both directly and indirectly throughout these pages.

There is considerable risk in writing a book that must engage another discipline in which the writer has limited familiarity. In addressing the subject of biblical authority as it relates to Christian ethics, I have had to inform myself of current developments not only in biblical studies but also in biblical criticism, and to some extent in the formidable realms of critical theory, literary theory, and contemporary hermeneutics. While my reading in these areas has been most interesting and personally rewarding, I am acutely aware that I cannot claim mastery of their content. My hope is that I have learned enough to give the reader a reasonable grasp of issues involved in the contemporary use of the Bible for Christian ethics, as well as to present a responsible—though admittedly brief—account of the ethical material one finds in Scripture. My purpose, of course, has not been to present an account of biblical ethics as such, but there is little question of the value for Christian ethicists to engage in serious biblical study for the sake of their discipline.[5]

This work begins in chapters 1 and 2 by addressing postmodern culture and responding to its relativistic impact on contemporary morality, as well as its pluralist character and what this means for the church in its relation to society. In chapter 3 the peculiar problems in approaching the Bible as an ancient text are discussed, as well as the nature of its authority. In chapter 4 we address more specifically an approach to understanding the ethical content and ethical authority of Scripture, with primary focus on the New Testament. Chapter 5 is devoted to an elaboration of spirit ethics, a constructive attempt to sketch a Christian ethical orientation that is both faithful to its Scriptures and responsible in its engagement with contemporary society. In the last three chapters of the book, I turn to specific social issues that pose substantial challenges to the church today, addressing them in a way that I believe is consistent with the orientation established in the preceding chapters.

A word at the outset may be appropriate for those not particularly familiar with usage of the terms *ethics* and *morality*. In contrast to *morality*, *ethics* denotes a discipline, or a second-order activity, that involves thinking about the terms and categories used to describe the moral life.

Although *ethics* and *morality* are often used interchangeably, Christian ethics as a discipline involves critical reflection on the nature of the Christian moral life, addressing such questions as: What does faith entail for the moral life? What standards do we hold to? What does it mean to make Scripture authoritative? Christian *morality,* on the other hand, would be a first-order description of moral behavior—the practices and virtues that are found in the Christian community. The use of *ethics* in the title of this book signals that our task involves not just description but also evaluation and critique, with the intent of bringing clarification and understanding to the nature of the Christian life and to the appropriate use of the Bible for Christian living.

Christians invariably will have strong convictions about the subject matter addressed in these pages. The perspectives I articulate will certainly offend some and bring satisfaction to others. That in itself is not the real issue, however. My hope is that this work will help the reader gain a clearer perspective on the issues involved in relating the Bible and tradition to the Christian life and to the church's mission in the contemporary world. This goal will in turn enable a more responsible and effective dialogue in the church concerning the issues it faces today. While no one is in a position to state the final word on these matters, together we can help each other in discerning the church's mission in an often confusing and threatening environment. I will be satisfied if what I have to say in these pages will make some modest contribution toward achieving that end.

1

POSTMODERNISM AND CHRISTIAN ETHICS

During the last half of the twentieth century, attention has increasingly focused on the transitional character of our times. The sense that we are moving from one epoch to another is strongly fixed in our consciousness, with common reference to concepts such as "postmodernity" and "postchristendom" expressing this point. These concepts refer to changes occurring in intellectual and cultural consciousness, the pervasive context in which Christians understand themselves, their message, and their mission as a community of faith. To grasp the meaning of these concepts is to understand something about our own self-awareness as children of these times, as well as to gain a perspective that enables us to critically assess the cultural changes we are experiencing. Any current treatment of Christian ethics and its relation to biblical authority must take this cultural setting into account if it would speak with some degree of cogency to the concerns and questions being raised in our time. Both ethics and the authority of an ancient text are subjects that raise peculiar issues for the frame of mind we have come to call "postmodernity," and thus it is appropriate at the outset to spell out what is meant by that term.

RESPONDING TO THE POSTMODERN CHALLENGE

To define *postmodernity* or *postmodernism* is a daunting task, for they refer to vast congeries of ideas that have been generated over the past century. Any limited description sketched here is bound to be challenged from the perspective of a differing dimension of postmodern thought.[1] It is fair to say, however, that one common denominator of most postmodern thinking is a critical reaction to the assumptions that have characterized modernism, by which is meant the dominant Western intellectual and cultural tradition identified with the Enlightenment. That tradition, which has profoundly shaped Western culture up to our own times, exalts reason as the essence of humanity and carries implicit confidence in its capacity to arrive at the truth. Rational philosophy in the early Enlightenment embarked on the quest for indubitable truth concerning humanity and its place in the universe, convinced that it had the key to open the truth once religion and superstition were set aside. It was an idealized view of reason, with many assuming that its triumph over the forces of ignorance would establish a new order marked by sanity and peace. The emergence of the scientific age in the nineteenth and twentieth centuries has been seen as a crowning achievement of human reason, enhancing the powers of the human community to create a more hospitable environment as well as to create immense material benefits for increasing numbers of people. Human progress itself has come to be defined in terms of technological achievements. The optimistic self-confidence of modernism also expresses a high degree of moral self-sufficiency. Belief in the human capacity to attain the truth has included the confidence that humanity would also use it to achieve what is good and desirable. The universality of human reason, moral autonomy, the orderly design of the universe, the rights of the individual, and a shared optimism concerning human progress and achieving a better world have all characterized the modernist mind.

The beginnings of disillusionment in late modernism of the mid-twentieth century have come into full bloom in our own time. The past century has seen two world wars and the emergence of the nuclear age, events that have destroyed for many the confidence and optimism of an earlier era. A sense of realism and, for some, a spirit of cynicism have prevailed, with reason no longer regarded as an unadulterated good but more often than not an instrument to achieve power for one's own selfish ends. Truth itself is not universal but particular, limited and shaped by one's historical location. Individual sovereignty is an illusion, for we are creatures of time and place. The impact of historicism set in motion by the Romanticism of the nineteenth century thus comes to decisive expression in postmodern thinking, leading to the rejection of any kind of overarching truth that transcends the historical flux. Whether it is the Enlightenment's myth of the ahistorical, sovereign individual, or the universal narrative concerning the God of Christian faith, or Karl Marx's philosophy of history, the attempt to present a "total" view of the nature of things exceeds the human grasp and ultimately leads to the exploitation of others in the name of one's own particular truth.

Terms often used to describe the emerging, postmodern era are *fragmentation,* in the face of rejection of every attempt to provide a meta-narrative or overarching story that gives meaning and purpose to human history; *privatization,* of ethics, and *moral relativism,* with the loss of universal standards; *eclecticism,* in which all options are possible without a dominating or prevailing truth; and *pluralism,* which describes the society of today, where differing historical expressions of culture, truth, and morality are living side by side.[2] For Christians in North America, these terms have increasingly described the realities of their cultural life and have had an inevitable impact on their understanding and communication of the Christian message, including Christian ethics and the nature of biblical authority for the Christian life. Postmodern thought challenges the idea that any community can base its faith and moral life, in any meaningful sense, on the contents of a book originating in ancient times. The message and ethos of Scripture is wedded to a language and culture that is far removed from our own, incapable of being understood today in any way that would replicate the meaning it had for the Bible's contemporaries. Postmodernism sees languages and cultures as heteromorphic, resisting any attempt to equate meanings from one culture with those of another. Any attempt to convey a tradition or an ethos from a previous era is to transform that tradition into language and cultural understanding that is distinctively our own, thus transforming its meaning into something new. This subject will be addressed at more length in chapter 3.

While the general impact of postmodern ideas appears overwhelmingly negative and challenging to the Christian community, there are also positive elements in the realm of social ethics that can be welcomed. For example, the critical response of postmodern thinking to the use of power in society, drawing attention to the manipulations of the power elite or of the majority population, has encouraged the marginalized in society to challenge the dominant culture. The relativizing of truths gives fuel to those who have been excluded by the dominant truths and assumptions of the culture. One sees this expressed, for example, in the feminist movement, which contests the governing interpretation of Western history as an expression of patriarchalism. Men have interpreted history in ways that have assumed and justified male dominance, and women now come to this subject armed with a "hermeneutics of suspicion" that would expose the ideology of the male class. This hermeneutics has been wielded by female scholars with particular effectiveness in

the realm of biblical studies, raising further questions about the understanding of biblical authority. Race is another realm in which this kind of
development has been encouraged, exposing racist assumptions that
have governed prevailing "truths" and the exercise of power in a society.
Developments of this kind carry a positive thrust, bringing greater
awareness of and sensitivity to sources of injustice and dehumanization.

Ideologies, seen as the "construction" of meanings that serve the purposes of those with influence and power, come into play in other realms
of human life as well, inviting the critical examination of postmodern
thinking. When science, for example, becomes "scientism," or a worldview that defines reality according to its own empirical assumptions,
some deconstructive analysis is invited not only on the part of postmodernists but from Christians as well, for it results in a positivistic worldview under the guise of science in which religion and morality are
consigned to the realm of feeling in contrast to the world of knowledge.
This postmodern challenge to science's confidence in its own closed universe prompts Diogenes Allen to observe:

> All people are now in the position in which it is sensible to
> become a seeker. If people are sensible, they will earnestly want
> to know whether this universe is ultimate or not. There is there-
> fore no need for Christians to continue to be defensive. Just as
> Socrates did in ancient Greece, we have a mission: to challenge
> the supposition that the status of the universe and our place in
> it have already been settled by science and philosophy.[3]

In feeding the breakdown of confidence in attempts to find a secular
basis for morality, postmodernism, Allen argues, opens interest in the
possibility of religious interpretation for the moral life. This interest is
intensified by the fact that society is concerned about a disintegrating
morality and the need of a secure moral basis. Dethroning a positivistic
reason that explains away one's moral experience may at least provide a
more level playing field to the benefit of religious belief concerning the
moral life. Indeed, the postmodern probing of cultural assumptions is
contributing in many ways to a more open environment concerning the
religious life and the realm of "transcendent" experience.

The more jaundiced view of human nature that postmodernism
expresses also finds some resonance in Christian thinking. While not
pessimistic, Christian anthropology reflects a profound realism concerning the human predicament, recognizing the devious and often uncon-
scious ways in which we establish and maintain ourselves in positions of
power and privilege. We have every reason to be sensitive to the ways in
which knowledge is exercised as a means of power. Where ideological

factors are clearly present and play an important role, including many expressions of religion itself, the capacity of people wielding power and influence to act in self-serving ways is virtually boundless. The fact is all the more apparent when we move from the individual to the corporate level, such as the tribe or nation, where self-interest can be expressed in particularly destructive ways. Reinhold Niebuhr is one theologian and ethicist of recent times who has driven home this truth with considerable eloquence.

The postmodern emphasis on particularity is another feature that need not be seen as detrimental to the Christian cause. From the beginning, Christians have recognized that the truths of their faith are embodied in specific cultures and subject to historical relativity. Anyone who grasps the biblical revelation recognizes its historical character; it has a specificity and singularity that resists generalizations. This understanding of truth was an offense to the Enlightenment mind, exemplified by the German dramatist and critic Gotthold Ephraim Lessing (1729–81), who disparaged any attempt to identify a historical revelation with universal truth. From the Christian side, we have displayed a mind divided on whether to find support for our claims of truth from the world of philosophy and metaphysical reasoning. The postmodern turn now invites Christians to a renewed appreciation of the historical character of their faith, challenging them to a "reunderstanding" of what it means to speak the truth in Jesus Christ. That truth is rooted in a historical tradition, as are all affirmations found in the religions of humankind. This carries implications for our understanding of truth and our capacity to dialogue with those who represent a quite different history and tradition.

One implication of this point that carries important moral significance relates to the common claim that Christians possess the ultimate truth. The meaning of that claim on the part of the church needs further reflection today, including the recognition that the church's claim to possessing an ultimate and universal truth has had catastrophic consequences, devastating to both the image and integrity of the church. Absolutism concerning its beliefs has made the church guilty, many times over, of "totalism," with the violence inherent to such a stance. When joined with political power, totalistic pretensions have had particularly ruinous consequences where the church has attempted to legislate and in other ways force its beliefs upon the unbeliever. In every age the church must keep in mind the eschatological nature of its faith and life, compelling the recognition that the church is always "on the way" and cannot claim divine sanction for its teachings or claim a divine prerogative for making ultimate judgments of unbelievers. Absolutist claims of this kind call for repentance and conversion on the part of the church.[4]

The question being raised here is the appropriateness of the church's claim to *possess* the truth. We can *affirm* the truth, *confess* the truth, and *profess* the truth, but we cannot claim to have it as a possession. To make that claim not only removes the eschatological future as the point of orientation for the Christian life, but removes the mystery of God's Word and intrudes on God's sovereignty. Such a claim inevitably becomes a curse, removing the capacity for self-criticism and turning the truth into a source of manipulation of others. It is no overstatement to observe that the sinful condition of humanity turns every claim of possessing the truth into an occasion for claiming one's superiority and the right to sit in judgment of everyone else. Christians who exalt themselves in this way deny the truth that God's Word first judges those who are of the household of faith. Unlike the postmodernist, Christians can and must speak of the truth of God, but it is a truth we know—as emphasized in the Pauline letters—when we are *in* the truth, rather than possessing it through an act of cognition (2 Cor. 5:17; Col. 2:6-7). Our efforts to present the truth in doctrinal statements share the provisional nature and contingency of all human constructions. Their purpose is not to justify our claims to having the truth but to witness to that truth and assist the church to be faithful in its discipleship. A proper sense of modesty and humility should come from the church's encounter with postmodernism precisely at this point, for even the atheism that is often apparent in postmodern thinking can be a fruitful source of Christian self-examination and self-understanding.[5]

ABSOLUTE COMMANDS VS. UNIVERSAL IDEALS

As we turn more specifically to the Christian understanding of the moral life, and ask both what Christians might positively learn from the postmodern spirit and where they should resist it, the subject of moral absolutes quite naturally arises. The one feature of our times that perhaps disturbs Christians the most is the pervasive sense of relativity, if not a thoroughgoing relativism, that appears to dominate popular thinking and attitudes. The postmodern suspicion of any claim to absolute standards would appear to be a major challenge to any religious person, and I focus on it here to illustrate both a current issue for Christian ethics and a possible response to it. Many in the secularized Western world who have no acquaintance with postmodern theory as such are likely to resonate with the suggestion that such concepts as good/evil and right/wrong are expressions of individual opinion or social custom rather than reflecting a transcendent moral order. For postmodernists it is axiomatic that our location in a particular culture in a specific time and place makes impossible any notion of an immutable and absolute moral truth. Some indeed would celebrate the "demise of the ethical," placing ethical judgments in the realm of aesthetics and concluding that ethics essentially is a matter of one's personal tastes. Others would recognize the validity of moral concerns but question the adequacy of traditional ethical theories to address them. Modernity's search for absolutes is seen as a dead end, a misguided search conducted under false pretenses and doomed to fail.

> The foolproof—universal and unshakably founded—ethical code will never be found; having singed our fingers once too often, we know now what we did not know then, when we embarked on this journey of exploration: that a non-aporetic, non-ambivalent morality, an ethics that is universal and "objectively founded," is a practical impossibility; perhaps also an *oxymoron*, a contradiction in terms.[6]

Contemporary suspicions about transcendent moral standards are often belied in the common use of values in reference to moral beliefs, which generally carries the understanding that such beliefs are subjective and relative, peculiar to the individual or to a particular group. They are seen as expressions of opinion whose validity is dependent on what they can do for the person who espouses them rather than due to any inherent truth or mirroring of reality, as in natural-law teaching. Social morality is understood as the moral consensus of the group, whatever that consensus might be. Ethics becomes a descriptive account of morality rather than an appeal to ethical truths that carry prescriptive force. The conspiracy theory seen in postmodernism invites the idea that values are also ideological tools manipulated by the establishment in order to control the populace. If values do not carry prescriptive meanings that hold everyone accountable, they become weapons of manipulation by which to achieve one's own purposes.

The impact of this kind of thinking is readily seen in the writings of ethicists, whether secular or religious. The loss of confidence in the rationalist, universal claims of the Enlightenment tradition has begun to reshape our understanding of the appropriate scope of ethical judgments. The new situation is succinctly described by philosopher Martha Nussbaum:

> Anglo-American moral philosophy is turning from an ethics based on enlightenment ideals of universality to an ethics based on tradition and particularity; from an ethics based on principle

to an ethics based on virtue; from an ethics dedicated to the elaboration of systematic/theoretical justifications to an ethics suspicious of theory and respectful of local wisdom; from an ethics based on the isolated individual to an ethics based on affiliation and care; from an ahistorical detached ethics to an ethics rooted in the concreteness of history.[7]

This characterization of contemporary ethics has been embraced by an increasing number of Christian ethicists. Their interest in narrative and story reflects the interest in historical particularity and specific traditions as the source of ethical discourse and judgments. "Narratives are grounded in history, in actions, enabling us to avoid thinking of Christian ethics in terms of universal abstractions, and instead to ground ethics in the contingencies of our historical existence."[8] The current emphasis on the believing community as the context for Christian ethics is the natural corollary to this interest in narrative, reflecting the movement away from the individualist, ahistorical reasoning that has been typical of Christian ethics.

What does this mean for customary references, particularly among Christians, to "moral absolutes"? Is it not the peculiar task and responsibility of the church to lift up absolute standards and to insist on their continuing relevance and importance? Are not the Ten Commandments the peculiar gift of the Judeo-Christian tradition to all of humanity, regardless of specific religious and moral traditions? These are serious questions that are often raised with a sense of frustration on the part of Christians who are puzzled by the apparent hedging they see among Christian academics and even clergy concerning absolutes. They deserve serious and carefully explained answers, for the problems raised by absolutist language are not that simple or obvious.

First we need to carefully define what is meant by *absolutes*. The term is used in many contexts and with different connotations so that it suffers from conceptual murkiness. One problem is that the debate over absolutes today commonly occurs in an ideologically charged atmosphere. The verbal battle shapes up as a hard either/or: either there are moral absolutes or everything is relative; either we recognize absolutes or we invite moral permissiveness that leads to societal collapse. In this overheated, ideological context, absolutes take on symbolic importance, becoming a primary point of contention in the culture wars that divide our society.

We understand absolutes here in accordance with popular opinion both within and outside of the church, which tends to identify absolutes with commandments that prohibit specific actions, as with the Ten Commandments. By this understanding, absolutes are commandments that allow for no exception—they are always to be obeyed regardless of circumstances. These commandments are regarded as immutable, meaning that they transcend the flux of history and thus are not subject to the changes and relativities that mark the human story. This means that absolutes leave little room for moral reflection and judgment on the part of the agent; the decision is made *for* the agent by a rule that stands prior to the situation one is addressing. Of course, we do in fact enter into circumstances calling for moral decisions with certain moral beliefs and assumptions that constitute a kind of "ground rules" governing our actions. We don't have to stop and think about whether this situation allows for adulterous activity or the possibility of stealing, for example, because our moral convictions rule out those options. There is, however, a different mind-set with a different set of implications between those who would establish the validity of moral proscriptions on the basis of their absoluteness and immutability, and those who understand their validity on the basis of their importance to the life of the community and to one's own integrity as a member of that community. The notion of absolutes easily discourages the appropriate grappling with the *why* of one's moral decisions, working against growth and development in ethical maturity. This fact, however, is regarded by the absolutist as well worth the price if the result is greater weight and force for the prohibition—and for the cause of absolutes.

The Christian is concerned not to diminish the importance of the law but to incorporate it into the distinctive context of the Christian life and understand it from a Christian perspective. This means that God's commandments are not abstract prohibitions that need to be reinforced by treating them as absolutes; they establish boundaries to the moral life that foster responsibility. The law is but one dimension of life "in Christ," and not the most distinctive aspect of that life (a subject to be addressed in subsequent chapters). It is also true, however, that the non-Christian is quite capable of recognizing a larger context of human relationships in which the purpose of the law can be understood. That context is the human community, which would resist destructive actions that jeopardize a common life of peace and good order. The law judges every one of the myriad ways in which self-serving humans are capable of exploiting others, and in doing that the law would keep us honest in all of our relationships so that community is served. This function of the law is not intended to shut off deliberation by the application of absolute commands but rather to direct us toward the morally responsible life.

I believe it is both more helpful and more effective to speak of universal ideals than of absolute commands in responding to the relativist argument. There are universal moral truths that are capable of capturing the moral imagination in every culture; they are ideals rather than specific commands, appealing to and inviting our aspirations. Jesus' admonitions to "love your neighbor as yourself," and "do to others as you would have them do to you," express a vision of our common life that reaches well beyond his own culture. Though expressed in the language of command, these exhortations can be appropriately understood as ideals in the sense that they express the goals envisioned by the coming kingdom. His language is abstract, keeping its distance from the nitty-gritty of actual living and thus avoiding the questions of application that would complicate the understanding of the ideal. Like the command, "Do good and avoid evil," the love command conveys no specific action until it is applied to concrete situations that initiate the process of moral judgment and weighing of possible actions, but one begins with the ideal and seeks to take it seriously. The ideal of love leads one to positive action on behalf of others, but it would also compel one to avoid and resist destructive actions of violence and deception. The Ten Commandments direct us to do the same by means of specific prohibitions—the negative form of moral exhortation.

Biblical faith sees these commandments as a gift of God, presented in the Scripture's Mount Sinai story (Exod. 19–20), and functioning as an enabler of community. Rather than treating the Decalogue ahistorically as an independent body of commands, rooted in a universal and rational human nature, we can understand it as a reminder of the realities of human relationships that hold us in obligation to each other. A fruitful way of understanding this structure of societal living is to recognize that it facilitates relationships of trust, which societies require to function effectively. This trust between people takes various forms and levels of commitment, depending on the nature of the relationship (it takes a considerably different level of trust between husband and wife than between customer and salesperson, for example), but each is important to the welfare of the common life.[9] The Decalogue lifts up the trust issue between people and exhorts us to be faithful to each other; it makes clear that human relationships involve obligations that are rooted not only in the very character of community life but in the will and purpose of God. The Commandments thus reflect the necessity and the desire of the community to live together responsibly. At the same time, their application on the part of the community is subject to particular social and cultural circumstances that are peculiar to a society and that also evolve with the changing nature of societal life. Thus we can recognize a "common morality" from one society to another in the effort of each to maintain trusting relationships, even as we see differences between them as a result of their distinctive religious and cultural beliefs and the peculiar stamp that those beliefs put on the character of trust in the varied relationships of life.

It is also true, of course, that when we relate an ideal to particular circumstances, we are faced with the need to make judgments about how loving one's neighbor, or doing good and avoiding evil, is appropriately expressed in this or that particular setting. These are judgments over which equally faithful and discerning persons may disagree. Holding to universals is consequently no guarantee of unanimity concerning what we ought to do, and thus it is not surprising that absolute commands with a higher degree of specificity are proposed as a way of identifying God's will. It is precisely that specificity, however, that raises problems when moral judgments become more complicated and nuanced, and when changing understandings of moral obligation and responsibility evolve with the passing of time. The symbolic value of absolute standards expressed in prohibitions will always remain strong, particularly in a time when people are fearful about eroding values and an apparently precarious public morality. In this kind of setting, lifting up absolute commands and rules can be an effective rhetorical device on the part of those concerned about the state of public morality. Nonetheless, moral responsibility is not dependent on the claim that our standards are to be obeyed *without exception*; on the contrary, responsible persons are those who recognize their obligations in light of their relationships with others. What serves the welfare of the neighbor constitutes one's moral obligation, and rules of behavior are to serve that end.

Some may find it arbitrary to identify the command of prohibition with particularity and the ideal with universality. The point is that ideals or moral aspirations relate to character and virtue. The ideal of truth-telling, for example, tells us to be truthful persons rather than devious in our relations with others. As a virtue this is a universal ideal, but when translated into specific commands, it becomes subject to the often warped and complicated conditions that mark human relationships. For example, to translate the ideal of truthfulness and veracity into the command, "Never tell a lie," is hardly possible, because we can enter into circumstances that remove the moral obligation to tell the truth. I am hardly obliged to tell the truth to someone who requests it in order to commit an atrocity. The ideal is valid and essential, but affirming it does not remove the necessity of moral reflection in order to determine its appropriate application. This is a strength in the nature of love *(agape)* as an ideal, which, as Paul Tillich notes, has a "listening" character that enables it to adapt to the situation. This does not imply, however, that duty and obligation are of less importance to the moral life. Because of human waywardness, cultivating a sense of moral obligation to one's neighbor is essential to responsible living. It is an indispensable feature of moral character, even if *what* I ought to do in any given circumstance may require considerable reflection and discernment.

One particular context that encourages people to reach out for absolutes in the form of concrete prohibitions is that of raising the young. We are understandably concerned that young people need to hear a moral trumpet that is loud and clear, which to the popular mind means "absolutes." It is thought that absolutes provide greater incentive for responsible living, and many are sensitive to the accusation that our society is turning the Ten Commandments into the Highly Tentative Ten Suggestions. One can certainly make the counterargument that a stronger moral environment for the child is one that, by example as well as by teaching, stresses responsibility in all human relationships and the importance of "being there" for the neighbor. One can and should stress the significance of ground rules that help each of us to be responsible, but perhaps the more essential task is to sensitize the child to the fact that we often seek to avoid hearing what we ought to do because we can be more interested in serving ourselves rather than our neighbor. This kind of moral nurture and honest insight is more likely to engender moral sensitivity than any emphasis on the absolute character of the Decalogue.

JESUS CHRIST AND MORAL RESPONSIBILITY

A distinctively Christian response to the question of moral absolutes is that of theologian William C. Spohn, who refers to Jesus as "the concrete universal."[10] He sees the entire story of Jesus as a norm for the Christian life, not the only norm but the determinative one that exemplifies the reign or the presence of God in the human story. By centering on the person of Jesus Christ, Spohn recognizes the centrality of the Incarnation to Christian faith and the peculiar Christian claim that truth is revealed in a person, which in turn unites truth with discipleship. The truth in Christ is also "the way" and "the life" (John 14:6), beckoning the believer to follow. This is not the language of prohibition but the language of promise, the language of invitation to a new life marked by commitment and faithfulness to a person. In terms of the language used here, Jesus is himself the ideal of agapeic love, which is universal in its appeal. He encounters the prospective believer with an invitation to believe, to trust, and to embody the story of his life in one's own. This leaves open to the believer and his or her community of faith the responsibility to make those decisions that concretize the universal in acts of love.

Thus Jesus Christ embodies both the particularity and the universality of the Christian revelation and its ethical demand. The good news of the gospel is no abstract, ahistorical message that is universally and immediately accessible to everyone in virtue of birth. Yet at the same time, this good news takes and transforms the noblest aspirations of love and altruism in the human heart, connecting them with God the Father of Jesus Christ whose love opens possibilities of repentance, forgiveness, and new life. To speak of God in the Christian context is to become as particular and concrete as the historical person of Jesus and as universal as the power of love to bring forgiveness and reconciliation into human relationships.

In addition to this central message of the Christian Bible, there are many powerful ideals embedded in its total witness—the exalting of social justice in the Old Testament prophetic literature, the emphasis on love of neighbor in the teaching of Jesus, and the "fruit of the Spirit" articulated by Paul are prominent examples. They come out of a specific history and tradition and yet can transcend those cultural boundaries, being recognized as moral wisdom in many different contexts. The moral claim they make, however, is not to be justified on grounds of a universal reason or intuition, nor on their prescribing a particular, God-ordained course of action for all times and places. Their claim rests on their capacity to inspire a more flourishing, humane life together, which is to say that they capture what it means to be human as children of God who live in community, creatures of God's covenant whose life together should be characterized by justice and peace.

The moral lesson to be learned in human relationships is our responsibility to others in seeking their welfare, expressed in the Christian context as loving one's neighbor. Insisting on absolute rules or laws of conduct can inspire fear but not necessarily a spirit of concern for the neighbor or the inculcating of a sense of responsibility for the other. Emphasizing absolutes may even discourage the fruitful engagement of the moral imagination in seeking the best moral solution to a situation in which all one can achieve is the relatively better rather than the relatively worse. The language of absolutes not only instills the false confidence that we can apply universal rules to every human situation without regard to circumstance, but also encourages a legalistic spirit that is too eager to rush to judgment without regard to mitigating circumstances. Thus we can conclude that while ethical ideals are essential as sources of inspiration and worthy goals to which we would aspire, the notion of absolute prohibitions is not as helpful or important as many would think. Instead of insisting on absolutes, Christians today would do better to speak of moral responsibility. It is a term that expresses our recognition that human beings are morally accountable. We live in relationship to others, and those relationships give rise to obligations that must be observed if we are to live in community rather than chaos. But what we ought to do here and now will always remain a matter for moral discernment, an exercise in responsibility with no absolute rule to make the decision for us.

Whether speaking the language of morality or of some other dimension of human life and experience, the Christian's faith in God does undergird the conviction of a common humanity that allows for common understandings and insights among peoples in spite of cultural differences. A justified critique of the Enlightenment's attempt to establish universal truth—including universal moral standards—on the basis of an ahistorical human reason does not deny this point. Every human being is a creature of God, bearing the divine image. As such we are dialogical creatures who are capable of speech and understanding and who seek to communicate with our neighbors, including those nurtured in cultures with quite different traditions and worldviews. While the obstacles to understanding and genuine communication can be significant, these differences are best understood in terms of degree rather than constituting an absolute divide that cannot be bridged. Empirically, there is far too much meaningful communication between people rooted in diverse cultures to dispute this truth.[11]

As to the moral life, the shrinking political world accentuates the challenge to find common values by which diverse peoples can live together in justice and peace. We assume a fund of common values that, though finding many diverse cultural expressions, still provide the basis for mutual understanding and recognition. Affirming the particular, historical origin of our values does not mean we are compelled to deny the logical and empirical possibility that they have universal significance as well. Belief in the creator God has moral implications for people of every race and culture, because it establishes the inherent dignity of the human being. While this faith is rooted in a particular community, its universal moral implications are capable of being recognized as valid and authentic by people in every land and culture. We can expect to see commonalities in ideals and moral expectations among peoples representing a variety of cultures at the same time as we recognize the peculiar impact of their traditions on the shape and form these moral ideals and expectations take. Wherever people enter into relationship and seek to maintain community, a case can certainly be made for the necessity of some common values being involved—a sense of responsibility, fairness, respect—however shaped and expressed by the dominant culture.[12] In regard to the biblical story of Israel and the emerging Christian community, the continuity embedded in the common faith and its traditions, as well as a common humanity, provide the elements of significant continuity with the church of our own time and place.

Among Christian traditions, Protestants generally have more readily recognized both the vulnerability of human reason to misuse by other human purposes and its limitations due to historical location. There is greater suspicion of any professed confidence in the capacities of human reason to arrive at clear and indubitable truths in spelling out the implications of the church's gospel for the life of faith. Roman Catholics, on the other hand, historically have been more confident in ascribing a transcendent, universal reason to humanity, and thus Catholic leadership has been more inclined toward a blanket repudiation of the postmodern critique. It is clear, however, that the traditional confidence of Roman Catholicism concerning the human ratio has seen some modification in recent years. Catholic theologian Gregory Baum notes there is more willingness to recognize that "sin, power and ideology distort God's gift of human reason." Nevertheless, "redemptive grace," or the saving work of God in humanity, enables people "to transcend the distortions and become open to the light of reason."[13] Baum appeals to Jürgen Habermas's notion of an ideal speech situation, free from dominance or oppression, as holding the possibility of a universal ethics. He argues that it implies the foundational notion of a common human nature as essential to communication. The contemporary turn to dialogue and cooperation, overcoming cultural boundaries, anticipates the possibility of a common ethics.[14]

A more traditional response is seen in Pope John Paul II's encyclical *Veritatis Splendor* (1993), which constitutes a stern reaction to postmodern thinking in its reaffirming of the absolute and immutable character of moral truth. The encyclical has drawn a critical as well as appreciative response, but it is fair to say that an increasing number of Catholic scholars are convinced of the necessity of rethinking their moral tradition in an effort to work out a more adequate understanding of the dynamic of both constancy and change. A notable example of this effort is the work of John Noonan, whose essay "Development in Moral Doctrine,"[15] challenges the notion that moral norms transcend history. In proving his point, he notes how the church's moral judgments on slavery, charging interest, and religious freedom have changed quite radically over the years. Drawing on the developmental theory of John Henry Newman, he sees a genuine growth in the moral life of the church through a mutual interaction with its culture, resulting in new insights into the meaning of the Christian story and, consequently, new stances taken on issues of morality. Alasdair MacIntyre is another scholar indebted to Newman, whose work has emphasized the dynamic character of a viable tradition that is able to absorb ideas from without as well as developing its own historic resources.[16]

This theme of change in the midst of continuity is one to which we will often return in these pages. It stems from the recognition of the impact of history and our inability to live in a vacuum, as it were, where we seek to deny the change and development that is inherent to life in all its forms, including the church and its moral teaching. The conclusion at which we arrive, however, is not a relativism that would deny the meaningfulness of moral standards and the possibility of moral truth, but rather the recognition that moral judgments are inherently contextual, reflecting both continuity with a moral heritage and the need to adapt and develop in interaction with the contemporary setting. Christians live with and in a tradition of immense "staying power," which has contributed to their identity as believers and from which they draw, discriminatingly, in defining a responsible moral stance.[17] But the continuity provided by that tradition also reveals significant change, in its interaction with culture. Given this fact, an obvious challenge in every historical setting is to avoid letting the expectations of contemporary society dictate what is normative for the Christian life so that the Christian response is no more than a mirroring of society. This is the challenge for every generation, one that can be met only if Christians are thoroughly rooted in the biblical story, letting it define their understanding and outlook on life. That outlook is defined here primarily in terms of loyalty to the person of Jesus Christ, which gives both substance and direction to the moral life at the same time as it recognizes its inherent open-endedness. The Christian life requires wisdom and discernment in making moral decisions, which in turn requires the presence of the Christian community and its tradition as a source of nurture, support, direction, and admonition.

The negative features of postmodernism are likely to impress Christians the most: its widespread atheism and suspicion of all God-talk as attempts to impose one's ideology on others; its radical relativism and rejection of any attempt to frame life within a larger story or metanarrative that gives meaning and purpose to human history; its rejection of any possibility of meaningful intercultural communication and dialogue because of the isolating character of distinctive worldviews and differing assumptions embodied in the language of each culture; and the moral relativism inherent to its individualism, which does not allow for meaningful consensus concerning moral beliefs based either on a belief in God or recognition of a common humanity that binds all people together.

It would appear that the only appropriate response of Christians to the postmodern spirit is wholesale repudiation, a stance of "Christ against culture," in the familiar language of H. Richard Niebuhr. In many respects this repudiation is altogether necessary, particularly in regard to the disintegrative features of postmodernism that leave humanity religiously and morally rootless. Yet we have already noted its anthropological realism and its historical reasoning, which is capable of bringing insight to Christians as they reflect on their own tradition, leading us to caution against a broad-brush response that prevents appropriate discrimination in the judgments we make. Also among the various strands of postmodern thinking are holistic and communitarian elements that can be seen as complementary to Christian theology and ethics. Moreover, the critique of an authoritarian church in postmodernism can help to keep the church honest in its relations with society, serving as a corrective to any absolutist pretensions in making theological and moral assertions. Too readily Christians have assumed that they see things from God's point of view, an assumption that has fed a harmful spirit of hubris throughout the church's history. Our task is to recognize and acknowledge the conditioned character of our knowledge of truth without denying that what we are affirming is the truth that both claims and warrants our faithful commitment.[18] One must also recognize the impetus in postmodern thinking toward a greater opening of society to people on the margins. This is a most significant development for the church in two respects, on the one hand challenging it to a more faithful discipleship in working toward an inclusive society, and on the other hand providing support to its own efforts toward fashioning a more just society.

One particular feature of postmodern society that calls for further discussion here is its pluralist character. This is a feature that has particular bearing on the status of the church in society and its appropriate role in addressing social issues. Given the conflicting voices within the church concerning its appropriate response to society, it is necessary to examine the issues and to suggest a response that is consonant with the church's mission. These matters are addressed in the next chapter.

2
THE CHURCH IN A PLURALIST SOCIETY

In the previous chapter I noted the cultural atmosphere that is skeptical of moral standards and encourages a spirit of relativism. In this chapter I consider the sociological and political dimensions of that development in the changing place of the church and its Bible in a pluralist setting.[1] For most people, perhaps the most notable aspect of postmodern society is its pluralist character, in which many and opposing viewpoints about life and meaning exist in close proximity to each other. Tolerance must be a high priority in order for this society to exist in relative peace. Indeed, as Stephen L. Carter has noted, our situation requires more than tolerance in the sense of "putting up with" people whose mores are perceived as not only different from but challenging to our own. What is required is a willingness to respect those who are different, which means a willingness to understand and appreciate their traditions and the ethos they have generated.[2] In regard to ethics, pluralism constitutes a particular challenge because of the gravity of the moral life for one's personal identity and the cohesiveness of society. To live with a spirit of respect toward those whose morality appears strange and even incompatible with one's own is obviously difficult, if not threatening, for most people.

Pluralism is not the equivalent of what we have traditionally understood as relativism; it simply describes a societal diversity—in philosophical and religious worldviews, cultural roots, races, economic classes—and a political environment that allows each group to thrive without coercion or oppression. Ideally it is a situation that encourages dialogue, based on the belief that the community is served if people listen to each other and are willing to take each other seriously. The respectful spirit that welcomes diversity does so in any meaningful sense only if it speaks from an organizing center of moral conviction. Indeed, respect and tolerance have little substance for anyone who believes that all views are equally valid, or that we can suspend our moral judgments at will for the sake of good relations. The challenge of a pluralist society is to take our own convictions seriously and at the same time to maintain respect for those who differ from us, recognizing the necessity of a self-critical spirit in order to avoid absolutistic pretensions that prevent our profiting from the insights of others.

The prevailing stance of Christians addressing pluralism has often been a defensive one, trying to make the best of a bad situation in which, unfortunately, the Christian ethos no longer has the influence it once had. Ian S. Markham challenges this stance with the refreshing notion that the God of Christian faith points us to diversity and should inspire a theology that "affirms plurality because God intended it."

> Theologically, cultural enrichment is grounded in the God who welcomes diversity. It is a God who created the planet with immense diversity; it is a God who demands respect for persons especially if they disagree with you. The fact is God has deliberately created the world in such a way that the truth is not obvious. God has given each one of us a perspective that makes it very difficult to see the truth. All our perspectives are limited, partial, and incomplete. God has done this because he welcomes the fact that we are forced to supplement our perspective with the perspective of others.[3]

Christians do need to recognize that cultural, religious, and ethical differences serve many purposes that are salutary for both individual and society. The curiosity that drives the quest for knowledge is often inspired by differences. The journey toward self-knowledge takes on a more challenging and potentially more rewarding character when one is faced by significant differences among those with whom one associates. Differing perspectives on substantive issues help to keep one honest in various ways, challenging any tendency to absolutize one's own ideology or to refuse to countenance differences. Openness, respect for differences, and willingness to take those differences seriously—because the quest for truth is a serious business—are traits necessary to a pluralist society. They express a humility that recognizes the truth as greater than any one person or group can claim to possess, a humility that challenges the all-too-human inclination to use one's truth as a self-serving means of judging others.

THE DISLOCATION OF BIBLE AND CHURCH

The optimism pervading the Markham quotation is important to a positive and forward-looking stance on the part of the church. At the same time, there are significant developments in a pluralist society that cause somber reflection for many Christians. Not least among these developments is the weakening of the Bible as a cultural force in Western society. Even where its message is not believed, the linguistic world of the Bible has profoundly influenced Western society by providing the stories and images that embody its cultural heritage and the language in which the human quest for meaning has been expressed. Though reliable documentation is difficult to come by, the impression of a loss of biblical literacy in society as a whole is undoubtedly accurate. Within the church itself there is general agreement that familiarity with Scripture has weakened significantly. The Bible is no longer as likely to interpret the worlds in which Christians live, because it is no longer being read and savored as it once was. Thus as society loses hold of its traditional cultural heritage and its common language in discussing questions of meaning and purpose, many Christians understandably wonder about the consequences for both church and society.

Theologian George A. Lindbeck argues the necessity of the church regaining its biblical literacy, not through objective, critical studies of the text, but by internalizing its stories and images and symbols. He sees the postmodern temperament as actually providing a positive environment for this quest in terms of an interest in texts and what the world looks like in and through them. It is a matter of entering into the world of Scripture so that "one proceeds to imagine and think scripturally." Christians can lead the way, and others may follow, because there seem to be no other effective alternative modes of public discourse.[4] The appropriate expectations of the church for society and for its own role within society is a matter addressed below, but an obvious prerequisite is that the church possess a clear understanding of both its own identity and its relationship to society. The Bible is intimately bound up with each of these issues. The church cannot exist without being nurtured by the Bible, and thus one can argue that whatever the church can accomplish in society is dependent on how well rooted it is in its Scripture.

Sociologist Robert N. Bellah argues in a similar vein, noting that our culture has lost its "biblical tongue." In a pluralist society, biblical language has been pushed to the periphery because there is a multiplicity of tongues we must learn. Amid the cacophony, the language of science has become dominant in the modern era and has succeeded in forming the prevailing worldview of Western society. In a postmodern age, Bellah sees the possibility of a more genuine pluralism, "one in which we would become genuinely multilingual, speaking the language of science and psychology where they are appropriate, but also speaking the language of the Bible and of citizenship, unashamedly and well."[5] Both Lindbeck and Bellah recognize the dislocation of the Bible from its position of prominence in the culture, but both affirm its potential to provide a truthful Word to a postmodern society. One may question the optimism in Lindbeck's desire for Scripture to return to a position of prominence in society, "helping to fill a cultural vacuum at the heart of national life." Yet we would at least desire and expect that the message of Scripture be effectively communicated and heard, whatever the consequences.

A pluralist society thus compels the church to do some serious thinking about the way it communicates, both in terms of its proclamation of the gospel and its witness as a participant in the public square; to reassess its place and role in society, recognizing that where it once spoke and communicated with authority it now must assume a more modest role, rediscovering itself and the nature of its calling in a new cultural setting. A pluralist society has in fact led the church and individual Christians into respectful dialogue with others, in a relationship of equality. This changing cultural milieu is providing an opportunity for the church to learn something about itself, the importance of humility and respect, and the privilege of reaching out to those who in the past have been written off or condemned. It is often not easy or comfortable for the church to adjust to the demands of pluralism, for the modesty it demands runs counter to the spirit of absolutism that the church often has been inclined to bring to its theological and moral assertions.[6] In a postmodern, pluralist era, Christians are being challenged to reunderstand the meaning of their deepest convictions within a worldview that has become intensely aware of the limitations of historical existence and the contextual character of its knowledge and moral decision making. As Ronald Thiemann notes, "Fundamental to the philosophical acceptance of pluralism is the conviction that we have no self-evident, incorrigible means of establishing the truth of our assertions . . . we cannot coerce others into believing as we do."[7]

The democratic character of our society also carries implications for the church's role in regard to social morality. The church as society's religious establishment has been used to exercising moral authority throughout American history, but Edward Tivnan argues that the spirit of our democratic tradition does not allow claims to infallibility concerning what stance society should take on a contested moral issue.[8] This does not mean that there are no sound and convincing moral positions to be taken, but in the public realm churches must realize that their particular positions may fail to win public consensus, to say nothing of their being legalized. The nation's democratic heritage and the new pluralism are exerting their impact also *within* the churches, where unanimity on moral issues often proves highly elusive and any attempt to establish a common position on a given issue raises considerable opposition. On contested issues the church as well as society is being challenged to maintain the dialogue rather than impose a position from above. Within both church and society this situation is creating much frustration and often dire predictions of moral collapse, because a spirit of openness signals for many a willingness to comply with a relativist point of view.

The increasing religious diversity in our society will continue to challenge many traditional roles once assumed by the church. Much has been written about the passing of Christendom, a society in which Christianity reigns as the establishment religion and dominates religious beliefs as well as the ethos of society. We are well on the way to a society in which this kind of influence and status is no longer exercised by the church, and how Christians respond to this change is important to the church's future role in public life. Whether it be the Christian tradition or some other, we no longer live in a society in which a religious institution is expected to deliver a code of conduct that claims to be the final word. An appropriate modesty concerning moral claims is essential to the integrity of the contemporary church, not in the sense that it has no moral convictions worthy of affirmation, but because it recognizes the conditions under which it can participate in a pluralist society. It is neither possible nor desirable for the church to "pull rank" on the basis of its long history and previous status.

This situation raises very difficult issues for American churches, with some resisting the degree of societal accommodation suggested in the above paragraph. Some seek a return to an earlier age and a cultural mentality in which the church was expected to speak with authority to the whole society. The current distress on the part of many in the church over what is perceived to be the weakening moral fabric of society can also encourage dogmatic statements about our moral direction. Often the Roman Catholic Church is cited as an admirable example of a church that knows where it stands and has the courage to state its convictions, regardless of the prevailing moral atmosphere. With its natural law tradition, Catholicism has been particularly confident in making moral judgments that it professes to be rooted in human nature. Since Vatican II (1962–65), however, the reservations among Catholics about spelling out precise moral judgments on the basis of broad anthropological convictions have grown in volume, stimulated by the negative response to the papal encyclical on birth control *(Humanae Vitae)*. Theologian Herbert McCabe expressed these concerns in 1967:

> The magisterium of the Church should not be quick as formerly to see in individual rules of behavior which either prevail in society or are laid down by itself, immutable principles of natural law valid for all times and places. It should be readier to see more of these as good guides for the time being, perhaps to be modified later. Indeed the magisterium…[should] be more of a pastoral guide to men, pointing out to them, under the inspiration of the love of God in Christ, the best means of living that it now knows, instead of a legal authority laying down universal laws and sanctions for them.[9]

Just as visible in recent years has been the political activism of many conservative evangelical churches and related parachurch organizations in an effort to steer the populace "back" to family values identified with the past. These voices have significantly increased in volume as their numbers have grown, often playing a dominant role in the public forum. The confident judgments of these churches are based on what they profess to be clear and indubitable pronouncements from the Bible. Whether Catholic or Protestant forms of moral absolutism, there is the issue of the church's honesty and integrity when it claims a God-given moral position—with its corollary of God-given certainty and self-confidence—concerning deeply contested and ambiguous issues. Rather than claiming to be indisputably right on these matters in virtue of a direct pipeline to divine truth, the church must rely on the force and cogency of its arguments, rooted in its theological convictions as well as its reading of the contemporary scene. Whether it is addressing abortion or homosexuality or euthanasia or genetic engineering, the church ought not pose as the final arbiter with an ultimate truth. To do so is not only dishonest; it also invites a loss of authenticity in the eyes of contemporary culture. When the church speaks out with strong conviction, which it certainly must, it should be in a way that invites dialogue and honest encounter with those with whom it disagrees.

Whether it be the claim of an emancipated reason that knows a universal moral order, or of a direct revelation that gives clear and uncompromising answers, both assertions take on the character of hubris. Our passion for certitude and security leads us to deny our limitations; we would transcend our finitude in an effort to know absolute truth from the vantage point of God. The quest for knowledge, as Kierkegaard noted, is a constant pressing against the intractable limits of our finitude; our reach exceeds our grasp. Thus one can argue from a Christian perspective that absolute moral claims rooted either in the rational nature of humanity or in the pages of a divinely inspired revelation, both untouched by the flow of historical existence, are expressions of human pride in its quest for absolute certainty.[10] From our existential situation we are driven to claim more for ourselves than is warranted in our quest for theological and moral certainty, a truth that we can more readily appreciate in a postmodern, pluralist age.[11] As Jeffrey Stout argues, in a time marked by disagreement and conceptual diversity in ethics, we must avoid the extremes of either maintaining a "God's-eye view" in our ethical positions, or coming to a "complete loss of confidence" in those positions.[12] Neither is warranted.

A conservative evangelical friend who read these first two chapters in manuscript form offered the comment that my emphasis on dialogue was in danger of being contradicted by my harsh judgment of Christians on the right who are in the habit of making absolute claims concerning the truth and their possession of it. It has to be admitted that a real danger for Christians in the historic, mainstream Protestant denominations is the demonizing of the Religious Right and fundamentalists in general. The acrimony directed by Christians toward others *within* the church is often the harshest and most mean-spirited, and judgments made of those on the right can be particularly uncharitable because they are usually mixed with disdain over what is assumed to be their ignorance and lack of sophistication. It is important to recognize that the concerns of these Christians have their legitimacy; efforts to maintain the tradition, whether pursued with cultural sophistication or not, constitute an important task for the church in every age. Those who are more inclined to stress the necessary engagement between church and culture are often in need of being jostled or prodded by those who are more tuned to seeing the contradictions between them. We need each other in order to arrive at a proper balance on these matters; only as we maintain an openness to fellow believers—however much we disagree with them—will that balance be achieved. At the same time, in a spirit of frankness in the pursuit of truth, we must be willing to both exercise and accept critique in our relations with each other.

The point made in chapter 1 that we do not possess the truth relates directly to the recognition here that we cannot maintain a "God's-eye view" of the truth. The turn to particularity and the historical drives home this truth, but it is important to recognize that we are making an epistemological point that does not deny the reality of the God of faith.

It acknowledges that our knowledge of God is inextricably bound to our traditions and expresses the faith of the believing and worshiping community, and no attempts at rational proof can compel the assent of one who is not part of that community. When it comes to matters of faith and the ethos by which people live, Christians as well as adherents of other faiths are creatures of the communities that nurture them. Thus there is no inconsistency in Christians affirming both the reality of God (and therefore an ultimate meaning and purpose to the human story) and at the same time the contextual nature of their faith and understanding in appropriating that truth. For morality this means that universal ideals can be affirmed even as one maintains a healthy recognition of one's limitations in knowing the will of God. For the Christian, postmodernity and pluralism do not mean the abandonment of an ultimate truth for a multiplicity of truths, or the repudiation of moral truths that can order and direct our lives. Rather, it should mean the recognition of our limitations of perspective and the necessity to listen to others both within and outside the community of faith in forging a responsible theology and a responsible moral stance.

INTERPRETING THE TRADITION IN A CHANGING SOCIETY

In light of the turn to tradition and community, it is not surprising that many theologians are emphasizing the inherent connection of Christian ethics with the Christian community.[13] The critique of Enlightenment assumptions has enlarged our focus from the decision-making individual to the ecclesial community as a context of moral nurture and direction. That community has its distinctive history and traditions that shape the moral convictions of its members. Rather than claiming a "divine morality" directly received from God, an immediate, trans-historical source of moral truth, this viewpoint places the source of Christian moral insight in the believing community itself, with its peculiar faith in the living God who is known in Jesus Christ. Just what this means in relation to biblical authority will be investigated in the next chapter; at this point I want to consider the continuing and necessary conversation that goes on between the church and a postmodern society, and the impact that conversation has on the thinking and developing tradition of the church.

Given the crazy-quilt character of American denominationalism, it may sound contradictory to refer to the tradition of "the church." Yet every denomination understands itself in some way as standing in the train of New Testament Christianity, justifying its existence in terms of its faithfulness to the tradition set in motion by the New Testament story. The particular history of each Christian community has shaped the understanding and interpretation of that story, however, accounting for distinctive differences among them. This fact is dramatically illustrated in American denominationalism, where the emergence of each new religious community reflects distinctive cultural, ethical, and theological issues that give the group its peculiar stamp and character. There are often significant differences among them in the prevailing ethos of each church and, consequently, on any number of moral issues addressed by the churches. We are not surprised to find both continuity and diversity among ecclesial traditions, common ground as well as conflicting stances. The two-way, ongoing conversation between church and society gives a dynamic and often distinctive character to the tradition of each community of faith, expressing both identity with society as well as varying degrees of tension and opposition.

The moral tradition of every church includes both continuity and change, reflecting a history in which shifting circumstances and relationships have demanded a rethinking of traditional responses. The temptation for many Christians is to suppose that the church's tradition itself has been and will continue to be an unchanging monolith that contains once-and-for-all moral answers for past, present, and future. Yet this belief is contradicted by any honest reading of the church's history. If we as Christians recognize that our moral convictions are not based on a transcendent moral order but emerge from the story of the believing community, we are then better able to recognize the nature of moral authority within the church. It develops from the often stressful dialogue that takes place among believers over changing circumstances in society. The ongoing conversation with society necessitates an ongoing conversation of the church with its tradition, giving rise to new understandings and perspectives.

Stanley Hauerwas has written that traditions "by their nature require change, since there can be no tradition without interpretation. And interpretation is the constant adjustment that is required if the current community is to stay in continuity with tradition."[14] In both Judaism and Christianity there is abundant evidence that creative interpretation of the tradition—including the biblical record itself—has been done not in an effort to change the tradition, but to remain faithful to its spirit and intent. Such interpretation emerges from an honest grappling with the tradition, taking it seriously at the same time as one consciously addresses it in light of contemporary knowledge and values. A wooden, legalistic interpretation of the tradition does not serve the faithful who are looking for insight from the past in addressing present realities, whether theological or ethical. The present always demands a creative application of past truths if the past is to serve us well. Thomas Ogletree makes this point in regard to the interpretation of Scripture:

> Every successful act of interpretation brings something new into being. It is never a mere re-presentation of something fully intact. The paradox of interpreting is that we are able to say the same thing as the text only by saying something different. The originality of the interpreter is to venture formulations which can contribute to the common mind toward which understanding reaches. The point is to gain a more adequate grasp of the moral life by way of an engagement with biblical materials.[15]

These observations do not imply that there are no moral "anchors" within the tradition on which we can rely. There are structures to the common life of every society, with moral ideals and rules and societal laws protecting that common life. As was previously noted, the Ten Commandments hold a special place in Christianity as a divinely sanctioned expression of such laws, relating them to the God who has created our life together. Nonetheless, we are compelled to recognize that how to interpret the Decalogue remains a continuing task in light of changing social structures. New moral insights emerge with new circumstances and expectations, and those insights become a part of our tradition. The conversation and sometimes lively arguments we carry on with our tradition lead to new moral insights, significant innovations, and sometimes even reversal of time-honored convictions.[16] While the notion of some kind of order and structure to our lives is essential, the implications for ethical behavior are not always as clear and neat as we would like.

Given this vital character of society in which our relationships to each other and to the world of nature are being changed at even a faster rate today by technological advances, and the corresponding emergence of new understandings of the world and our place within it, there should be little surprise over the changing moral landscape of our lives. Every instance of moral ambiguity and conflict in society becomes an occasion to raise new questions of the tradition and prompt new interpretations of it, and possibly generate a healthy reassessment of its limits. We are helped in cutting through the ideological polarities created by these issues when we are capable of affirming the importance of both continuity and change in the traditions by which we order our lives. It involves respect for those who have gone before us and who have helped to define the church's identity in the world, but at the same time it involves the recognition that we honor their contribution by rethinking and reformulating the truths at which they arrived. In that process, we discover that new perspectives bring new power and insight from the tradition in addressing issues we face today. It may also lead to perspectives on given issues that do not fit into the customary framework in which those issues have been understood in the church's tradition. Obviously, there is both risk and promise for the church in this continuing responsibility to relate its tradition to the changing moral scene.

The church's conversation with society also raises the question whether society can be a teacher of the church. The Old Testament witness clearly recognizes God at work among the nations, sometimes using them to exercise judgment of Israel. In the New Testament, Gentiles were recognized for their faith (Matt. 8:5-13) and a Samaritan is pictured as the model of compassion (Luke 10:29-37). Any theology of culture not willing to recognize the presence of the "righteous Gentile" and serious moral aspirations in the surrounding society, no matter how secular, fails to see the presence of God in the common life of all people. While there is no place for sweeping judgments that would maintain an inexorable moral progress in the human story, there are certainly areas of secular life where moral sensitivities have been raised and where immoralities and injustices once ignored are now challenged. The impact of the Christian ethos may readily be seen in the sharpening of conscience on issues of racial justice, for example, but society often has exercised a more conscientious effort than the church to address and challenge efforts at undermining the realization of that justice.

With its self-awareness as a community of forgiven sinners, the church should not be interested either in posing as a model of moral rectitude, or in shutting itself off from what it can learn from the rest of society. In the spirit of the Gospel, the church's critical engagement with society necessarily involves its capacity to observe the moral struggles and achievements of society and to learn from them. If our involvement in the public square is to be honest, we will need to be open to those outside the church and to engage in a process of *mutual criticism*[17] in an effort to further the cause of a more humane society. While the church in a pluralist environment can no longer assume the role of the moral teacher of society, it still has the responsibility to take its place in the public forum and not be afraid or unwilling to make a witness there. That witness includes honest listening and openness to dialogue with the disparate elements that make up a free society like our own.

This conversation and involvement with public life is always subject to the danger of the church's politicization. This occurs on the one hand when the church's involvement takes on a partisan character in which it identifies with a particular political party or particular candidates, and on the other hand when it fails to act or speak out on grounds of theological and ethical principle, being swayed instead by political goals and arguments of expediency. This is a realm of the church's life that calls for much vigilance and a high degree of self-criticism, for the dangers of self-deception are great. If it becomes apparent that political and ideological convictions are motivating the public involvement of the church, its faith is trivialized as well as abused. Then the political tail is wagging the theological and ethical dog, and the church does no more than reflect the values—usually solid middle class—of its members.[18]

The Current Debate Concerning Church and Society

Concerning the church's conversation with society, there is currently a lively debate on the appropriate stance the church should take toward society and the political order. A prominent participant in this debate is ethicist Stanley Hauerwas, who challenges the assumption (reflected here) that the church has a distinctive and important role to play in the public square. His argument is that the church's role in society is simply to "be" the church, living out its distinctive life in society and thereby making its witness. The challenge he raises is whether the church that becomes active in the public square can be true to itself in a liberal, democratic society. While its freedom and independence are constitutionally protected, it is nonetheless subject to the subtle control involved in having to participate according to the rules set by the political establishment. By stressing the contradiction between Christian and liberal democratic understandings of justice and freedom, Hauerwas makes any genuine conversation between them exceedingly difficult, if not impossible. It rules out the possibility of Christians working with non-Christians for a more just social order, because justice in the context of the gospel is radically different from secular justice. To work for justice in the realm of politics, says Hauerwas, is to make political power the end goal of our activity—a contradiction to which the church ought not subject itself.[19]

Hauerwas is a notable example of a Christian response to postmodernity that would lift up the turn from universality to particularity as an opportunity to recapture the true nature of the church and its relation to the moral world surrounding it. His acceptance of the postmodern repudiation of claims to universal moral discourse is reflected in his conviction that there is no point to the church's engaging society in dialogue, for it leads only to misunderstanding between them and to society's co-option of the church. The church must recognize that it has a unique faith and a unique ethics that will only be sacrificed to the secular establishment if any kind of dialogue is maintained. The impact of Karl Barth is evident in this stance, where church and society are understood as natural enemies. The result for Hauerwas is a skeptical judgment of democratic society and a purist conception of both the church and its relation to the state. While his writings contribute significantly and admirably to the espousal of a countercultural stance on the part of the church, his understanding of church-state relations would limit the extent and expression of that stance.

There is also the postmodern conviction—seen noticeably in such writers as Lyotard and Baudrillard—that the "megastructures" of modern society are deeply rooted, a situation that does not encourage the belief that the church or any other group can make a meaningful difference in effecting change.[20] Many Christians have bought into this conviction, but it creates a significant contradiction for those who share at the same time the traditional Reformed conviction that the church's mission is to "transform" society. One understandable reaction to this contradiction is to emphasize the opposition between church and society and turn inward to the cultivation of a distinctive Christian ethics among the believing community. This in turn raises the obvious danger of sectarianism, in which the church washes its hands in relation to society and retreats into its own ghetto.

In opposition to this kind of thinking, I believe the continuing task of the church is to maintain a lively awareness of its identity at the same time as it maintains a lively engagement in the public square. The two are interdependent and feed on each other. "To be the church" must include the desire to maintain a vigorous engagement with the powers that be, not based on expectations of making an impact as much as exercising faithfulness. Such activity is not marked primarily by proclamation but by the mission to bring principle, compassion, and inclusiveness into societal structures, a humanizing of the common life. The life of politics is fundamentally an ongoing debate over values, and churches bring a distinctive voice to that debate. Their mission justifiably embraces a concern for the common good, exercised with a prophetic judgment of the establishment, an emphasis on responsibility, and the fostering of works of mercy. In the kind of society in which we live, it is persuasive theologically and politically to recognize the dialectical relationship of the church to the state, with both resistance and support being appropriate according to differing contexts.[21] The church does not have the luxury of relating to the political establishment on its own terms without withdrawing into its own world, an outcome repudiated by Hauerwas and yet one that certainly expresses the thrust of his argument.[22]

At question in these differences is how much weight Christians should give to the postmodern turn. Hauerwas accepts it as a defining moment with far-reaching and permanent implications, while others take a more skeptical view. Theologian and ethicist Max Stackhouse questions the denial of any possibility for "universalistic arguments," claiming that "the purported breakup of meaning in our 'postmodern' era is overstated, and that humans have the capacity to learn one another's languages and to engage in meaningful cross-cultural debate on such matters as human rights, sound ecology, fair trade, good technology, quality medicine and just law." Whether one speaks of a common grace, or a common humanity, there is the possibility of faith claims being publicly assessed and debated in conversation with those who do not share the faith. "Indeed, this is what makes serious theology possible and necessary."[23]

With its Thomistic heritage, Roman Catholic moral theologians have been particularly critical of an ecclesial ethics such as Hauerwas represents because of its sectarian direction. They see its accent on Christian particularity as an acknowledgment of the validity of postmodern skepticism concerning reason, rejecting the possibility of a common morality that transcends cultural boundaries. Lisa Sowle Cahill argues:

> It is no real solution to the truth question to locate truth and its criteria within the believing community in such a way that external or "objective" criteria become irrelevant to its own confidence in the message it bears forward out of its internally coherent traditions. This is not to say that *faith* in God can be justified or produced on rational grounds, but only that the *morality* that goes with Christian faith is intelligible on reasonable as well as on religious grounds.[24]

Cahill and Hauerwas, the one a Roman Catholic and the other a Protestant from the Reformed heritage and strongly influenced by Mennonite theologian and ethicist John Howard Yoder, represent two classic polarities or tensions always present in theology and ethics: the drive toward universality that relates Christian faith and theology positively to culture, seeking the points of connection between them, and the drive toward particularity that would conserve the distinctive character of the Christian message in contrast to culture. These polarities are perennial themes because they both capture an element of truth. Both Christian mission and Christian identity are inherent to this debate, and the question becomes whether that twofold quest in a given context can best be pursued by emphasizing openness and points of connection between church and society, or emphasizing points of contrast and discontinuity between them. Obviously, it should not be a question of either one or the other in any exclusive or permanent sense.

I have noted that postmodern themes have accentuated this debate, encouraging a withdrawal mode on issues of church and society and emphasizing the church's need to tend to its distinctive character as a community of faith with a peculiar, identifying tradition.[25] Instead of understanding the church's social mission as simply "being" the church, however, we must recognize that an active stance toward society and culture is not only more responsible to the church's mission but essential to the church's life. The church's identity must be forged in relation to society as the necessary setting in which the church moves and has its being, relating its tradition to the times through critical engagement and by that very activity maintaining its identity as the body of Christ. This is part of the church's mission imperative, based on the conviction that it is governed by its Creed's First Article concerns as well as its Second and Third. Whether based on the sovereignty of divine love and justice that would encompass all people, or on specifically covenantal thinking between God and the human family, Protestant churches have rightly understood the church's mission to include a responsibility for the larger society. The social dislocation of the church does not remove that responsibility, but only changes the setting and the mode and character of the church's response.

It was H. Richard Niebuhr who eloquently insisted that the radical, monotheistic faith of Christians has a direct bearing on the capacity of a society to maintain an open, egalitarian stance. Wherever there is belief in God who alone is absolute Truth, no particular group can claim a divine or secular warrant for elevating itself above the rest of us. Before the One who holds all of us to account, we are equal at the most fundamental level of our existence. It follows from that conviction that no one segment of society can make absolutistic claims for itself. Any grasp for power on the part of an elite, and the consequent injustice that ensues, stands under the judgment of biblical faith.[26] The church has a responsibility to hold that message firmly before the consciousness of society and its political leadership, also in a postmodern, pluralist age.

Thus the church renders an authentic expression of its faith when it critically affirms both the egalitarian, democratic ideals of a liberal democracy and the attempt to maintain a genuinely pluralist society.

While the church must keep a proper distance from the centers of political power, this should not blind Christians to the merits of a system in which the church is free to speak out in the public square. Max Stackhouse puts it well:

> While no single political system is necessarily more "Christian" than others for all times, decisive biblical and theological principles press Christianity in a democratizing direction. I take democracy, with all its weaknesses, to be the best expression of basic theological principles in modern social life in this sense: any political or economic system that does not support the possibilities of pluralistic democratic governance under laws that protect basic human rights, minorities, and dissent is not theologically or ethically defensible in modern public discourse.[27]

The church properly concerns itself with matters of justice, commending efforts to realize a more just society and challenging conditions of injustice. This is not a matter of seeking power for the church, but rather appealing to the best instincts of those in positions of power to exercise their authority responsibly. The fact that the church lives in a post-Christendom society, with an appropriately chastened sense of its status in the public square, only compels it to be more diligent and innovative in bringing its witness to public attention. That witness bears integrity to the degree that it avoids being identified with privilege and status, motivated instead by the sole desire to make a responsible witness. That witness will always include the courage to take a stand on behalf of the marginalized in society.

The identity, mission, and integrity of the church are at stake in these developments. An ideological response from either the left or the right that would identify the church with either liberal or conservative forces in society would constitute an assault on the distinctive identity and integrity of the church. It must exercise discernment and a spirit of self-criticism, both in reference to itself and in its engagement with centers of power in society. This challenge is obviously more pronounced with a church in active engagement with society than with a church in withdrawal, but accusations of ideological bondage will be heard whatever stance it takes. The church must not give up its claim for the right to be heard and to make its case on behalf of a more just and humane society, but this activity ought not carry the expectation of a privileged status in relation to other religious groups. Acknowledging this point is also to recognize the truth that an egalitarian, pluralist society is a gift to the church, a reminder that it lives in dependence on the grace of God rather than on the favor of any public authority.

3
DETERMINING
"WHAT THE BIBLE SAYS"

In this and the following chapter, I focus attention on the Bible to consider the nature of its authority for the moral life of the Christian community. This chapter must consider some preliminary issues to the subject of biblical authority, which have a bearing on the conclusions at which I arrive. Those issues have to do with our appropriation of the biblical text in the first place, and the possibilities for understanding the text. In other words, prior to the question, "What is the ethical authority of Scripture?" we need to ask, "How do we approach the Bible in order to discern its message?" This question has become increasingly complicated in the last century.

The word *hermeneutics* (the study of interpretation, in Greek *hermeneia),* though now a much-inflated philosophical term, historically has been used in biblical and theological discussion to refer to the complex of issues arising from the contemporary attempt to understand and interpret a text—such as the Bible—originating in the distant past and reflecting a culture quite different from our own. In the nineteenth and twentieth centuries, the hermeneutical task has included critical historical work in clarifying and determining the meaning of the text. This has involved exegesis, or the withdrawing of the content of the text, as a first step, and then relating the content to our own times through critical engagement with the text, as ones who live in a different cultural milieu. This inevitably is an interpretive activity in which our appropriation of the meaning of the text is shaped by the assumptions we bring to it. As an academic and critical enterprise, the hermeneutical task has not developed without resistance within the church, particularly when its conclusions have contradicted traditional understandings of the text. Now from the outside as well, the rise of postmodern hermeneutics has occasioned a lively debate concerning the historical critical method as an appropriate means of getting at the scriptural message. This constitutes a significant challenge, because it attacks critical methodology at the level of its assumptions, questioning whether those assumptions are legitimate.

THE BIBLICAL CRITIC UNDER ATTACK

The historical critical method[1] is a child of the Enlightenment in that it assumes the capacity of reason (in contrast to religious belief) to determine the truth about historical evidence, both as to what has actually happened and what the event means. It operates with a critical spirit in that it seeks self-evident truth, in distinction from mere opinion or conjecture. It raises the critical "what" questions in regard to the historical evidence, and when or if the larger question of meaning is raised (the "why" question), it seeks an answer offered by the historical context and governed by the assumptions of the critic. This means that historical criticism is not a monolithic phenomenon; while it is appropriately recognized as a critical method, treating the Bible "like any other book," the range and degree of critical perspective and skepticism brought to the text will vary considerably from one critic to another. The presence or absence of faith in the critic will have a bearing on the range of possibilities the critic will recognize in understanding the text. Nonetheless, the critical orientation of the method has often placed it in the role of an antagonist to the church, whose approach to the biblical record is governed by the conviction that it is a medium of divine self-revelation, the Word of God.

In the late nineteenth and early twentieth centuries, there was notable reaction within the Christian community to this critical approach to Scripture, as well as to the larger cultural atmosphere of religious skepticism. It repudiated the historical critic and absolutized the transcendence of the Bible as a work that comes directly from God, apart from any significant human mediation. Through a theory of divine inspiration, the Bible was lifted up as a source of indubitable truth. This viewpoint, which we identify with Christian fundamentalism but whose roots are clearly present in sixteenth-century Protestant orthodoxy, claims that the Bible essentially is a book of propositional statements that are either true or false, and that a foundational document for the church's faith cannot contain what is false without undermining both itself as God's Word and the faith of the whole church. Thus foundational assertions about the perfection of God as absolute Truth, and the perfection of the Bible as God's truthful Word, result in a book in which we can have absolute confidence. Not content to let a belief in the Bible's veracity or dependability rest in the witness of the Spirit, fundamentalists claim the ability to prove the perfection and therefore the divinity of Scripture through a theory of inerrancy. The foundational ideal of rational, scientific proof is boldly applied here in support of traditional religious belief.[2]

This attempt at guaranteeing certainty concerning the Bible as Scripture betrays both a theology of glory that claims the ability to make God transparent in a human vehicle, and the Enlightenment assumption that at the basis of our knowledge must lie an indubitable truth. We have already challenged the latter assumption, and the former must be repudiated on theological grounds. An inerrant Scripture represents one of many theological attempts to guarantee the truth and consequent authority of the Christian message in an effort to escape the uncertainty that is inherent to faith. It is understandable that Christians are tempted to find every means of support for the Bible in a skeptical, relativist age, but the quest for absolute certainty makes them particularly vulnerable to false arguments and specious assumptions.[3] This vulnerability is the attempt on the part of fundamentalists to establish their argument by returning to a previous age, oblivious to the historical and cultural dynamics of today. As a consequence, rather than genuinely engaging the issue of biblical authority, fundamentalists in our time are often dismissed as irrelevant.

During the last several decades, however, discontent with historical criticism as a method of biblical interpretation has moved well beyond the attacks of fundamentalists. Theologians who in the past have valued the contributions of historical, critical scholarship, assuming its validity for their own biblical and theological work, are now expressing their disillusionment with it. Over the years there has in fact been a kind of love-hate relationship between the church's theologians and biblical scholarship. Those identified with mainline churches have generally affirmed the necessity of a critical orientation in addressing the historical record; they have recognized the contribution of historical scholarship in cutting through various assumptions and biases that quite naturally attach to religious piety in its approach to and understanding of its Scripture. Historical seriousness and a spirit of objectivity appeared to ensure a responsible reading of the Bible and a defense against its misuse. That confidence has now been challenged not only by theologians but from within the community of biblical scholars itself.

Walter Wink has been a particularly eloquent critic of the historical critical method. He sees it as essentially bankrupt, bound to a scholarly intellectualism that actually gets in the way of a genuine encounter with the text.[4] While biblical critical methods claim objectivity, Wink contends, they are not at all "value free"; critical methodology alienates the reader from the text, turning one into a functional atheist who is unable to integrate with one's own assumptions the world and message of the Bible in which God addresses sinful humanity. Wink sees the purpose of Scripture aimed at personal and social transformation, while the critic's work is aimed at analytical dissection of the text to the point that it no longer speaks to human beings in their existential situation.

Despite the thrust of his argument, Wink is not willing to give up the critical tools of historical investigation. He seeks a new paradigm where critical methods are "transposed into a wholistic context in which questions of technique have been subordinated to the overarching purpose of enabling transformation."[5] Such a paradigm relates the reader to the text in a way that transcends the subject-object dichotomy established by Enlightenment thought, enabling the reader to be addressed by the text at a level of depth that promises a new life-orientation. Wink himself finds an effective means of accomplishing this purpose by going outside of the world of biblical theology, finding support in psychoanalytic theory and practice as a way of bringing the whole person into relation with the text.

In many ways the critique of Wink is representative of the criticism being heard today. He pictures the nature of biblical criticism as inherently atheistic and secularized, incapable of an open and responsive approach to the text. With such generalizations, Wink understands the biblical critic as one who by definition is in bondage to a worldview that repudiates the worldview of Scripture. At this point, I believe he overstates his case. He can be appreciated, on the one hand, for challenging a prevailing worldview that posits a closed universe, with no room for the mystery and surprise of God's presence. In this he is exercising his own postmodern critique of a scientific worldview that seeks hegemony over all competing views. On the other hand, he conveys the idea that critical historical work can be *identified* with an atheistic viewpoint, failing to recognize that it can be judiciously used by persons of faith. To say that there are biblical critics who are not believers is one thing; to say that all of them are bound to assumptions that do not allow them to believe is something else.

In point of fact, from the beginning there have been biblical scholars of considerable renown who have been motivated by faith and who have used the critical method as a tool to better understand the scriptural witness. They have recognized both the usefulness and the limitations of historical criticism in grasping the whole picture of human life and destiny, or of grasping the full meaning of the text. Its work is indispensable in addressing the historical record, but the assumptions of those who use the method will differ in regard to the meanings and possibilities that emerge from that work.[6] A more appropriate perspective is expressed by the New Testament scholar Robin Scroggs, who, while acknowledging the concern of critics such as Walter Wink, also recognizes a more interrelated and complementary relationship between critical methods and the end goal of biblical understanding.

> Biblical criticism is crucial in helping to form the mature understanding of the biblical heritage we wish church people to have, an understanding that can provide a basis for impetus to transformation. . . . *But,* and this is the crucial word in [this] entire essay, biblical criticism is not enough, for it is not an adequate and in itself sufficient agent of *transformation.* It helps set the stage for transformation, but it is still at a distance, like Moses looking into the promised land. Along with the communication of critical insights must go tools that permit a more direct encounter with the challenge of the text.[7]

In the present environment of discontent with the tradition of historical criticism, Daniel Patte likens the historical critical method to fundamentalism in that both exhibit—each in its own way—a one-dimensional approach to Scripture that is alienating in its effects. Each claims a universality for its own, true interpretation of Scripture, and a degree of confidence and finality that estranges those who propose a different view.[8] Patte's drawing this kind of correlation can be helpful in pointing to the limitations of the historical critical method, but it fails to appreciate the resources that characterize the critical tradition. An individual critic can be guilty of excesses in what is claimed as objective, critical judgment, but the tradition itself serves to balance such judgments with other, opposing perspectives. The compelling assumption in this kind of critical work is the necessity to listen to judgments that differ from one's own, letting each view stand on its own merits. In this respect, relating biblical criticism to fundamentalism in terms of a common mind-set is misleading. A more cogent comparison between them would recognize their similarity in the sense that both would recognize the text as a set of objective truths that are available to public analysis, but beyond that their methods of approaching Scripture are quite different.

The notion of an objective text with its meaning to be discovered by the reading subject has been a presumption of modernism that clearly stands behind the work of the critic, who believes there is an original meaning to the text and that it can be discovered with the appropriate methodology. With the application of tools provided by scholarly disciplines—history, archaeology, anthropology, philology, comparative religion—the original meaning of the text can be ascertained. This scholarly approach has proven its usefulness many times over by challenging irresponsible interpretations originating from a credulous piety, dogmatic fervor, a closed mind, or simple ignorance, but its limitations are now more commonly recognized. While it embodies a critical principle that will always have an important role to play in biblical interpretation, the emergence of postmodern hermeneutics has been helpful in focusing on the interpretive assumptions that even the most "objective" methodology will reveal.

FROM TEXT TO READER

It is instructive to note that the shift from text to reader in postmodern hermeneutics has an analogous development in the discipline of biblical hermeneutics itself.[9] There is a tradition of biblical and theological reflection that has stressed the involvement of the reader as essential to an appropriation of truth. Here the theologian Friedrich Schleiermacher (1763–1834) is a pivotal figure with his distinction between general and biblical hermeneutics, focusing on the art of understanding and its implications for understanding Scripture. This involvement of the reader in the appropriation of the text takes on a decisive, existential character in the writings of Søren Kierkegaard (1813–55), who likens the biblical message to a letter from one's lover. We are existentially involved or the message does not reach us. Karl Barth's *Commentary on Romans* lifted up the subjective encounter with the Word of God and challenged the objectivism of the liberal scholarship of his day, while Rudolf Bultmann stressed the existential encounter with the text and the role of the reader's "preunderstanding" in addressing the text. Truth is understood as event and process in which the subject is involved, with revelation *occurring* rather than simply being identified with the text. The text, in the language of Gerhard Ebeling, becomes a "word-event."

The work of critical theorists such as Hans-Georg Gadamer, Jürgen Habermas, and Paul Ricoeur has also been influential for contemporary theologians in their approach to the biblical text. Gadamer stresses the "enculturation" of biblical readers, which in turn shapes one's preunderstanding in approaching the Bible. He proposes the model of "conversation" as a means of getting into the text, a process of question and answer in which the cultural horizons of text and reader are joined or "fused" so that a meaningful encounter takes place. It involves interpretation, giving rise to new knowledge and insight made possible in the fusion of cultures. While historical critical work is essential in order to avoid forcing the texts of an alien culture onto our own, it is but one part of the process that makes possible a genuine conversation with the text.[10]

To its critics, postmodern theory often appears to accentuate the reader-centered dimension beyond its necessary role in *appropriating* truth to an active role in truth for the reader. This results in the past (text) being lost in the reader's present, threatening the sense of historical continuity that has entered into and shaped our contemporary context and self-understanding. This disjunction between past and present would appear to pose a greater threat to the church's Bible than historical criticism. The biblical critic at least takes the text seriously as a source of objective information that holds the church accountable. Determining "what the Bible says" is not only a legitimate but a necessary enterprise. Postmodern hermeneutics, as we have seen, questions whether we can regard the text as conveying any determinate meaning at all, thus making the reader rather than the text the critical source for arriving at what the text means. "No meaning is already 'there' in a text, or at least 'there' in some objectivist sense, apart from a horizon of expectations brought to a text by the reader."[11] The reader plays the critical role, not simply in interpretation but "even in the birth of meaning."

A reader-oriented criticism thus prefers to read the text as a final product rather than attempting to pursue the process by which the text came into being. "Let the text speak for itself" in its encounter with the reader, rather than getting involved in a dubious quest for an original meaning. There is no final determination of the truth for us to make; there is no one meaning that remains to be uncovered. This viewpoint raises serious questions about the attempt to approach the text in an objective, disinterested manner, because it sees every such attempt as prone to overlook its own determining assumptions that enter into the "truth" at which one arrives. Thus the whole program of historical criticism is seen as fundamentally compromised, because the critic's own set of beliefs and commitments color and shape the results of one's critical investigations.

One positive result of this shift to the reader is the challenge to historical critics to be more self-critical about the supposed objectivity they bring to the text. This does not imply that all biblical critics are seriously lacking in bringing a self-critical perspective to their work, but at the same time there has been an implicit confidence in the assumptions of critical methodologies that ought not be taken for granted. Critics represent a tradition of interpretation that assumes the validity of certain concepts and models; they operate within a framework of meaning (what Peter Berger has called a "plausibility structure") that influences their understanding of the text, giving rise to particular interpretations that fit within the limiting parameters of what they regard as plausible. There is also the illusion in our contemporary outlook that we have put the worlds of superstition and false assumptions behind us as we attain scientific and rational objectivity. This leaves us oblivious to the blind spots and distorted perspectives we harbor. It reflects the basic human problem of thinking we are the open-minded explorers of reality, "that the real questions are the ones we formulate and put to the universe, and that our minds have a sovereign freedom to explore a reality waiting to be discovered."[12]

Reservations about seeking an original or definitive meaning in a text are also encouraged by the profusion of meanings and interpretations that scholars will find in the same text. This would indicate that establishing an "objective," final answer to the meaning of these ancient texts is often a problematic exercise. One dimension of the problem is indicated in Edgar McKnight's observation that the historical critic will typically work with the belief that the most original sources of the data concerning the history of Israel and of Jesus provide the authentic meaning, while any development of the tradition (whether within Scripture or beyond) is seen "as a progressive falsification of the data, which must be discounted." A reader response view sees it differently: "Sense was made of the 'events' of Israel and Jesus Christ by succeeding generations so that their meaning and significance were extended and made more available in the later tradition."[13] The issue becomes the proper use of historical imagination, or looking for the *meaning* of the text in its widest sense. Thus the Christian necessarily looks at the work of the historical critic with a sense of ambivalence: It cannot only protect the church from irresponsible uses of the text, but also prevent the church from seeing the larger dimensions of meaning embedded in the text.

In contrast, a reader-oriented theory can appreciate and even celebrate the unlimited potential meanings of the text. We recognize that readers in every instance bring their own life-experience and self-understanding, their particular religious and cultural traditions, and their own purposes and goals to the reading of the text, all of which enter into what is found there. Within particular contexts in which biblical reading and interpretation occur, one can even glory in the multitude of meanings texts are capable of generating when approached by a variety of readers. Amid the tremendous diversity of scriptural material, including poetry, parables, and stories, imaginative minds are capable of running in most every direction in their engagement with the text.

The justifiable concern in biblical interpretation, however, is not simply to let the mind run where it will in its encounter with the text, but to bring its interpretation into conversation with the tradition of the faith community and allow itself to be informed by that tradition. In this way the agendas and mind-sets that individuals bring to the text can be addressed and possibly challenged and judged by the wisdom of the tradition.

> A responsible hermeneutics will do something to prevent a shallow skimming from the text of the preformed viewpoints of the interpreter, now deceptively and dangerously clothed in the vestments of the authority of the text. Since in actual practice communities have sometimes shaped their lives and beliefs on the basis of what purport to be "biblical" truth but in fact have turned out to be bizarre distortions of it, biblical hermeneutics is of necessity a more anxious, more cautious, discipline than literary theory.[14]

This is an important point, well worth emphasizing. By its very nature, biblical hermeneutics demands close attention to the text because the life of a faith community is inspired and nurtured by the Bible. We can recognize that what each of us brings to the text has a bearing on what we receive from it, but for the sake of the community, it is essential that the text not disappear in a jumble of self-interested interpretations. There is an inevitable tension here that requires of the responsible reader a willingness to balance what she believes the author is saying with what other members of the community believe the author is saying. Often a consensus is reached, but the more rich with meaning and allusion the text, the more ambiguous or obscure, the greater the variety in meanings that will be perceived in it.

One can justifiably conclude that the significance of reader-oriented theory is not unrelated to the character of the text. The more elusive the text's meaning, the more weight is exerted by the reader's perspective and the greater the variety of meaning that will be found in it. It is the ambiguity in the text—or in any art form that invites our reflection—that inspires creative interpretation. But the text and the interpretive tradition surrounding and mediating the text provide a center of orientation that the responsible interpreter of Scripture does not ignore. Thus reader-oriented theory is no alternative to biblical critical work as such;

careful exegesis with the tools of the critical tradition, while subject to misuse, are indispensable to a responsible handling of the text. In using the critical tools of research, the exegete takes into consideration the historical distance of the text, but also presumes that this distance does not in itself preclude every attempt to establish a responsible grasp of the context and intent of the writer. An appropriately self-critical scholar, subjecting his own assumptions and predilections to scrutiny and evaluation, is equipped to make a significant contribution to our understanding of the text.

At the same time, a discriminating approach to reader response criticism can be helpful in encouraging a fresh expectation in the church's approach to the biblical text. Recognizing the inevitably contextual nature of our approach to Scripture should help the church to maintain greater openness to what it may find and profit from in its reading of Scripture. The tradition should not automatically reign supreme in determining the church's response to the text, for the church's experience in the present moment may be decisive in shaping a responsible approach to it. The church is always "in the middle," listening to both the past and the present, and knowing that it cannot listen uncritically to either. This interplay between past and present has obvious implications for the ethical tradition of the church; it is not a stable, unchanging tradition but a dynamic one that is in continual interaction with a changing cultural environment.

These observations lead one to conclude that historical criticism and reader-oriented theory should be interpreted in ways that make them complementary to each other rather than exclusive alternatives. This viewpoint means both a rejection of absolutist assumptions harbored by advocates of either approach and recognition of the important moment of the hermeneutical process captured by each. The one recognizes the importance of the historical context of the text and seeks to capture it to the extent this is possible; the other recognizes the inherently creative moment formed by the contemporary context, providing a fresh and meaningful appropriation of the text and challenging every attempt simply to replicate historical meaning rather than to interpret it in light of our own times. Where new understandings of the text challenge and conflict with earlier interpretations, the fitting response of the church is not automatically to reject them but to encourage a continuing process of listening to the text and engaging in dialogue.

An appropriate term for capturing the process we are describing here is *recontextualization*, a term used by Darrell Jodock in his *The Church's Bible*.[15] It involves the recognition of historical distance, or the significant difference between the governing assumptions of social and cultural life in the original context of the text compared to our own. At the same time that distance calls forth a disciplined commitment to understand those assumptions as a framework of meaning in comparison with our own beliefs, so that a correlation of setting and impact between then and now is achieved. That possibility is enhanced where there is an empathetic openness to the text, a resonance between the people of faith at that time and our own time, a listening to the Spirit that guides the church in its response to the biblical message. This kind of response occurs where there is faith in the biblical message, which means that the church as the community of faith is the indispensable setting for grasping "what the Bible says"; it is where recontextualization occurs as a natural and necessary task because of the impact of the text on the believing community. The essential role of the faith community in understanding the message of Scripture and recognizing its authority merits further exploration.

THE CHURCH AND BIBLICAL AUTHORITY

As noted previously, much of the current criticism of the historical critical method castigates the method as such instead of exercising a more discriminating critique. It tends to polarize the world of scholarship and the church, arguing that scholars are guilty of removing the authority of the Bible and rendering it useless to the church. An example of such an attitude is seen in the following quote:

> What needs to be reclaimed for the church is the Bible as authoritative Scripture....The methods of critical reason have tended to take over the entire operation of biblical interpretation, marginalizing the faith of the church and dissolving the unity of the Bible as a whole into a multiplicity of unrelated fragments. The academy has replaced the church as the home of biblical interpretation.[16]

While the destructiveness of an unwarranted historical skepticism in the hands of particular scholars, or the dangers of a false confidence in finding a clear and definite meaning in the text, cannot be denied, equal if not greater danger lies in castigating historical scholarship as such and creating a polarizing antagonism between the scholarly guild and the community of faith. A better response is one that recognizes the limitations of critical work rather than either repudiating it or absolutizing it. A more discriminating approach is preferable, one inviting a meaningful engagement between the church's theologians and biblical scholars.[17]

The fact that the message and authority of Scripture are appropriately understood from within the believing community finds support in postmodern thought. The community of faith as the interpreter of Bible and tradition assumes greater importance when significant cultural distance is recognized between reader and text. If we acknowledge the appropriate role of biblical scholarship in understanding the text, as well as the inevitable role of interpretation, then a peculiar responsibility is thrust upon the church in understanding and mediating the message of Scripture: the church nurtures competent scholars who will pursue the meaning of the biblical message in a way that is accountable both to the church and to the scholarly guild. As persons of faith, they will, in the language of H. Richard Niebuhr, perceive both the "internal" as well as the "external" history of Scripture, and be capable of participating in it as well as critically studying it.[18] Of considerable importance to the church is the fact that scholars of faith, as previously noted, have used the tools of historical critical scholarship to challenge the results of excessively skeptical critics. The church's scholars are also expected to conduct their biblical investigations in a self-critical manner, acknowledging the limitations of their discipline. They will recognize their dependence on the church's tradition as well as the canons of scholarship. They will acknowledge that their work neither destroys nor establishes faith, but where faith is present the Bible is recognized as a living witness rather than simply a historical document.

The focus on the church's interpretive role in relation to Scripture also has implications for the doctrine of biblical inspiration. Traditionally the authority of Scripture has been rooted in its being divinely inspired; as was noted earlier, fundamentalists argue that inspiration establishes the Bible's authority by guaranteeing an inerrant text. Mainline Protestantism, while rejecting inerrancy, has taken seriously the fact that the Bible affirms its inspiration by God (2 Tim. 3:16; 2 Pet. 1:21), with varying ways of interpreting what that means in regard to the Bible's authority. The discussion typically has made inspiration the means of establishing biblical authority, locating the presence of God in the book in contrast to an often wayward and fallible church. The focal point is an all-sufficient, if not perfect, text located in the distant past, with inspiration typically identified with the writers who are moved by God's presence in their lives to produce a body of material whose content testifies to its authenticity as the Word of God. The counter argument to this viewpoint would not limit inspiration to the book as a historical object, but would expand its meaning to include the ongoing and renewing presence of the Spirit of God that is experienced in the continuing dialogue between church and Scripture.

Here once again, a proper balance is needed to avoid a dichotomy between past and present in the form of an ancient Scripture and the contemporary church. The Bible is not just like any treasured book in the life of the church, of which there are many. It has a unique role because of its theological content, its constituting function in the life of the church, and its continuing impact among the faithful. It is understandably regarded by the believing community as the written form of the "Word of God." Not any formal qualities as such, but its substantive role within the church makes the Bible indispensable, an enduring resource in shaping the identity of the church. Properly understood, divine inspiration should embrace this whole dimension of the church's life, from inspired writers to the receiving community of believers. Faith recognizes the activity of the Spirit of God in these events, and that is the proper focus of divine inspiration.[19] That truth also broadens the notion of inspiration beyond the realm of the church's beginnings to embrace all of the faith-determined actions of the church in responsible engagement with the world.[20]

As Bruce Birch and Larry Rasmussen point out, understanding inspiration in terms of God who is active in the world serves to bring out the common ground between exegesis and ethics. "Both seek to discern the disclosure of God's will for the people of faith."[21] Exegesis does it by interpreting the biblical record, while Christian ethics attempts to read the signs of God's activity in the present world, turning to Scripture and tradition as resources in developing a faithful response. Thus the one moves from past to present and the other from present to past, but exegesis and ethics meet in the life of the church they serve. It follows that Bible and praxis must not be compartmentalized in the church's life, for they need each other and serve each other in the quest for faithful biblical interpretation and faithful discipleship in today's world.

Our rejection of formal characteristics of the Bible (such as inerrancy and perfection in all of its content, from historical to scientific to religious assertions) means that the concept of canon assumes all the more importance in the church's understanding of Scripture. Coming from the Greek word meaning *rule*, the canon denotes the books of the Bible as "the area in which the church hears the word of God," thus assuming an authoritative status for the faith community and a normative body of tradition.[22] In stressing the importance of the canon as a hermeneutical principle, the biblical theologian Brevard Childs has challenged what he sees as the failure of historical criticism to present a unifying, theological understanding of what the Bible is about. As witness to God's activity in the life of the church, the Bible cannot be imprisoned in the historical past, but brings the presence of God into the life of his people today. In acknowledging the Bible as canon, the church recognizes it as the rule or norm of the community's faith, bearing witness to the impact of the Bible on the life of the community.

While this concept of the canon has an appropriate use in the church and ought not be jettisoned (as some have argued in recent times), we must avoid interpretations that give it an authoritarian cast. The Bible's authority to the church is not as an external rule or norm that coerces one's agreement without honest engagement. Our emphasis on the continuing dialogue of the people of faith with their tradition excludes this understanding. At times the church may see no relevance in some portions of Scripture, but the continuing dialogue leaves open the potential of all of Scripture to speak to the church. Thus there is a certain openness and adaptability inherent to our relation to Scripture, based not on a lack of loyalty or reverence toward it, but on the recognition that the biblical witness is not simply an end result; it is finding its fulfillment in interaction with believers.

With the biblical theologian Walter Brueggemann, I would maintain that the Bible as canon is "minimal but crucial." By minimal is meant that the canon is not a norm that definitively settles every doctrinal or moral dispute in the church; it cannot function effectively as a legal standard by which to decide every contentious issue. Yet the Bible is "crucial" as an identity-forming and identity-sustaining source for the church today, providing the authoritative tradition from which the church takes its inspiration. It is a formal norm, with its theological and ethical substance a continuing invitation to interpret and understand. We are tempted to arrive at final conclusions and carve them into rock, but we are jolted again and again into new and fruitful understandings. Brueggemann is particularly sensitive to the cultural currents of post-modern times, stressing the importance of the cultural context to the church's understanding of Scripture. He argues that the loss of objectivity and a sense of certitude in contemporary society constitutes an indelible mark on the psyche of the Christian as well as others, making the biblical canon appear more as a "field of authorized possibility" than a "field of certitude."[23] The situation is all the more volatile with voices from the margins of the church—women, minorities, the poor—threatening the hegemony of those at the center, pointing to the association of prevailing interpretations with ideological power. Our task today, says Brueggemann, is to enlarge the conversation, to listen to those at the margins and not dismiss them.

This understanding has implications for relating the Bible as canon to the moral life of the Christian community. Brevard Childs does not regard the canon as a solution to "the central problem" of biblical ethics: "the question to what extent God's will has been made clear and unequivocal for his people."[24] It remains the task of the community to discern the will of God in regard to the moral issues of the day. While the church appropriately recognizes a closed canon, this does not mean its content is no longer subject to interpretation and reunderstanding. This is an ecclesial task that admits no simple or easy "technique"; it involves the resources people of faith bring to this task in their desire to be faithful. Individual Christians hope to find in their faith communities a level of discernment and counsel that will bring Scripture and tradition to bear in authentic ways, enabling a faithful response to the ethical challenges they face.

I referred earlier to the emerging consensus that Christian ethics is best understood as an "ecclesial ethics," recognizing the definitive role of the believing community in fashioning the Christian's moral response.[25] The discussion of current attempts to determine "what the Bible says" reinforces that perspective. We know Scripture as part of a community, making illusory any attempt to claim a direct dependence on the Bible apart from the contemporary experience of the church and the manifold witness of its tradition. It is important to recognize, however, that this fact does not deny the peculiar role of the Bible for theology and ethics as a primary element of the tradition by which the church defines itself. That tradition is vital to the lives of the community members, both as a theological source for self-understanding and a moral source for the formation of the community.

While the emphasis in chapter 2 was that the church must be in continuing conversation with society, the corollary truth in this chapter is that the church must be in continuing conversation with its Scripture. The need of the former is relatively obvious, given the changing nature of church and society; the need of the latter has become increasingly evident in the dawning of postmodern consciousness with its critical appreciation of historical understanding and the role of interpretation. While recognizing this truth, the point to be stressed in approaching Scripture is that there is an objective text to be interpreted with its own peculiar history. It may give rise to a variety of interpretations, but not without laying claim on the Christian interpreter to unfold its meaning as a book of faith that speaks to a faithful community. To do this responsibly will entail a necessary, if limited, role for historical critical work. While tending to such work does not insure an adequate theological interpretation of the text, ignoring it may seriously skew that interpretation.

An indelible insight from the discussion of what Scripture is saying to us is the necessity of maintaining in proper balance the objective reality of the biblical text and its importance to the church as text, and at the same time the necessarily contextual and dynamic character of the church's appropriation and interpretation of the biblical text. This balance is not achieved by the application of a rule that results in an obvious answer or direction we should follow. It involves, rather, questions of judgment that demand a strong sense of the church's identity and of its mission and responsibility to the world. An analogy can be drawn to the task discussed in chapter 1 in relating moral standards to the concrete circumstances of life. In both cases we are challenged by the task of relating a heritage and tradition to the historical context in which we stand and which in turn exerts its impact on what we perceive to be the responsible relating of past to present.

Our discussion to this point has affirmed the dynamic, "living" character of the church's involvement with its heritage. The church is not simply the recipient of a tradition but participates in it and seeks to embody it for our times, making its contribution to that tradition for times to come. Protestant Christianity rightly affirms the primacy of the Bible, compelling its continuing conversation with it. This conversation requires a careful listening to Scripture, but that listening takes place with "ears"—or minds and hearts—that bring to bear the concerns and perspectives of the church's own cultural and social world. In this process, the moral issues of the time stimulate new perspectives in understanding what Scripture and tradition have to say in relation to those issues. This process constitutes a hermeneutical circle, in which an authoritative Scripture is dependent on the community of believers from past to present in interpreting and applying that authority. This necessitates a prayerful and open approach in every age in listening to "what the Bible says." The next chapter will address more specifically the ethical material in Scripture as I attempt to spell out its responsible use and application by the church today.

4

THE ETHICAL CONTENT
AND AUTHORITY OF
THE BIBLE

No area of biblical interpretation has likely caused more confusion than the attempt to find biblical warrants for controversial moral positions. Throughout modern history in the West, the more important the issue to the general welfare of the populace, the more necessary it has been for interpreters to find biblical support for their positions. In seventeenth-century France, Bishop Bossuet's *Politics Drawn from the Very Words of Scripture* gave a spirited defense of the divine right of kings on the basis of Romans 13 and a variety of Old Testament passages. "The title of christ is given to kings, and everywhere they are seen to be called christs, or the anointed of the Lord."[1] A few years later, John Locke in England turned to the Bible to find arguments with which to refute Bishop Bossuet and support the Glorious Revolution of 1688. It was a tempestuous, revolutionary century where deeply controversial issues compelled a religious response. Locke's contemporary John Hales was moved to comment, "It is no hard thing for a man that hath wit, and is strongly possessed of an opinion, and resolute to maintain it, to find some place of Scripture which by good handling will be wooed to cast a favourable countenance upon it."[2]

In American history the Civil War poses a notable example of contradictory appeals to Scripture on the part of abolitionists in the North and clergy in the South, the latter often waxing eloquent about the divinely ordained order of Confederate society in which blacks were destined to serve whites.[3] Perhaps more than any other instance, this use of the Bible on both sides of the slavery issue has generated skepticism about attempts to find scriptural support for one's particular moral or social viewpoint. As John Hales observed, one comes to the Bible with a strongly held view and massages selected passages in a way that elicits support for it.[4]

The discussion of the hermeneutical issue in the preceding chapter provides a context for understanding this problem. There is in fact no reference to the message of Scripture, whether theological or ethical, that does not involve interpretation. The problem in arriving at a consensus concerning biblical authority is due to the prior problem of disagreement over how to interpret Scripture in the first place.[5] As Christians we bring our moral and social issues to Scripture, together with deeply held convictions about them that have been shaped by a variety of influences from within the culture, including the ethos of our churches. From within this context we then draw our conclusions as to how the message of Scripture should be understood and applied, and where we disagree, the issue of scriptural authority becomes important. The inevitable reliance on an interpretive framework does not immediately disqualify every use of Scripture as hopelessly biased or irrelevant to what the text actually says. It does, however, point us to the dialogical character of our use of Scripture, compelling self-awareness concerning the assumptions we bring to the text and recognizing that what we receive from it reflects the cultural orientation and the questions and concerns—the particular agenda—that we bring to it. In this situation the task of the church is not only to be in continuing conversation with Scripture, but to maintain a trustworthy theology of the Word that will assist the faithful in a responsible use of Scripture that avoids the false expectations commonly brought to it.

The distinction between biblical ethics and Christian ethics may not be all that apparent at this point. The fact that we bring an interpretive framework to Scripture means that we tend to give its ethical content a "Christian reading." This can lead one to the false conclusion that biblical ethics and Christian ethics are one and the same. Biblical ethics involves the uncovering of all the ethical content of the Bible with the purpose of determining, in all of its variety, what it meant for the believing community of that time. It is essentially a historical task, involving the tools of historical scholarship as well as theological and ethical interpretation. One may or may not conclude that biblical ethics bears a fundamental unity, or that it conveys at least a polyphonic rather than cacophonic ethical message. As a historical task, spelling out a biblical ethics will involve more attention to differences and disparities in the material, and careful attention to the assumptions one brings to any synthetic interpretation one might make. When one turns to Christian ethics, one is more interested in finding a coherent ethical message in Scripture that reflects the Christian conviction as to what the Bible is really about, or what its organizing center is. On the basis of this conclusion, one prioritizes the relative importance of the various strains that constitute the Bible's ethical content and relates this material in a coherent fashion for the contemporary Christian community. Thus Christian ethics claims a continuity with biblical ethics but has its eye on the challenges to discipleship in the contemporary world. Its purpose is to present a biblically inspired ethics with the necessary coherence and cogency that effectively brings it into conversation with the culture of our time.

TYPES OF ETHICAL CONTENT IN SCRIPTURE

In the previous chapters, the intent has been to sketch the historical and cultural setting in which we are raising the question of biblical authority and Christian ethics. While the discussion has included the *hermeneutical* issue, or the task of interpreting the content of a document far removed from us in time and cultural distance, the focus now turns to the *descriptive* task in which I spell out (in admittedly cursory fashion) the ethical content of Scripture. Inherent to describing this content is the *synthetic* issue to which I have already alluded, asking the question whether there is an internal consistency or coherence in the ethical content of Scripture.[6]

To describe the ethical content of the Bible is immediately to be reminded that it is neither a textbook on morality nor a systematic treatment of the topic. Its moral or ethical content is embedded in a variety of writings, so that to describe that content is at the same time a literary, historical, and theological task. One is describing both ethical content and mode of ethical reasoning in arriving at that content. One might proceed in different ways, but the following types or models, while not exhaustive, do capture most of the Bible's ethical message:

1. Law or commandments, embodied in codes or related hortatory material.
2. Paradigms or models of conduct, found in narrative material.
3. Principles or ideals, expressed primarily in a variety of teaching material.

    4. Exhortations and imperatives, based on theological affirmations
    concerning the gospel of Jesus Christ.[7]

Each of these categories or types will be elaborated on in the paragraphs
that follow:

    1. *The law or commandments.* The major concern of this type is to
provide clear and definite boundaries for moral conduct. The focus is on
avoiding immoral and destructive behavior, a legitimate concern for any
human community, and yet one that is particularly vulnerable to legalism. The ethical imperative is not expressed in ideals or personal models
of conduct that inspire emulation, but in rules of prohibition that maintain boundaries and seek to direct good works within clearly structured
channels of human activity. This type is clearly impressed with human
waywardness, seeing the primary ethical requirement as one that curbs
and limits our disobedience. The Bible as a holy book, bearing the signa-
ture of a holy God, is the primary source for insuring that we live in holiness and righteousness.

    This type of ethical material is often embraced by Christians today in
a way that would make of Scripture a kind of moral handbook, with little attention given to the impact of historical context on the laws and
rules that appear in the Bible. The major interest is in establishing
absolute and universal laws for moral behavior as clear and definite
direction for the believing community as well as for the larger society.
The Old Testament figures prominently in this type, with the more general prohibitions of the Ten Commandments providing the basic framework. At the same time, all rules of the Israelite community are
potentially of interest. Obviously much of the Holiness Code in Leviticus
19–26 is irrelevant to Christian relationships, and yet even that material
offers certain regulations that most people would regard as God's law for
today, such as prohibitions of incest and homosexual activity (Lev. 20).

    Laws and commandments can quite easily be treated in oracular fash-
ion, with direct applications being made to contemporary situations. It
often involves the search for "chapter and verse" to prove one's moral
point. Nonetheless, to the extent that a command from Scripture does in
fact capture the current situation, compelling a "moment of truth" for
the individual involved, it clearly carries out an important moral function. For that to happen with any consistency, however, a process of
moral discernment and understanding is occurring in the application of
the text. Many who are intent on keeping a strong prescriptive character
to the Bible will acknowledge that its rules and laws cannot be applied in
codebook fashion but should be understood as underlying principles

that are sufficiently flexible to be applied to changing situations.[8] In none of these types can the Bible be treated as an "external" body of texts, apart from that engagement that tends to the original context of the text as well as to the dynamics of the contemporary situation to which it is being applied.

2. *Paradigms or models of conduct.* This type conveys the essentially narrative character of Scripture, finding in the stories about God's people those models of conduct that are intended for our edification and emulation. The assumption is that the moral life is most effectively communicated through stories that stimulate the moral imagination. One is morally engaged by stories that dramatize the challenges of responsible moral choice, portraying resistance to temptation, holding to one's convictions, and maintaining a moral course in the midst of the concrete activity of everyday life. Thus the Bible provides "flesh and blood" examples that are much more inspiring to the moral life than the distillations expressed in moral laws. Lifting up biblical models accentuates the moral imagination in which we relate our own situation to that portrayed in biblical stories and see ourselves in light of those stories.

With this use of the moral imagination the distance of time, place, and culture is no serious obstacle to understanding, for example, the story of Joseph and Potiphar's wife (Gen. 39), of David before the prophet Nathan (2 Sam. 12), of Ruth and Naomi (Ruth 1), of Matthew the tax collector turned disciple (Matt. 9), of Jesus in conflict with the Pharisees (Mark 7). By juxtaposing these stories with our own circumstances, we experience the same moral realities of temptation, personal integrity, judgment, loyalty, grace, hypocrisy, and faithful discipleship. Paul himself lifts up exemplary lives of faith from the Old Testament for believers of his time to consider, such as Abraham (Gal. 3:6-10); or, in a negative vein, he points to the Israelites in the wilderness as a warning "not to desire evil as they did" (1 Cor. 10:6). The primary model for Paul, of course, is Jesus himself, who models servanthood and obedience even "unto death" (Phil. 2:5-8).

Particularly important to moral education are those narrative portions of Scripture that take the form of stories and parables told with the specific purpose of conveying a truth related to the life of faith and to human relationships generally. Jesus was the master storyteller, lifting up themes inherent to human life and experience to which people respond from all times and places. The Good Samaritan (Luke 10) and the Pharisee and the Tax Collector (Luke 18), for example, lift up the challenge to love one's neighbor and to look critically at one's own moral pretensions,

themes that get to the core of human relationships and convey a fundamental moral demand. Such parables have contributed substantially in
forming a Christian ethos.

3. *Principles or ideals.* This type covers a variety of moral teaching
stretching from the Old Testament prophetic and wisdom literature to
the New Testament teaching of Jesus and Paul. The prophetic literature
is lifted up for its strong emphasis on social justice and its challenge to
those in positions of influence and power. The wisdom tradition, in contrast, emphasizes personal virtues with concrete reference to everyday
relationships. The books of Proverbs and Ecclesiastes in the Old Testament and James in the New contain a variety of wisdom sayings, usually
reflecting the moral wisdom of the larger society. This is also seen in the
Household Codes *(Haustafeln)* in Pauline letters (Col. 3:18—4:1; Eph.
5:21—6:9), which focus on order in the family and social stability.

Jesus' teaching includes an element of moral wisdom (Matt. 6:19-34;
Luke 12:16-21), but even here his teaching of the kingdom of God incor-
porates new meaning and gives a future direction to it. Allen Verhey
characterizes Jesus' moral teaching as "eschatological wisdom," shaped
by the coming kingdom and reversing the older wisdom tradition,
breaking through conventional mores with the radical expectations of
self-giving love.[9] The particular distinctiveness and power of Jesus'
moral teaching is captured in his emphasis on love (agape) that
embraces even one's enemies (Matt. 5:43-48; Luke 6:27-36). This love
expresses an ideal of self-giving that is willing to go out of its way to
serve the neighbor in need. It presumes the experience of judgment and
grace created by the recognition of God's presence in the proclamation
of Jesus himself.

Pauline moral exhortation usually arises from situations or incidents
related to the congregations he founded. His teaching at times, as in the
Household Codes, will reflect the ethos of the surrounding culture. This
creates a tension in Paul's ethics between his exhortations reflecting the
hierarchical and patriarchal nature of his society, and those exhortations
reflecting the radically egalitarian message of the Gospel (Gal. 3:28).
Some would emphasize the contrast in this polarity, while others note
the modifying impact of Paul's gospel ethics upon the cultural mores to
which he appeals.[10]

Those who stress the importance of this type of ethical material will
recognize the variety and even disparity in biblical moral teaching, but
rather than attempting to forge some kind of uniformity will generally
take a contextual approach that helps one to understand differences in
the moral perspectives one finds there. The teaching of Jesus, however, is

recognized as definitive, and where there appear to be contradictory teachings, his own perspective provides the appropriate direction. His emphasis on the coming kingdom of God conveys clear and powerful imperatives concerning the love of neighbor and reaching out to the poor and vulnerable of society (Matt. 25). While the decisive impact of eschatology in his teaching is typically seen as a strength in contributing to the urgency and radical power of the love imperative, it has also raised questions about the applicability of Jesus' moral teaching for our own time.[11]

4. *Exhortations and imperatives.* This type is exemplified in much Pauline moral discourse, in which the major motifs of Christian faith that result from reflection on the biblical story give rise to ethical imperatives for the Christian life. The decisive element in Paul's ethical teaching is the deed of God in Christ Jesus that stands at the beginning of the believer's life and provides the basis for a distinctively Christian ethics. The cross and resurrection become central images in capturing the love of God and in presenting the example of Jesus for his disciples to follow. These imperatives are drawn at both the individual and corporate level of Christian relationships, beginning with the indicative, which refers to what God has done, and ending with the imperative, which refers to the appropriate response of faith. This movement from the indicative to the imperative gives the formal structure to this particular dimension of New Testament ethics.[12] Major motifs such as the Incarnation, the cross, redemption, resurrection, the sacraments, and the eschaton are lifted up as bearing distinctive moral imperatives for Christian life in God's world. For example, the Incarnation portrays humility and servanthood that believers are to follow (Phil. 2:1-11); in the cross, our old selves have been crucified with Christ so that "we might no longer be enslaved to sin" (Romans 6:5-7); the baptized have been united with Christ in his death and consequently have died to sin and are called to walk in "newness of life" (Romans 6:1-4); and the coming of Christ in the end time inspires hope and persistence under oppression (Revelation 3:11-12).

While the ecclesial tradition in which one has been nurtured bears an influence in the understanding and application of each of these types of ethical content, its influence is especially obvious in this particular type as one moves from theological convictions to one's moral stance. Thus one who identifies with the Mennonite tradition, for example, will conclude that a stance of nonviolence or pacifism is inherent to the Gospel as well as the teachings of Jesus, while one raised in an evangelical or mainline denomination typically will be swayed by arguments justifying the use of force under certain conditions. In the Pentecostal tradition, there is likely to be more emphasis on apocalyptic literature, with a corresponding accent on the moral purity of the congregation as it waits for the Lord's coming. We are reminded of the point made in the previous chapter that interpreting Scripture is a two-way street, bringing our convictions—shaped by a variety of sources, including Scripture and our church traditions—into play with the text.

In delineating the above types, one has to be impressed with the variety and diversity of the ethical content of Scripture. Rather than lifting up one or two types as exclusive criteria in determining the nature of biblical ethics, one can argue that in fact each of these types has a contribution to make in presenting the richness of the Bible's ethical content. It follows that each part of the canon should be allowed to speak and to be heard for its particular contribution to this richness and depth of content. It all reflects the variety of contexts in which one encounters the ethical demand, as well as the variety of moral vision that is present in Scripture. One's choice of a particular type as primary will reflect one's synthetic conclusions in arriving at the distinctive moral vision of Scripture in light of its theological message. Whatever the type, however, it is essential that one keeps in mind the context of each biblical text, for without this awareness the meaning one gleans from any particular text can be fundamentally skewed.[13]

As the ethical content of Scripture is examined more specifically, the primary focus understandably becomes the New Testament in light of our Christian identity. This does not mean, however, that the New Testament stands in isolation from the Old Testament. The New Testament cannot be understood apart from the total story, beginning with the creation accounts, continuing with the story of Israel and the development of Judaism, from which Jesus and the Christian gospel emerged. Nonetheless, Jesus for Christians represents a new beginning with a new life marked by faith in the risen Lord, developments that in turn have given the distinctive stamp and character to Christian ethics. Thus our focus on biblical ethics becomes New Testament ethics, but a New Testament enhanced by ethical themes from the Old Testament that are continuous with the Christian gospel and that consequently will continue to play a role in the discussion.

THE DISTINCTIVE ETHICAL CONTENT OF SCRIPTURE

I believe we can summarize the distinctive ethical content of the New Testament in a number of salient concepts that capture the major motifs that emerge from the above discussion. The fourth type we delineated is most promising as a framework by which to proceed, for it begins with the distinctive theological message of Scripture as a basis for its ethics. For the Christian this renders without question a Christologically oriented ethics because the distinguishing message of Scripture for Christian faith is the revelation of God in Jesus Christ. It means that warrants for ethical action are theological, rooted in God's deed and summoning loyalty to Christ. These distinctive Christian imperatives rooted in the biblical narrative also turn us to the eschaton, which becomes a source of promise and hope for the moral life. While the focus here is Jesus Christ as God's deed rather than Jesus as a moral teacher, his identity as God's Word gives special importance to his teachings. Thus the third model of ethical teachings takes on particular significance, as does the second model of narrative example. Of least relevance in expressing the distinctiveness of biblical ethics is the first model of rules and laws, and yet that model has its place in recognizing the fallen character of human beings and the need of protecting the community from destructive actions. Law and gospel together are continuously pertinent both to the human condition and to the challenges of the moral life.

A recent attempt of extraordinary scope and erudition to present a New Testament ethics is that of Richard B. Hays, who argues that the unity of New Testament ethics is to be found in certain key images that emerge from the text. He maintains those focal images to be three in number: Community, Cross, and New Creation.[14] Because no one image "can adequately encapsulate the complex unity of the New Testament texts," he finds this cluster or sequence of images to be more satisfactory as a matrix in which that unity can be recognized. The church is the countercultural, covenant community to whom the imperatives of the New Testament are addressed; the cross of Jesus Christ is the paradigm for expressing the community's faithfulness to God in this world; and the new creation expresses the eschatological dialectic that runs throughout the Christian message. That dialectic expresses the new life in Christ as present and yet not present in its fullness because Christians live in that "now but not yet" time between the resurrection and the fulfillment of existence in the parousia.

Hays argues that the concept of agapeic love and of liberation, both of which have been used extensively to capture the ethical message of the New Testament, are inadequate for that purpose. In regard to love, he cites Mark, Acts, Hebrews, and Revelation as four major New Testament witnesses that resist the attempt to capture their moral visions with that term. His use of the term *image* also militates against the use of love because that word is actually an interpretation of an image rather than an image itself. Finally, Hays sees more of a hermeneutical problem today in the use of love, given its debasement in contemporary culture; it has become "a cover for all manner of vapid self-indulgence."[15] The appropriate image for love is the cross, which expresses the suffering inherent to genuine love that is willing to sacrifice and go the second mile. Hays's argument carries substantial weight, not least in his point that a cluster of images is more successful in capturing the complexity of New Testament ethics than any single one. One can certainly maintain, however, that agapeic love is so central and so prominent both to the teaching of Jesus and to Paul's and John's formulation of the meaning of the gospel, that it carries a solid claim to inclusion in any expression of the distinctive content of biblical ethics. If we move from image to concept, which is a quite natural transition as one moves from biblical ethics to Christian ethics, one can translate the meaning of New Testament ethics with another cluster of terms: *freedom, agapeic love,* and *responsibility.* These concepts overlap in part with Hays's images, as we might expect, and it is important to emphasize that as abstractions used in a multitude of secular contexts, these terms within the Christian context need to be clearly defined in light of the biblical message.

Freedom signifies the essential gift of the gospel that emerges from the profound experience of *repentance* and *forgiveness,* terms that are central to the new life in Christ. Forgiveness brings liberation from bondage to sin and guilt; it stands at the beginning of life in Christ or the life of the Spirit—what Hays would associate with the image of new creation. This freedom *from* the "old Adam" within us opens up new possibilities of commitment and service, or freedom *for* a larger life made possible by the liberating message of the Gospel. Thus it is a freedom peculiar to life "in Christ," made possible by the grace of God, which invites the sinner into a new relationship with God, oneself, and the neighbor, based on the empowering acceptance of the sinner by a gracious God. *Agapeic love* is the imperative inherent to the new life of freedom in Christ, calling us out of ourselves and directing us to our neighbor. This self-giving love defines the meaning of life in terms of service, giving a cruciform character to the faithful life (thus corresponding with Hays's image of the cross). Agapeic love is inclusive, ignoring human distinctions such as class and race and accepting the neighbor as a brother or sister in Christ. The third concept, *responsibility,* is a term that recognizes the life of faith as *response* to what God is doing in the world. It also expresses our continuing accountability to the law of God and our freedom to express that accountability as children of God, blessed with gifts of faith and discernment. It recognizes the whole realm of relationships in which we live in both the human and natural worlds, in both individual and corporate relationships, as a theater in which we are responsible, ultimately, to God.

Hays's use of community is significant as the context for our receiving the ethical message of Scripture, a point emphasized by many contemporary Christian ethicists and often expressed in these pages as well. Christian ethics and the life of discipleship is not a possibility for isolated individuals divorced from the believing community. It is not inappropriate, however, to caution that efforts to emphasize the ecclesial community ought not ignore the necessary polarity, tension, and interdependence involved between community and individual. These are natural polarities that must be defined in relation to each other. Both poles are integral to Christian ethics, resisting any definition that would simply subsume the one under the other. There is always the danger that one pole is emphasized at the expense of the other, a mistake that occurs with the frequency of a pendulum swing throughout our cultural history. While challenging an individualism run amok in contemporary culture, Christians must not be blind to the reality of individual responsibility for moral decision making, recognizing at the same time that individual identity is inextricably interwoven with community and culture. The ongoing challenge for the church is to guide, support, and sustain the individual within a self-consciously Christian community.

It is instructive to note the implications of biblical ethics for the post-modern, pluralist society discussed in the opening chapters. The life in Christ, which we have described in terms of freedom, agapeic love, and responsibility does not remove the Christian from the historical flux, providing a vantage point above history that can transcend the conditioned, relative character of historical existence. But from within history, life in Christ sees the meaning of history in terms of its future, culminating in the kingdom of God. The gospel of Jesus Christ turns history into a story of promise, orienting the believer toward the future in a spirit of expectation. Living in this "forward direction" that is appreciative of its past but based on trust in God's future, the Christian can live with a humble yet firm confidence in the lordship of Christ and be open to cultural pluralism and change rather than fearful of it.[16] Life that is lived "in Christ," or life under the guidance of the Spirit of God, is not chained to the past but is willing to be a creative participant in shaping the future.

THE ETHICAL AUTHORITY OF SCRIPTURE

The hermeneutical problem has impressed some biblical theologians to the extent that they see no purpose in turning to Scripture at all for ethical guidance, consequently denying the Bible's authority for the moral life. Jack T. Sanders is quite explicit about the futility of deriving an ethical position from Scripture, as in this oft-cited quotation:

> The ethical positions of the New Testament are the children of their own times and places, alien and foreign to this day and age. Amidst the ethical dilemmas which confront us, we are now at least relieved of the need or temptation to begin with Jesus, or the early church, or the New Testament, if we wish to develop coherent ethical positions. We are freed from bondage to that tradition, and we are able to propose, with the author of the Epistle of James, that tradition and precedent must not be allowed to stand in the way of what is humane and right.[17]

Sanders reflects a postmodern skepticism concerning the possibility of communication across temporal and cultural differences; biblical answers to contemporary issues prove "alien and foreign to this day and age." This viewpoint does highlight a genuine issue for any reference to the Bible in support of contemporary ethical positions, but ultimately it is too pessimistic, denying the possibility of responsible reference to the Bible's ethical content for Christians today.

Sanders's concern is often united with the argument raised by other biblical scholars whose study of the ethical content of Scripture has convinced them that there is no consistent ethical message to be found in the Bible. They see disparities and contradictions that appear to make impossible any reference even to an ethics of the New Testament, to say nothing of an ethics of the whole Bible. This diversity in the Bible's ethical content has been emphasized recently by those scholars who have used tools of the social sciences to develop an ethnography of the early Christian community, focusing on the forms of culture within which the moral customs and sensibilities of Christians were shaped and took on meaning. Wayne Meeks, a prominent representative of this approach, draws the following conclusion:

> What the ethnographer of early Christianity finds is only a record of experimentation, of trial and error, of tradition creatively misread and innovation wedged craftily into the cracks of custom, of the radically new mixed up with the familiar and old, of disputes and confrontation, of fervent assertions of unity amid distressing signs of schism, of opposite points of view on fundamental matters, of dialectic and change....There has not ever been a purely Christian morality, unalloyed with the experience and traditions of others.[18]

It follows from Meeks's conclusions that any reference to a New Testament ethics involves creative selectivity in order to establish a consistency that is not present in the text. It becomes a matter of honesty in acknowl-edging the assumptions one brings to Scripture and the consequent direction one sees in the ethical content presented there.

Given the significant disagreement among scholars concerning the ethical content of Scripture, as well as other factors associated with post-modernity that have accentuated our perception of the historically con-ditioned character of Scripture, it is hardly surprising that voices are being raised today questioning whether the Bible can be regarded as a meaningful authority for the moral life. New Testament theologian Robin Scroggs is one such voice, arguing that it would be better to rec-ognize the Bible as the *foundational* document of Christianity rather than the authority for Christian faith and life. As the foundational docu-ment, the Bible is "absolutely indispensable" to knowing what Christian-ity is about and must be considered in any matter of importance coming before the Christian community, but in reality it does not serve as the final word.

> The question thus lies heavily upon us: Does the claim that the Bible has authority any longer make sense? If assessments about biblical faith and ethics are made from contemporary sensitivi-ties about what is right or wrong, *then it is our contemporary perspectives that are authoritative.* Where the Bible agrees with those sensitivities, it is invoked to support what one already knows to be correct. Where the Bible disagrees, it is relegated to its historical context and becomes something we have overcome in our struggle for the truth. This is, I would argue, how the Bible is in fact used *by both evangelicals and liberals.* What we need is a new understanding of the role of the Bible in the church today that acknowledges the actual reality of our situa-tion—an understanding that takes the Bible as a foundational document but not as authoritative, that is, an understanding that does not assume that the Bible determines all that we are to think and do.[19]

There are clearly legitimate issues that Scroggs and others raise on this matter, but it would be a mistake to give up the concept of scriptural authority, because too much would be lost. The Bible is indeed the foun-dational document, but that in itself does not recognize its contempo-rary significance for the Christian community, which believes and confesses that the witness of Scripture is a "living Word" through which the Spirit brings an authoritative message. Scroggs's argument is served by his definition of biblical authority in terms of "legal authority" that "determines all that we are to think and do." This is an understanding that imposes authority on the community. On the contrary, scriptural authority is recognized when its message brings faith and healing to the believing heart, and while its foundational character in the history of Christianity enhances the importance of biblical authority, it is not equivalent to it. Scroggs maintains that qualifications brought to the understanding of biblical authority have resulted in a piecemeal erosion of that authority, but it is more accurate to say that such qualifications are necessary in reaching an authentic understanding of biblical authority.

I have already noted the attempt of some Christians to resist what they perceive as erosions of biblical authority by claiming an *absolute* authority for Scripture through a theory of inerrancy that guarantees a perfect and complete expression of a divinely bestowed ethical message. This view encourages the use of the Bible as a transcendent codebook without reference to context, resulting in all kinds of misuse. It is a viewpoint that is also incommensurable with the understanding of biblical revelation and inspiration presented in these pages. A more qualified view is one that claims the *sufficiency* of Scripture as a source of moral direction, but this also raises problems, because it mistakenly suggests that Scripture is all we need to reach a responsible moral position on any given subject. As we shall note below, this is hardly true to our experience in making moral judgments. Another way to qualify the authority of Scripture is to understand it to mean the *primacy* of Scripture for moral decision making. This expresses a legitimate Christian conviction about the Bible, but it needs to be explained to avoid misunderstanding. It does not mean that the Bible can be expected to be the primary source in determining an ethical response to every moral issue we encounter (as Scroggs would understand it). Its primacy must be understood in terms of our identity as a community of faith, in which we affirm that the faith orientation we bring to each moral situation should be decisively informed by the gospel of Jesus Christ. Thus the Bible is primary as the written Word of God, which, through the interpretation of the community of faith, informs and shapes our moral understanding.

An approach that I believe is quite helpful in understanding the Bible's ethical authority is offered by the biblical theologian Luke T. Johnson, who distinguishes between the New Testament as Author, as Authorizer, and as *Auctoritates*.[20] The New Testament as Author refers to its ability to author or "to create a certain identity in its readers, to bring a Christian community into existence or renew it." This "identity-formative function," reflecting the primary purpose and intention of the New Testament writings, is the area in which we find the most unanimity. It centers on Jesus Christ, the crucified and risen Messiah, and the life-giving power of the Spirit. As to the second category of Authorizer, the New Testament "provides its readers with examples of ways in which authoritative texts can freely be reread in light of new experiences and the working of the Spirit—without thereby ceasing to be normative." This is an expression of the Bible's authority that recognizes the dynamic, changing character of the church's life and its responsibility to interpret and reinterpret the normative witness, just as in the New Testament itself we see the development of interpretation between Paul, the Synoptic Gospels, and John. Third, as a collection of *Auctoritates*, or specific authoritative judgments on issues of moral concern, the New Testament displays a wide diversity of opinion. "On any number of issues it is simply impossible to reconcile what New Testament writers have to say on the same subject." For example, what should the Christian attitude be toward the state? It depends on whether one is reading Romans 13 or the Book of Revelation. What about the Christian stance toward the world? It depends on whether one is reading, for example, the Johannine literature, which tends to demonize the world, or Luke-Acts, with its clear and confident affirmation of the world.

By making these distinctions, Johnson can affirm the authority of Scripture at a fundamental level in which there is a basic unanimity in terms of the intentions of the authors, and also allow for a variety of understandings concerning specific issues. Our emphasis on the continuing interpretation of Scripture on the part of the church, bringing forth new insights and new conclusions in addressing changing circumstances, is affirmed in his concept of the Bible as authorizer. It gives the Christian community the warrant to reread given texts in light of its own experience and apply them in new ways without destroying their normative impact. His conclusion is that we need to make a clear distinction between Christian identity and the variety of its expression in the world:

> If the New Testament writings agree so powerfully on the shape of Christian identity but differ so much on the specifics of its articulation in the world, this might mean two things: The first is that identity is more important than ritual consistency; the second is that the New Testament actually legitimates a healthy pluralism of practice within the same basic identity.[21]

These observations are pertinent to the constitutional or confessional statements of Protestant churches in which Scripture is lifted up as the norm for the Christian life. A typical example is the constitution of the Evangelical Lutheran Church in America, where the assertion is made that this church "accepts the canonical Scriptures of the Old and New Testaments as the inspired Word of God and the authoritative source and norm of its proclamation, faith and life."[22] This in fact is a way in which churches acknowledge their identity as inextricably tied up with the record of God's revelation in the Old and New Testament, as well as affirming the unity of faith and life. But it clearly raises formidable problems if it is understood to refer to Johnson's third category of *auctoritates*, which introduces divergent and conflicting viewpoints. As Johnson observes: "Every Christian community, like every Christian, stands to one degree or another in disagreement with some part of the New Testament. Anyone who claims otherwise is simply lying."[23]

Thus the authority of Scripture in the moral realm has its peculiar character, requiring careful definition and a more restricted understanding along the lines that Johnson suggests. Biblical authority does in fact play differing roles depending on the subject one is addressing. One obvious subject is the story of salvation culminating in Jesus Christ that is the centerpiece of Christian faith. The Bible is the primary record of that narrative and, consequently, has a direct bearing on our understanding of it. That record is indispensable to the theological formulations of the church, which claim a continuity with the story. The faith of the church literally rests on that story, with obvious implications for the importance of its theology being faithful to it. This is one clear and important context in which biblical authority is affirmed and recognized.

The Bible's authority in this confessional context is clearly theological. The church affirms Scripture's authority for the theological act of confessing its faith in Jesus Christ, an act essential to Christian and ecclesial identity. When we turn from this act of theological confession to the realm of morality and the individual and corporate life of believers, the meaning of biblical authority must retain its essentially theological cast. Faith and life are inextricably united; the moral character of one's life is also a confession of the lordship of Christ, a truth implicit in Paul's words, "For one believes with one's heart and so is justified, and one confesses with one's lips and so is saved" (Rom. 10:10). Focusing on this theological center of the Christian's moral life will help to avoid any notion that Scripture is intended to provide a comprehensive prescription for the content and boundaries of faithful living. The authority of Scripture for the moral life finds its center in Jesus Christ as Lord who summons believers to a life of repentance and faith, taking up their cross and following him. This is the identifying and formative center for the Christian life, establishing an orientation toward the world that is marked by loyalty to Christ and faith in God's presence rather than by a particular moral casuistry. Relating one's Christ-commitment to the demands of the moral life calls for faithfulness to the spirit of Christ's life and teachings and openness to guidance from the Christian community, without expecting Scripture to bring closure to each moral issue of the day.

SCRIPTURAL AUTHORITY
AND MORAL DECISION MAKING

There are a number of other factors in the Christian's moral response that we can profitably relate to scriptural authority. One is the inherently contextual character of our moral decision making. While this relates to all human action, it takes on a more decisive and critical role in the realm of moral activity, where we seek to determine standards of conduct. The context becomes decisive because it defines the often diffuse and ambiguous, or sometimes restricted, options that are available for moral choice. In other words, the level playing field presupposed by the application of moral standards is often missing, requiring the interpretation of standards for particular situations and the recognition of moral ambiguity in the often complicated relationships of life.[24] Orthodoxy is considerably more focused and manageable than orthopraxy! The question is further complicated by the realities of sin and grace that shift the crux of the Christian moral life from moral righteousness and obedience to repentance and forgiveness. All of these factors make it both impossible and inappropriate to understand the Bible's authority for the Christian life in terms of specific directives for moral action.

Another point germane to this discussion is that appeal to the Bible as an authority for the moral life never takes place in a vacuum. There are too many dimensions to the process of making moral decisions to think that any one source can function exclusively. We have noted the importance of the church's tradition, which serves as a kind of lens through which the Bible is apprehended and understood. The contemporary experience of the Christian community, expressed through its publications and through conversation with other Christians, is also a decisive factor.[25] The ethical perspectives of philosophical views in the larger society may commend themselves to the Christian, supported by insights from the biblical message. In addition, any responsible decision making must take into consideration "the facts of the matter," the empirical information that defines the moral situation and that cannot be ignored if one would act responsibly. This factor in itself often requires considerable analysis in order to ensure responsible action. In light of these complicating factors, it is quite possible for a single-minded attention to Scripture to actually get in the way of moral discernment, precipitating a "tunnel vision" that fails to recognize the full range of resources that can contribute to responsible decision making.

The critical issue in making the above point is whether these elements entering into moral decision making—Scripture, tradition, the contemporary experience of the church, insights from normative thinking in society, and the impact of circumstances that define the empirical situation— stand in hierarchical relation to Scripture so that in every moral decision each element that contributes to one's decision is subordinated to Scripture. Richard Hays argues that this is in fact the case when he says that "extrabiblical sources stand in a hermeneutical relation to the New Testament; they are not independent, counterbalancing sources of authority."[26] The discussion up to this point, however, should make it clear that such a position needs to be carefully defined. Using the language of Luke T. Johnson, the hermeneutical primacy of Scripture applies in the sense of the Bible as Author or as an identity-formative source, not as a norm for every ethical decision made by Christians, whether corporately or individually. The traditional language that designates Scripture as *norma normans* ("the norming norm") and all other sources from the church's life as *norma normata* ("the normed norm") has its validity in this basic sense of Scripture as the transmitter of the identity-forming message of the Christian community.[27] In regard to specific moral decisions, however, it is generally the case that the ethical witness of the Bible is neither sufficiently clear nor consistent to give it a blanket hermeneutical primacy. Contested moral issues will always require the deliberation of Christians together, addressing the various facets of the issue with the clear consciousness of who they are as followers of Christ.

There is yet another hermeneutical assumption behind these considerations that reflects our discussion in the previous chapter: the Bible does not function morally by issuing commands or insights immediately or directly from God. The Bible is not a divine "problem solver" whose texts can be directly and immediately applied to the social issues of the day or to every circumstance in one's personal life, a notion encouraged by the Bible's long history as a "holy book." This expectation of clear and timeless rules in Scripture that can resolve our moral issues carries momentous implications for the Bible's authority. It is a view that turns the Bible into an external, heteronomous authority without respecting the ongoing experience of the church. Its authority becomes authoritarian or legalistic, denying the wisdom and discernment of the believing community and making impossible its meaningful engagement with the Bible. In contrast, our hermeneutics of engagement, which places the church in active conversation both with society and with its own tradition beginning with Scripture, would allow for contemporary experience to provide new insights and understanding to social issues as they assume new shape and form, as well as to discover new insights and imperatives from the tradition as it speaks to a changing society.

The Bible itself provides examples of historical change and adjustment occurring within the Christian community in regard to perplexing moral issues (the "authorizing" function of Scripture, in Johnson's language). One instance often cited is divorce, in which we see modifications and changes as we move from Jesus' rigorist stance to the judgments of Paul and Matthew. According to Mark 10:2-12, Jesus clearly says that divorce and remarriage are contrary to God's will and are therefore prohibited, while the reading in Matthew 19:9 allows for one exception to this rule: sexual infidelity. Scholars generally agree that the Markan version is more characteristic of Jesus' teaching, while Matthew's version likely reflects the pressures of reality in the early Christian community. Paul's advice to fellow Christians, which he explicitly refers to as his own counsel and not a word from the Lord, makes a distinction between Christians and non-Christians on this issue. He allows for divorce if an unbelieving partner "desires to separate" (1 Cor. 7:15).

Is Jesus' position on this matter to be understood in terms of a divine law that ought never be broken? Or is it the statement of an ideal to which we are to aspire, but too often without success in a broken world? Or is Paul's counsel the final word on the matter? Christian teaching has generally recognized the importance of the fact that Jesus' teaching on this subject is positive, holding up marriage as that union in which two persons become one, a relationship marked by fidelity to each other. He is not intent on imposing a law as much as conveying a vision of what is to be, a vision that too often we do not allow to empower and direct our lives as believers. In dealing with this reality, the church has been challenged to forge a stance in which marriage is both exalted and yet not absolutized as unbreakable, maintaining the demanding task of affirming the vision without turning it into an oppressive law. In this process the church has been compelled to work out its position on divorce as responsibly as possible, not as a perfect realization of a particular scriptural position but in light of the realities with which it has had to live.

My conclusion is that the ethical authority of Scripture is expressed within an ongoing process of dialogue and conversation by the community of believers among themselves and with their Scripture and tradition. The cultural and temporal distance between the contemporary church and its authoritative documents, a subject discussed in previous chapters, is particularly significant in the realm of ethics. While a church's confession of faith will require continuing attention to the shifts in meaning of various concepts important to the content of that confession, the realm of ethical judgment and the responsible moral life introduces yet more obvious dynamics of change. The ethos of early Christian communities was formed in relation to the ethos of the societies in which they lived. This fact of history not only contributed to the particular character and distinctive features that emerged in Christian understandings of discipleship and the responsible life, but also subjected those understandings to further modification and change with the passage of time. While churches maintained continuity in their visions of discipleship by holding to what they understood as the moral witness of the New Testament, the understanding and application of that witness is far from uniform in the unfolding history of the church.

These considerations contribute to the conclusion of many ethicists today that the ethical message of the New Testament is not to be identified primarily with imperatives relating to issues of our time. Because the New Testament writings are directed to first-century churches and only secondarily to twentieth-century American churches (or tenth-century Coptic churches or seventeenth-century Russian Orthodox churches, each living within a distinctive cultural ethos), there are obvious limitations to securing directives from the Bible relating to particular moral issues contemporary to those churches. This is not to say that one cannot glean ethical insights from Scripture that are relevant to current issues, as though the Bible were totally mute in regard to the major social concerns of the day. It is, rather, a recognition that we cannot expect meaningfully to address current issues by citing chapter and verse, nor can the Bible be expected to provide a clear and final answer to each of these moral issues. If we follow the example of Paul, the major intent of ethical admonitions is to strengthen and edify the community of faith through the encouragement of faithful discipleship (Rom. 12; 1 Cor. 12; Eph. 4, 5). That task can certainly be understood as including both the nurture of personal character and virtue, and the furnishing of moral insight and perspective, which can contribute to the understanding and evaluation of moral issues in the larger society.

5

SPIRIT ETHICS AND A
RESPONSIBLE CHURCH

The discussion thus far has recognized the centrality of the church as
the necessary context for hearing the message of Scripture and appropriating its theological and ethical content. A hermeneutics of engagement
appropriately describes the church's task as a community of faith and
moral deliberation, engaging in conversation with its Scripture and tradition as well as with its cultural and social world as it seeks to live
responsibly in its own time and place. The discussion has also determined that the distinctive ethical content of Scripture derives from God's
deed in Jesus Christ, who goes before us as both model and teacher. Amid
the variety of ethical themes and perspectives in the Bible, the church
becomes the critical focal point in interpreting Scripture and defining the
responsible life of faith in today's world. Now it is necessary to describe at
more length the nature of the church's ethical life and social responsibility as a community rooted in the message of Scripture. By making both
the believing community and Jesus Christ central to Christian ethics, we
are recognizing the presence of the Spirit in Christian faith and life and
are moved to speak quite naturally and appropriately of an ethics of the
Spirit.

An Ethics of the Spirit

To speak of a spirit ethics is to adopt the language of Scripture itself, in
which a Christocentric ethics is described in terms of God's presence in
the Spirit. A spirit ethics thus reflects the life of faith in Christ in which
the reality of God and the reality of God's relationship with us is

affirmed as fundamental to Christian ethics. Spirit ethics expresses the conviction of new life in Christ in which one knows oneself as a sinner and claims through repentance the empowering forgiveness of God. Thus to speak of a spirit ethics in the Christian context is to speak of life "in Christ" and to reveal in our lives "the mind of Christ" (Phil. 2:5-7; 2 Cor. 2:12-16). The Spirit is active where faith confesses Christ as Lord and where the story of Christ gives nurture and direction to one's life.

The author of Luke-Acts gives a particularly decisive witness to the centrality of the Spirit in the life of the church. At the outset of Jesus' ministry, Luke tells the story of his return to his hometown of Nazareth as a modern-day Moses, empowered by the Spirit to liberate the oppressed (Luke 4:16-21). With the Pentecost experience, the church is now empowered to continue the ministry of Jesus, proclaiming the good news of deliverance to the poor and challenging the rich and the powerful. Luke tends to mute the imminence of the anticipated eschaton, giving more emphasis to the ongoing responsibility of the church as it embarks on a journey of unknown length and with the clear prospect of suffering and risk. Luke sees the Spirit-empowered life as life in community, where people of faith and a faithful people are formed.[1]

A spirit ethics necessarily focuses attention on the community of faith as the matrix in which ethical people are formed and nurtured. Trinitarian theology recognizes in the Spirit the active presence of God, at work in the community of believers through the Word, which is planted in people of faith and embodied by them in the world. Spirit can be spoken of both in terms of God's presence in the world and in terms of empowerment that God's Spirit effects in the lives of believers. That empowerment expresses itself individually in the life of each believer and corporately in the church as the body of Christ, with each dependent on the other for effective witness and discipleship in the world. When Paul emphasizes one body, one Spirit, it is clear "that [his] understanding of the Spirit has its roots in the bond between the Spirit and the community."[2]

Together with Luke, the apostle Paul lays particular stress on the Spirit in understanding the life of discipleship. For Paul, the Spirit of God fulfills an eschatological promise, rooted in the Old Testament, that is now fulfilled in Jesus Christ, the "Chosen One" who has come in these last times. Paul accordingly uses the *Spirit of God* interchangeably with the *Spirit of Christ as Lord* (Rom. 8:9; 2 Cor. 3:17). It is an empowering Spirit that has far more to do with the life of believers than occasioning extraordinary and miraculous happenings. Ecstatic visions, speaking in tongues, and other phenomena of this kind can dominate and skew Christian understandings of the Spirit. These kinds of "fireworks" impress the human penchant for the dramatic and extraordinary, tempting even the devout to think that here is positive proof of God's presence. What is forgotten is that throughout history the more powerful and continuing expression of that presence is found in the "still, small voice" (1 Kings 19:12) that modestly works in the minds and hearts of believers everywhere. While the "gifts of the Spirit" Paul discusses in 1 Corinthians 12 include the more notable and distinctive *charismata,* it is also clear that he is particularly concerned to identify the Spirit with the core life of faith—issues of faithfulness, service, and obedience. One indeed can argue that the apostle is intent on transferring the emphasis on gifts of the Spirit to those traits of morality and character he calls "fruit of the Spirit." Thus Paul lifts up agapeic love in 1 Corinthians 13 as the "more excellent way," showing his readers that the Spirit empowers a self-giving life that is much more essential to the common life of the church than these other, more remarkable, gifts.[3]

Making this point is not intended to deny an authentic diversity in Christian experience, or to repudiate every expression of Pentecostalism in the church. There is, after all, the very real opposite danger that churches stifle the Spirit's presence through institutional organization and the need to control. As creatures of the Enlightenment, we are normally much too suspicious of every expression of ecstatic or mystical experience that testifies to the mystery and otherness of God in the midst of life. From a spirit ethics perspective, however, the sense of intimacy and emotional intensity that can mark the Spirit-relationship does not translate into an ethics that features direct and immediate commands from God. This is because what distinguishes the Christian experience of the Spirit from other religious experience is the person, Jesus Christ. The Spirit gathers the community of faith in the name of Christ, and our response to the Gospel is shaped by that context of a community that worships Jesus as Lord. Thus Paul lifts up Jesus as the model of divine love (Phil. 2:1-11)and, in language that is both practical and profound, spells out some of the meaning of this love in the thirteenth chapter of 1 Corinthians.

A spirit ethics distances itself from a literalistic frame of mind in approaching Scripture and from the inclination to glean a code morality from the Bible. As Paul observes, "The letter kills, but the Spirit gives life" (Rom. 7:6; 2 Cor. 3:6). Rather than a complete set of answers, faith claims the presence of the Spirit to guide and empower. Here the community plays a particularly important role in relation to the individual believer. Through the Spirit the community serves to steady and guide the individual by providing both a supportive and critical context that contributes perspective and gives aid in the process of moral discernment. The emphasis on individual autonomy in North American society makes this role of the community all the more important, for it challenges the illusory character of individualist ideology at the same time as it turns us toward each other, helping us recognize our dependence on others. The individual's capacity to live faithfully and to interpret the Spirit's presence is closely related to the presence of the community of faith in which the individual believer is living and interacting. The lives of other believers whom one has come to know and appreciate are essential to one's faith as living witnesses to the work of the Spirit.[4]

The Book of Acts provides an excellent model for Christian understanding of what it means for the community of faith to act in confidence of the Spirit's presence as it addresses a new and threatening situation. The Jerusalem Conference (Acts 15) had to settle the issue whether Gentiles must become Jews in order to become followers of Christ and join the young church. The church's Scripture and tradition up to this point reflected its Jewish heritage; now a creative decision, arrived at through the confidence of the Spirit's presence, was called for. That decision occurred through earnest listening and honest dialogue, resulting in new perspectives and changed minds within the community of faith. A similar kind of situation has been repeated many times over in the history of the church, as expressed in the words of John Howard Yoder:

> The gathered community expects Spirit-given newness to suggest answers previously not perceived. The transcendent appeal to authority is moved away from the inspiredness of holy writ and from the centralization of an episcopal magisterium, as well as from any personal, unaccountable "fanaticism" (what Luther called *Schwärmertum*). The community pulls back as well from catholic generalizability and infallibility, yet it is believingly, modestly ready to say of consensus reached today, "it seemed good to the Holy Spirit and to us," and to commend this insight by encyclical to other churches.[5]

The emphasis upon the Spirit in Christian ethics focuses attention not only on concrete decisions to be made, but primarily on the quality and character of one's life as a follower of Christ. It both commits the believer to struggle confidently with the demands and temptations surrounding the moral life, and to understand and interpret those encounters in light of God's presence. Paul's language of "fruit of the Spirit" is a recognition that the moral life generated by faith in the triune God is not a human achievement but the work of the Spirit of God. To speak of ethics in terms of the Spirit also puts considerable responsibility on the individual: The relation to community does not strip the individual of responsibility for decisions by *forcing* obedience to authority, whether expressed in Scripture or in the tradition or laws of the community. Thus Paul exhorts the Christians in Rome to "prove what is the will of God, what is good and acceptable and perfect" (Rom. 12:2). This testing of the spirits challenges individual discernment at the same time as it takes place within the context of community guidance and support.

Particularly in Paul the language of Spirit in describing the life of faith is contrasted to life governed by "the flesh." In Galatians 5, Paul's list of "works of the flesh," including immorality, impurity, enmity, strife, anger, selfishness, and the like, is contrasted to the "fruit of the Spirit," including love, joy, peace, patience, kindness, goodness, faithfulness, gentleness, self-control. How is the church to understand the relation of life "in the flesh" to life "in the spirit"? One temptation is to understand these two poles in moralistic terms, defining the Christian life as one that has attained a higher moral status by entering the realm of the Spirit and leaving behind the works of the flesh. The Christian life is then defined in terms of the success one has achieved in eliminating the works of the flesh from one's daily life. This invites the understanding that people can be divided into two groups, those who manifest the fruit of the Spirit and those who do the works of the flesh.

This kind of dualism, however, is both ethically and theologically suspect. To focus on "works" is to encourage a surface understanding of the Christian life, or one that sees life in linear rather than organic terms. It fails to understand the depth of character of the moral life, where people can struggle with demons of various kinds and live heroically but with little obvious moral achievement. The moral life is in fact permeated with ambiguity, making it difficult if not impossible to compare people on the basis of any kind of moral calculus. Evidence of moral transformation is often a matter of recognizing a sincere effort to live responsibly more than the achievement of morally exemplary deeds.

Beyond this inherently questionable attempt to separate people according to moral standards, the Christian insight into human nature as "fallen" also recognizes that faith does not result in a moral transformation that in effect abolishes evil and makes one good. The insight of Luther, that the believer is *simul iustus et peccator*—both justified and a sinner—enables the recognition that the divide between the moral and immoral life runs *through* rather than *between* each person, whether one is "in Christ" or not. This insight correlates with the truth that is paramount in Jesus' teaching, namely, that repentance and forgiveness are at the center of the life of faith. The distinctiveness of that life is its dependence on divine grace and mercy rather than any claim to moral achievements.

Having made this point, one cannot deny that life in the Spirit does engender moral seriousness; if true to oneself the Christian will not be careless about discipleship. We do in fact encourage faithfulness in each other and rejoice with every expression of love, joy, peace, faithfulness, goodness, and the like—in other words, a turning from self-centered behavior and an earnest desire to walk in the way of Christ. New Testament language concerning the Spirit is that of a sanctifying presence; the Spirit "makes holy," consecrating the lives and work of believers (Rom. 15:16; 1 Thess. 3:13). Profession of faith without evidence of commitment to discipleship betrays a lack of authenticity as a follower of Christ. The sanctified life expresses the expectation that one will "walk, and not just talk" the life of faith. One's commitment to Christ will indeed loosen the power of sin to govern and control one's life, without denying the point already made concerning the continuing reality of temptation and moral failure in the Christian life.

The critical truth is that the reality of the new life in Christ is based on what God has done in justifying the sinner, not on any proof that sinner is able to demonstrate through a changed life. The struggle of the faithful life is expected, but not the expectation that one has "arrived." That is properly identified with the coming of the kingdom, which indeed has broken into the present through the life and ministry of Christ but still bears a "not yet" character as we await the final consummation. This "not yet" character is appropriately identified with the life of every believer. At the level of abstraction we can and must contrast life in the Spirit with life under the law, but at the level of concrete living or human embodiment, there are no absolute or exclusive divisions to be made. The reality for every believer is that one lives as "both saint and sinner." Repentance and forgiveness in the Christian's life mark a decisive turning point in self-consciousness as a forgiven sinner, and this in turn puts the moral life in new perspective without removing the struggle and failure inherent to it.[6]

Life in the Spirit invites the understanding that the present life of the believing community carries a definitive role in determining the moral decisions and directions that it takes. It does not remove the church's tradition as integral to its identity, but it places the emphasis on a creative handling of that tradition rather than relying exclusively on past understandings. It places emphasis on discerning the times and testing the spirits that compete for our allegiance, recognizing that this kind of contemporary experience brings its impact to our engagement with the tradition. Our trust in the guidance of the Spirit can never simply be equated with the direction the church receives from its past, important as that may be. The Spirit's leading will instead often create tension in dealing with the tradition, for confidence in the presence of the Spirit gives substance and importance to the contemporary experience of the church as it grapples with the moral issues of its time. Christians will look for evidences of the Spirit in the lives of those who call for reassessment of the tradition and for striking out in new directions, keeping in mind that whatever course the church takes should lead to the building up of the "communion of saints."

Some may conclude that a Spirit ethics leaves too much to the subjectivity of the individual and lacks concrete direction from external sources, such as laws and principles found in the church's moral tradition. On the contrary, the understanding of the Spirit in these pages leads one to embrace the long tradition of ethical reflection in the church, not as immutable directives or ready answers, but as a gift from our past that merits discriminating consideration.

> [A]s a lone criterion for judging good and evil, the leading of the Spirit is a dangerous guide....Anything, from the Jonestown massacre to the robbing of a gullible TV audience, can be claimed on the basis of the leading of the Spirit. Fortunately, many Christians who have been renewed by the Spirit also love the Scriptures, respect their theological tradition and show a healthy common sense.[7]

In any consideration of the Spirit's leading, the individual or group involved cannot isolate themselves from the Christian community, which establishes a more inclusive context and brings broader resources for one's moral deliberation. The church as a whole thus functions as a necessary conversation partner in the process of discernment, helping to prevent people from taking aberrant directions.

A spirit ethics must also speak of prayer and communion with the triune God in individual and corporate worship. This is the necessary context in which the Spirit of God is known, where people's lives are marked by trust, humility, and confidence that "in everything God works for good with those who love God" (Rom. 8:28). Any reference to the church as the body of Christ, engaged in moral nurture and formation, must begin with worship through Word and Sacrament. Through Word and Sacrament, the consolation and exhortation of the gospel is proclaimed, shared, and experienced with each other. It is also true, though not sufficiently recognized, that in addition to the Scripture and teaching traditions of the church, its sacramental practice bears important implications for the church's moral witness. From the core activity of proclaiming the Word and participating in the sacramental life of the congregation flows all the life of the church, including its occasions for moral deliberation in classes and forums that bring Word, sacraments, and society together. In this activity the body of Christ nurtures in each of its members the quiet confidence that the Spirit of God is present and ministering to them in their struggle for discernment. There is no expectation of a miraculous word from above, but a willingness to listen and to be satisfied with the admonitions and counsel received from the faithful who have gone before us and from the faithful now struggling with us, as we read the signs of the times and deliberate together concerning our response. We can speak of a "creative responsibility" (Bonhoeffer) that emerges in this process in which the Spirit empowers us in a serious engagement with the issues of our time. All of this takes place in the spirit of worship, with a lively awareness of our dependence on God's grace and mercy.

In John 14-16 Jesus promises the coming of the Spirit, telling his disciples that the future would bring fuller understanding of what he had taught them and what he had done. "When the Spirit of truth comes, he will guide you into all the truth . . ." (John 16:13a). The uniting of truth with the future is significant for Christian faith. The "Spirit of truth" expresses our Christian conviction that God *is* Truth who brings both a truthful Word that judges and redeems us, and a light and direction to our lives as the truth we are to follow. The "Spirit of truth" witnesses to Jesus Christ as the One in whom this is happening. The Spirit gives Jesus his finality both as the Word who reveals the will and purpose of God, and the Word in whom we find our own purpose and fulfillment. Because this Word is an event occurring in history, it is subject to the limitations and restrictions of the cultural understanding and ethos contemporary to it. As the Spirit unfolds that Word of God in history, the Word takes on new meaning and new direction for the community of faith, at the same time as that community seeks an appropriate continuity with what has gone before.

The language of Spirit points us to the future, inspiring confidence that the meaning of God's Word in Jesus Christ will continue to unfold in new and powerful ways. This futurist orientation bears confidence that the truth in Christ will continue to be revealed and teach us new insights about who we are as children of God and what we are to do. If this were not true, we would be bound by the letter of the tradition rather than being liberated by the truth of the Spirit. Thus there is a fundamental openness to an ethics of the Spirit, recognizing the inherently dynamic character of the moral life that is future-directed. Furthermore, this future orientation helps us to "sit lightly" in regard to the cultural ethos of our own day, keeping us alert to ways in which it can restrict our understanding of responsible discipleship. In every age the witness of the Spirit encounters a dominant culture and ethos that will test and threaten to corrupt the church's understanding of the faithful life.

SPIRIT ETHICS AND ETHICAL THEORY

Christians bring to the moral life a vision that is distinctive, generated by faith in Jesus Christ as Lord and marked by "the mind of Christ" that led him ultimately to the cross. This vision, however, does not remove the Christian from those modes of reflection that are characteristic of moral decision making. In the history of ethical theory, two modes of decision making have been dominant, often referred to as deontological and teleological (or formalist and utilitarian): the former lifts up the notion of duty or obligation as central to responsible decision making, pointing to laws, rules, and principles as the concrete expressions of duty in the moral life; the latter emphasizes ideals and values, with responsible decision making characterized by the effort to realize those values in the outcome or consequences of one's decision (thus this theory is often called "consequentialism").[8]

In addition to these two modes of decision making, a third view, which has seen renewed interest in recent years, focuses on the agent making the moral decision. Variously characterized as virtue or perfectionist theory, this view stresses the importance of character and virtue in the person making the decision. It does not offer another kind of decision-making procedure, but reminds us that decision making does not occur in a vacuum but engages the judgment and discernment as well as the moral character of the individual. It recognizes that acting on the basis of duty or of an ideal to be realized is subject to the moral discernment and discriminating judgment of the individual making the decision. It also would emphasize the truth that a primary task of ethics is the long-range formation of virtuous persons, or people of character. Within the Christian context, the church as a community of faith is directly engaged in this task, providing Christian nurture of the young and establishing an ethos that contributes moral stability and purpose to the life of society.

Much debate has occurred concerning the relative merits of deontological and teleological approaches to moral decision making, but rather than seeing them as competitive, we should recognize them as complementary to each other, with contextual considerations bearing considerable influence on their appropriate application. From a Christian, spirit ethics perspective, the stress on duty and obligation recognizes the moral nature of humanity, one important dimension of our being created in the image of God. It further recognizes the fact that human life is lived in relationship, and relationships introduce moral obligations and expectations that are fundamental to life together. The complexity of these relationships can often create dilemmas in which we struggle with competing obligations. We are then compelled to make a hard decision on what constitutes our primary obligation in a given situation, even though it may not be a fully satisfying resolution to the issues involved. In other contexts, we are often reminded that a sense of duty is needed to counter the self-centered character of our existence. This sense of duty, expressed in laws, rules, and principles, can be critically important to the moral life, a salient line of defense against human weakness and waywardness that jeopardize responsible human relationships.

At the same time, a spirit ethics recognizes the inherent limitations of law-centered ethics, the function of which is to protect the neighbor by prohibiting harmful deeds rather than defining moral action in terms of human purpose and values. The abstract, general character of law is both a strength and a weakness, suggesting on the one hand the weight of universality to one's moral duties, but on the other hand failing to recognize the role of personal judgment and moral wisdom that often must claim sovereignty in reading and responding to the nuances of a particular moral situation. The reaction of law-centered ethics in this kind of complicated situation is to create still more rules of a more specific nature, encouraging a legalistic mind-set in which the moral life is understood as subservience to an external set of rules. Thus deontological thinking needs the balance of a broader, purpose-oriented way of thinking that brings ideals and values to bear.

A spirit ethics appreciates the positive, goal-oriented character of teleological thinking as yet another reflection of the image of God in our moral life. Purpose and intentionality are distinctive to human activity, expressing the futurist direction of human life. We are capable of imagining and intending noble goals that contribute to a more just and livable existence for a greater number of people. While deontologists would call us to account, teleologists would beckon us to a vision concerning the good and urge us to realize it. Clearly the focus of each of these aspects of moral experience is important and necessary to the moral life, with deontology reflecting human "brokenness" in its stress on duty in the face of temptation and self-centeredness, and teleology reflecting our capacity for idealism and the desire to create a more humane social order.

There are, however, reservations that a spirit ethics would also bring to teleological thinking. At the level of individual action, the more distant in time the goal to be achieved, the more dubious becomes the motivation for action and the likelihood of achieving the goal. This is a situation that invites rationalization. There is also the element of hubris, or an excessive self-confidence in thinking that one can engineer a good result with little appreciation for one's limitations in controlling future events. When one moves from the individual to corporate action, the attempt to control future happenings in order to ensure the desired outcome takes on still more ominous possibilities. Serious conflicts can arise between a desired goal and the means pursued to meet that goal, posing a critical ethical issue in itself. The end, no matter how desirable, does not justify every means. Here deontological thinking would protect the individual from destructive effects of a broader, societal goal. A spirit ethics would also caution that while teleological thinking can accomplish much good when united with responsible ethical vision, it does not promise the ushering in of the kingdom. That future comes to us in grace, rather than through human achievement.[9]

Finally, a spirit ethics clearly resonates with the focus on personal character and virtue. Here the content of virtue is shaped by the gospel and expressed by Paul in terms of "the mind of Christ" and "the fruit of the Spirit." In the history of Christian ethics, Thomas Aquinas cited the three virtues Paul refers to in 1 Corinthians 13—faith, hope, and love— as the "theological virtues," in distinction from the Platonic or philosophical virtues of temperance, courage, wisdom, and justice. While all virtues that enable the individual to flourish and contribute to the common good are important to Christian ethics, faith places all these virtues under the lordship of Christ and relates them to a discipleship that bears the marks of the cross. It is also essential to recognize that any reference to virtue in the Christian context must be understood in terms of process rather than achievement, of becoming rather than being, and of God's work rather than our own. The Christian mind-set does not encourage continuing attention to oneself—a moral "pulse taking" in view of standards we impose on ourselves—but is instead ruled by trust as a follower of Jesus Christ.

The emphasis on personal virtue is often appealing to conservatives, who are interested in individual integrity but are highly suspicious of any attempt to "engineer" social goods. Thomas Ogletree notes that perfectionist theories tend to be aristocratic rather than democratic: "They may as a result have a certain tolerance for human misery, inequality, and servitude provided the possibility for the accomplishment of human excellence is present for the worthy."[10] When the personal virtues of which one speaks turn the individual to the need of the neighbor, however, this separation between individual and social welfare is fundamentally challenged. In exalting love that tends to the neighbor's welfare, Christians are also exalting justice as a virtue that love seeks in promoting the welfare of society as a whole.

A spirit ethics thus brings a vision to moral decision making but uses a variety of methods according to the context one is addressing. While there is no one ethical theory that can be identified as "Christian" or labeled as "biblical," there is the insistence that the moral discernment and mature judgment of the individual maintain sovereignty over the application of rules or ideals according to the context. In other words, wisdom and character are essential to ethical activity, conditioning every application of moral standards. In specifically Christian language, the person who is "in Christ" would be expected to demonstrate the character that is consonant with that commitment, with faith giving responsible direction to one's decisions.[11] Yet also here, human weakness compels the recognition that no one is perfect and that individual sovereignty is therefore never absolute; it will be challenged and judged by laws and ideals whenever that sovereignty is misused. Those whose lives are marked by personal confession of sin in the presence of God should be acutely aware of the human capacity to act in self-serving ways, even in the name of what is true and good. This chastened self-consciousness is the first line of defense in keeping the individual honest with oneself in the exercise of moral judgment and decision making.

This emphasis on the importance of discernment and judgment on the part of the mature individual, with context playing a determinative role, will impress some as too subjective and as vulnerable to the charge of relativism. Our questioning of absolutes in chapter 1 would be seen as further corroboration of that charge. Yet we have acknowledged the structures of societal life created by human relationships and the importance of duty and obligation occasioned by those relationships. Contrary to the situationism of Joseph Fletcher, love does not stand alone but guides the individual within the restraints of the community's law and traditions. The issue centers more upon absolutist applications of the law rather than a repudiation of law itself. The stance argued here seeks an appropriate balance in which the claims we make for the law's imperatives do not require the denial of the necessary sovereignty of the responsible individual when addressing the complexities of the moral situation.

Spirit Ethics and Social Ethics

How does one relate life "in Christ" to the social issues Christians as individuals and as the church are facing in society? What role does the Bible play in giving form and shape to the individual and corporate response of Christians to the challenging and often divisive issues of our time? Our discussion to this point would lead us to reject a general expectation that biblical passages can be found that provide a definitive answer to contemporary social issues. On the other hand, the defining orientation of what it means to be a Christian and what it means to be the church, based on the witness of Scripture, does provide an orientation or stance from which to address the issues of society. The witness of Jesus concerning the kingdom of God, or of Paul concerning life "in Christ," or of the Old Testament prophets concerning the rich and the poor, do not form a public theology or a social ethics as such, and yet there is much in their teachings that shape a Christian perspective and bring insight and understanding to contemporary issues.

There are of course a variety of traditions in the ecumenical church, each with its distinctive reading of Scripture that gives rise to differing implications for the church's relation to society as a whole as well as to specific issues. There may be a common confession in the lordship of Christ, but how that is understood and applied to the church's relation to society leaves room for considerable disagreement. Thus the minority "peace churches," for example, are convinced that the radical ethics of the Sermon on the Mount is directly applicable to contemporary society and should be embodied by the believing community as a persuasive, nonviolent model for the rest of society.[12] The major Protestant as well as Roman Catholic churches, on the other hand, are more intent on addressing the concrete challenges facing those who wield political and economic power because they see this as their responsibility before God. Until now, at least, they have themselves been identified with the establishment as majority churches, and consequently they have been committed to that more nuanced struggle to maintain their distance from secular power at the same time as they acknowledge its God-ordained purposes.

As soon as the church takes seriously the importance of the secular realm, with the complex arrangements of its social, economic, and political institutions, it is committed to address those institutions in responsible ways. This involves both the recognition of the social context in which they function and the imperative to challenge them to responsible actions and just policies that contribute to the welfare of society. This point was made in chapter 2, but here I address some of the issues at more length. The question facing the church throughout the ages has been how to interpret Scripture and the message of the gospel so that the economic and political powers are appropriately and authentically addressed in light of the church's faith.

To illustrate the problems that arise with this subject, it is helpful to raise some concrete questions: Is it appropriate for the church to apply the Sermon on the Mount to the corporate ethics of a business institution? Or does the radical love ethics of the kingdom of God in Jesus' teaching apply directly to the nation state as it considers the prospect of going to war against an aggressor nation? If the realities of corporate relationships in the secular world make the ethics of agapeic love appear naive and inappropriate, what should be the response of the church? What course should be taken if we reject as inadequate the answer of those who believe the church should not be addressing the power issues of the secular realm at all, but should focus instead on its own responsibility to live out its ethics and to let that life serve as a paradigm to be emulated by others?

In one way or another, what most churches have done is to find those resources in Scripture and tradition that enable them to connect with the realities of corporate life so that the moral issues faced by institutions and their leaders are cogently addressed from a stance of faith. This "correlation" recognizes that the ethics of Christian faith cannot be reduced or restricted to the cruciform life as a kind of universal standard for every individual or group without regard to context. The faith is also capable of relating to the secular realm with other resources from its ethical teaching, such as the law and a keen sense of social justice. One might cite the classic two-kingdom teaching—or, better expressed, the two-realm teaching or twofold rule of God—found in the Lutheran tradition as a notable illustration of one church's attempt to relate the Christian message to the public order.[13]

Many would regard Luther's teaching of the two realms—the secular, public realm of politics, commerce, and culture, and the realm of faith centered in the church or religious community—as little more than a historical relic with no possibility of fruitful application to contemporary society. In fact, however, there is an unfortunate history to this teaching that reveals significant distortion of its intent. This occurred during the nineteenth century in particular, when the challenge of science and a spirit of secularism contributed to a tendency to privatize faith, divorcing it from the public world. The two-realm teaching was often understood along these lines, where God and faith were identified with the "inner life" and divorced from the world of *Realpolitik*.[14] In contrast, the intent of Luther was not to absent God from the public realm but to understand God's presence within that context in terms of the law, which fits with the purpose and function of the state. In the language of today, it was an attempt to be "contextual." Because the state is responsible to God in its responsibility for providing a political framework for a just and viable society for its people, the law serves a providential purpose in helping society carve a realm of order out of the continuing threat of chaos. The context of political and economic life is the context of law that maintains structures of justice and order. In contradistinction, the realm of the church is appropriately captured in terms of the gospel, the peculiar message that defines and constitutes the community of faith. Here the governing themes that identify the life of the community are rooted in its faith—repentance, forgiveness, reconciliation, agapeic love, and the cruciform life. In this context, love inspired by the cross of Christ is sovereign in contrast to the sovereignty of law in the public realm. Two-realm teaching would reject any social ethics that attempts to "Christianize" the state by expecting public life to recognize, if not demonstrate, the themes inherent to Christian faith and life. This does not deny that the Christian's faith commitment and theological and ethical convictions will influence one's approach to law and justice—indeed, such convictions will challenge the spirit of vindictiveness in the exercise of law and will temper justice with mercy. Nonetheless, the governing motif for public life remains justice, not love.[15]

Any direct application of Luther's two-realm thinking to our present-day situation would overlook the fact that the reformer lived in a quite different world of religious and political relationships. He can hardly be cited as an advocate of church and state "separation" in current understandings of that idea. Nonetheless, the direction of his teaching contributes to the drawing of boundaries that help to avoid confusion in the relation of church and state and in the expectations that Christians bring to public life. A particular strength lies in its challenging both institutional religion and the state from claiming a sovereignty that does not belong to them. It is basically a "defensive" teaching, drawing boundaries and keeping institutions honest concerning the proper limits of their authority. Its continuing relevance for contemporary American society is clearly seen in the present-day phenomenon of the Religious Right. While these Christians have their urgent agendas and sincere reasons that would justify their actions, they are plainly intent on imposing their understanding of Christian social ethics upon society through manipulation of the political process. It is the contemporary American version of the church making a questionable attempt to exercise political power.

These Christians lose the distinction between speaking out to encourage a majority of citizens to agree with one's political point of view, and engaging in partisan politics in order to control political parties and candidates as a way of legalizing one's viewpoint, regardless of the will of the majority. Religious Right advocates are often guilty of the latter in their use of parachurch organizations that wage aggressive campaigns to give legal status to their moral agenda and thereby to control public morality. Two-realm teaching would challenge any attempt inspired by religious beliefs to impose those beliefs on the public, either through manipulation of the political process or through establishing a voting majority that ignores the rights of minorities.

Despite the continuing relevance of two-realm teaching, it is not an adequate structure on which to build a positive social ethics for the church—a lesson Lutherans have been slow to learn. Drawing boundaries, while necessary to any understanding of religion and the public realm, is hardly adequate as a means of depicting the full scope of that relationship. Too often a boundary mentality has discouraged a creative and positive involvement on the part of the church in society.[16] When one considers the full scope of the church's relation to society, it becomes a matter not of drawing lines but of determining space. As Fr. J. Bryan Hehir has observed, it is a matter of recognizing the gifts religion brings to society and allowing it the room to function as a distinctive and legitimate participant in the public square. Hehir notes "three fundamental gifts of a religious tradition to the wider society in which it functions: ideas, institutions, and community."[17] The "ideas" of a church or any religious tradition will include basic tenets of its faith that distinguish its adherents from the rest of society and will not be believed or shared by society as a whole (the church's gospel, for example). But there are also ideas in religious traditions that can provide the possibility of a shared vision with the larger society, ideas of a moral nature that recognize a common humanity among all people and lift up the ideal of justice and community (the realm of law in Lutheran language). They are not ideas generated specifically by the church's gospel (though they are clearly related to that gospel), but are derived from its convictions concerning the God of creation.

This means that the involvement of the church and of individual Christians in public life includes convictions that both promise positive connections with others and that harbor the potential for disagreement. Christians will discover their differences from others in the distinctive convictions that identify them as Christians, but they will also discover their unity with others in the ideas and goals they share in light of their common humanity and their common calling as responsible citizens. There is clearly much in moral decision making and in addressing the social issues of the day that calls for knowledge and discrimination in reading the situation, mattering little whether one is Christian or atheist. There are insights in secular philosophy and in humanist ethics, as well as in the Christian moral tradition, that can be profitably shared, just as the wisdom tradition in Scripture, with its secular roots, makes its contribution to the ethics of the Bible. Yet there remains the distinctive character of faith in the triune God that exalts agapeic love and creates a powerful desire to serve the neighbor.

The Christian potential for contributing to the public good lies in the whole realm of human life and experience, involving both being and doing. There is much in its theological and moral traditions that one can refer to at this point, such as ethical teachings that encourage responsibility and enhance the common life; the ideal of equality, rooted for Christians in their belief concerning the *imago dei;* the quest for social justice that is inspired by the image of God, maintaining that we are all creatures of the one God; the conviction that life is ultimately meaningful, disallowing any temptation to become pessimistic or cynical concerning the human prospect; respect for the structures of life that maintain and enable peace and community; and a profound sense of responsibility for the environment as God's creation. Beyond their traditions of belief and practice is the social reality of Christian communities, including their many institutions of mercy. By their very presence, these communities and institutions make their contribution to the public good and to the possibility of a common discourse that will unite people of goodwill. These kinds of interaction with society bring witness of the Spirit's presence, who inspires the believing community to reach out in responsible actions that address the needs and injustices that cripple and dehumanize society.

SPIRIT ETHICS AND THE BIBLICAL VISION

A primary task of the church in relation to the social order is to articulate its vision concerning the purposes of God and what those purposes mean for human life and destiny, and then to draw implications from that vision for the task of the church in society. Essential to that vision is the image that captures the message of Jesus himself—the kingdom or reign of God. This is an image that is "at home" in an ethics of the Spirit, for both express the reality of God's presence in the midst of life and call for a human response. Throughout the church's history there have been a number of tensions if not conflicts concerning the proper understanding of the kingdom in relation to three polarities: the present and future, the individual and community, and the church and society. The danger has always been to address these polarities in terms of either/or: either Jesus is speaking of a present, "realized" reign of God in which the future is collapsed into the present, or he is speaking of an exclusively future reign, which makes it transcendent and removed from the present; either Jesus is speaking of a reign of God in the heart, a spiritual and essentially private, individual reality, or he is speaking of a communal reality known only in the relationships of the community; either Jesus is speaking of a reign to be exclusively identified with the believing community, or of a reign that also stretches into the affairs of the larger society with national and international implications.

These expressions of either/or must be rejected in favor of a dialectical approach capable of holding these opposite poles together for the sake of a deeper truth. In Jesus' own teaching, there is a "temporal dialectic" that brings together both present and future. It means that "people can speak of [the kingdom] as imminent and pray for its coming (as in the second petition of the Lord's Prayer), but can also proclaim its dawning in the present with Jesus . . . as the proleptic presence of the future."[18] Jesus understood his own ministry as a sign of the kingdom's presence at the same time as it remained a future, though imminent, reality. A spirit ethics recognizes the close relation of the kingdom with the Spirit also in the life of Jesus himself. At his baptism "the Holy Spirit descended upon him" (Luke 3:21-22), and when he came to Nazareth he opened the book of Isaiah and read from chapter 61: "The Spirit of the Lord is upon me . . ." (Luke 4:18). Jesus' preaching of the kingdom and casting out demons was testimony to the presence of the Spirit of God in his life and ministry. With Pentecost, the church was created and the Spirit's presence was known for the first time well beyond Jesus, with thousands embracing the resurrection faith. Because of the Spirit's work, countless believers through the years have come to know themselves as sons and daughters of the living God. Yet the tension between present and future remains, with the Spirit's presence today a "guarantee" (2 Cor. 5:5) of the fullness of God's presence that awaits the final coming of the kingdom. The very nature of their faith places Christians in this "now–not yet" tension in their relation to the Spirit and the coming kingdom.[19]

Turning to the other tensions in our understanding of the kingdom, a passage like Luke 17:21 (which would translate: "For behold, the kingdom of God is with you") has been interpreted as limiting the kingdom to the inner life of the individual. But Jesus' ministry clearly contradicts this understanding; his exorcisms are signs of the kingdom and the preaching and healing of the disciples also "share secondarily in mediating the presence and reality of the kingdom of God" in the midst of the community.[20] Our recognition of the interdependence of the individual and community ties in with the close association in the Synoptic Gospels of the Spirit and the kingdom, for where the Spirit is at work, the kingdom is present. By necessity, this embraces both the individual and community. Nor can the church limit God's reign to the believing community in contrast to community. Just as the Spirit of God cannot be domesticated or harnessed through careful definition that would maintain ecclesiastical control of God's presence, so the kingdom of God is not subject to human limitations. The church is indeed a sign of the reign of God, but that reign moves far beyond the church itself. As a sign of that reign, the church has a particular mission that sets it apart from society, but God's presence and purposes stretch beyond the church to embrace the whole of society. It is true that Jesus refused to interpret the kingdom of God in the political or nationalistic terms that many of his hearers undoubtedly wanted to hear, but he does not hesitate to give social and political dimensions to the kingdom as he relates it to the needs of society, as in Matthew 25.

Focusing on church and society in view of the reign of God proclaimed in the coming of Jesus, one point of enormous importance is the fact that this vision denotes human destiny in terms of community—the kingdom of God. In Pauline language, the Spirit is the community-building presence of God, primarily in the community that recognizes Jesus Christ as Lord, but not to be separated from every expression of community in which people are known and renewed in constructive, life-serving relationships. This biblically inspired vision allows no place for self-completion of the individual or for human flourishing apart from community. The Christian message makes it difficult to talk about any kind of "self-realization" that does not imbue a sense of responsibility for one's neighbor. Increasingly we have come to appreciate the fact that our personal identity is a social identity and that we know ourselves only in relation to others. The ethical reality of this truth is that we are literally "all in this together," bound by a web of obligations and promises that constitute much of the substance of our lives. To know ourselves as moral beings is to recognize our interdependence with our neighbors. This certainly means for the church that it can never understand itself apart from the larger society in which it is planted; it is called to be a witness in the world, not only of the saving gospel of Jesus Christ but of the providential justice of God who holds us all to account for the sake of a just and viable community.

The image of the kingdom also conveys the eschatological nature of biblical and Christian ethics. It roots ethics in the biblical story of God's deeds in the life of Israel culminating in the story of Jesus, but that story turns us to the future in anticipation of a yet more comprehensive goal that embraces the whole of history.[21] The magnificent scope of this story includes everyone and excludes no one. It points believers to the future, conveying the promises of God and engendering hope and confidence. It unites the people of God with all of history and all of humanity, a vision that defies both comprehension and description. It is essentially an act of faith that places our destiny in the hands of the God of creation, redemption, and new life, whom we know in the biblical story. A clear expression of that faith is the church's responsibility to the larger society, seeking ways to strengthen community and taking a stand on behalf of the excluded and oppressed. While the church is not society's problem solver, its integrity as a community of faith requires that it make a witness that both challenges injustice and generates hope in the lives of the desolate. Whether by voluntary acts of mercy or by acts of confrontation of those in power, the church is called to be a witness of the Spirit's presence through activity that renews and enlarges community.

Another essential element of the biblical vision is expressed by Paul in Galatians 3:28: "There is neither Jew nor Greek, there is neither slave nor free, there is neither male nor female; for you are all one in Christ Jesus." Richard Longenecker refers to this passage as the "great Magna Carta of the Christian faith," bearing major social implications of the gospel.[22] Both the doctrine of creation, which recognizes every person as bearing the image of God, and the gospel that makes possible the new life "in Christ," bring a radical egalitarianism into human relationships. The Galatians passage was particularly helpful in making this equality explicit in regard to particular religious and social divisions in Paul's time. The task of the church in every age is to do the same thing, addressing division and oppression in light of its faith in the triune God. This is a potentially revolutionary task in virtually every setting in which the church finds itself, but it is basically a matter of the church being true to itself and to the biblical vision rather than making any effort to "meddle in politics." The church simply keeps faith with its message concerning the God of creation, the kingdom of God, and life in Christ when it challenges the exercise of power on behalf of privileged groups. Today in our own society that quest for justice continues in the attempt to challenge the misuse of power and to bring healing to such divisions as those between ethnic groups, between genders, and between the rich and the poor.

One might argue that the church is inherently conservative and not likely to be at the cutting edge of any movement that would challenge injustice and lead to significant social change. Is it an exercise in self-deception to identify the church with the cause of social justice? Is the church so wedded to the establishment that its ability or even its willingness to challenge structures of injustice have been fatally compromised? It is true that significant social movements in the recent past—those relating to civil rights, the Vietnam War, women, and the environment— have not been spearheaded by the church, and yet churches have exerted a significant moral impact that in some cases, particularly in regard to the civil rights movement, has been essential to the movement's success. In many instances the efforts of individuals and groups generated from within the church have contributed substantially to the success of social causes. Often the impact of the church on efforts toward social justice may be more intangible, related to the ideas expressed in its tradition that exalt equality and justice; those ideas give implicit, if not explicit, support to those who are working for a more just and humane society. Given the privatizing tendencies of many in the church today, there is particular need to make clear the importance of the church's witness in the public square and to point out the obvious connections of the church's ethical tradition with the plight of the poor and all those who suffer from exclusion and discrimination.

From this discussion it should be clear that the church's responsibility to society is not based on its likely success or lack of success in making a difference in a society often characterized as post-Christian. The ultimate question we must address as a community of faith rooted in the biblical revelation is the nature of the God who is proclaimed there. For the moral life as well as everything else, the question Scripture poses is always the same: "Who is your God?" Christians, whether individually or as a community, will answer by confessing the triune God, Father, Son, and Spirit, with the moral life taking on particular shape in response to that confession. Reflecting on the nature and implications of that confession as it is embodied in the biblical story, Christians have centered on the importance of love and justice: the God of love enters into a broken world by bringing possibilities of forgiveness, reconciliation, and healing, as well as challenging that world with a prophetic call to justice and integrity. Thus the truth that God is love and desires justice is to be reflected in the lives of Christians as they express love and seek justice in their own lives and relationships, both as individuals and corporately.

The chapters that follow address three subjects that pose important and divisive moral issues for our society, deserving the careful attention of the church. My purpose in addressing them is twofold: to illustrate an approach to these issues that is consistent with the biblically based ethical orientation described as "spirit ethics," relating its understanding of biblical authority to each of these controverted subjects; and to offer substantive conclusions that may be of help to Christians as well as others in their consideration of these topics. While particular theological and ethical assumptions will be brought to bear that are based on convictions of faith, I believe that the conclusions at which I arrive have merit for the public discussion and deserve consideration on the part of others, whatever the theological or philosophical convictions they bring to these topics. It is in this spirit of dialogue rather than one of dogmatic utterance of final truths that I offer my reflections on these topics.

6
EUTHANASIA
AND ASSISTED SUICIDE

An initial concern in each of these three chapters that address a current social issue is to reflect on those convictions rooted in Scripture and tradition that provide the Christian community with an orientation and perspective on the particular issue. What are the distinctively Christian presumptions that churches bring to the subject of euthanasia and assisted suicide? Furthermore, what import should those theological and anthropological presumptions have in shaping the conclusions that Christians arrive at in addressing euthanasia and assisted suicide? These questions properly recognize that the believing community has a distinctive witness to make in regard to these subjects. At the same time, they are questions raised in a particular cultural environment that enters into and shapes the response that Christians make to them. There is always the temptation to foreclose discussion of this changing scene by simply reiterating traditional Christian thinking, or by appealing to selected Scripture passages as a way of wielding a conclusive biblical authority on the matter. As a preferable alternative, it is first necessary to discuss the changes taking place in the care of the dying in order to better understand the situation we are facing, and to help us shape and relate Christian convictions to that situation in a way that effectively engages it.

Christian Convictions Relating to Death

The secularized, pluralist society described in preceding chapters brings some notable attitudes and beliefs about death and dying that both challenge Christian faith and provide rich occasion for Christian witness. Alluding to Walker Percy's imaginative novel *The Thanatos Syndrome*,[1] Vigen Guroian argues that a real-world "thanatos syndrome" has now emerged, in which a figure such as Dr. Jack Kevorkian functions as a high priest, proclaiming the absolute autonomy of the individual over questions of when and how to die. This viewpoint, says Guroian, has developed quite logically in a "postmodern environment no longer pervasively informed by the life-affirming principles of biblical faith."[2] Kevorkian urges society forward to a new age of "medicide" and "obitiatry," terms he coins in order to articulate a view of medicine that is divorced from religion, no longer restricted by the latter's taboos, and free to exercise its rightful sovereignty over death and dying.[3] The medical establishment would assume the character of a priesthood in Kevorkian's vision, providing therapy and guidance that would remove the "sting" of death of which Paul writes. Faith in God is replaced with faith in the capacity of humanity to resolve the threat and mystery of human mortality.

This secular worldview is united with the changing character of medicine in our society, brought about not least by the massive developments in medical technology. These changes in worldview and technology are together creating the new moral and cultural landscape in which euthanasia and suicide are being addressed today, making it necessary for Christians to take a fresh look at these topics.[4] One significant development resulting from medical advances has been the lengthening of the human life span, which has also changed the way people are dying. Infectious diseases that ravaged society up to seventy-five years ago, bringing death quickly, have now given way to degenerative diseases that stalk the old—such as cancer, stroke, and heart disease. The World Health Organization warns that this development will bring a huge increase in human suffering and disability as people linger on during the process of dying, gradually losing their capacity to function at the most rudimentary level. While basic Christian convictions concerning life and death have not changed, the developments taking place have made it more difficult for Christians to agree on the appropriate application of these convictions to the new circumstances now arising.

A fundamental Christian conviction stemming from the biblical witness and the church's tradition is that human life is a gift from God. We are creatures, not the Creator, profoundly dependent on the God of creation, who bestows value and purpose to human life. Therefore we are not autonomous beings who can claim absolute sovereignty over our lives; we are accountable to God. Life is not ultimately at our disposal, for we are stewards rather than sovereign possessors of our lives. This biblical insight clearly has implications for euthanasia and suicide, challenging the popular notion of a human sovereignty over death, often expressed in the language of "rights." There obviously are appropriate contexts for insisting on human rights, including the right to be protected from harm and injury that may be inflicted by irresponsible and intrusive medical care. But that right, as it has been understood in the church, does not extend our sovereignty to the point of deciding when and how we are going to die. To claim that kind of sovereignty for Christian faith has always been regarded as usurpation of the sovereignty of God. Thus Christians, in addressing those problems arising from medical practice in the care of the terminally ill, quite naturally would want to seek a solution by other means than by legalizing euthanasia and assisted suicide. Yet those problems today have inspired a massive chorus of voices calling for legalization, and one obvious challenge is to understand the nature of those problems and the concerns being raised so that they can be addressed in a responsible manner. Indeed, the church has something important both to learn and to contribute in addressing the new moral landscape created by these developments.

A second Christian conviction that has a bearing on euthanasia and assisted suicide is resurrection from the dead. The resurrection of Jesus Christ is at the center of this conviction, conveying the power and sovereignty of God over both life and death. Paul is particularly eloquent in proclaiming the resurrection, which he lifts up as God's deed in the face of humanity's archenemy, death. In 1 Corinthians 15 the apostle comes to grips with the threat of death, claiming victory over that threat—the "sting" of death—through the promise of the resurrection:

> Lo, I tell you a mystery. We shall not all sleep, but we shall all be changed, in a moment, in a twinkling of an eye, at the last trumpet. For the trumpet will sound, and the dead will be raised imperishable, and we shall be changed. For this perishable nature must put on the imperishable, and this mortal nature must put on immortality. When the perishable puts on the imperishable, and the mortal puts on immortality, then shall come to pass the saying that is written:
>
> "Death is swallowed up in victory." "O death, where is thy victory? O death, where is thy sting?" The sting of death is sin, and the power of sin is the law. But thanks be to God, who gives us the victory through our Lord Jesus Christ. (1 Cor. 15:51-57)

Paul addresses death here in apocalyptic mode, equating it with mortality, which constitutes the ultimate boundary of human life and raises the question of human destiny. The awareness of death that permeates human existence casts a deep shadow over life; it is the great void, threatening to swallow life in a sea of nothingness. Thus all religions address death in some way or another, seeking to incorporate it into a larger vision that brings meaning to human existence in the face of our mortality. Paul sees existence as future-oriented; we are creatures who live by hope. We look at life in terms of purposes and goals and find meaning in the horizons of life that beckon us into the future with a spirit of expectation. Death brings the end not only to biological life but to our hopes and dreams, and thus comes as a robber and an enemy. The Christian gospel addresses us at this ultimate boundary with the news of the resurrection of Jesus Christ, proclaiming to the world that the God of Christian faith is Lord over both life and death. Death is not ultimate defeat but transition into the mystery of new life.

This resurrection faith stamps every Christian consideration of death, whether it be in the courage of the martyr who faces execution, the agony of the parents whose child has been snatched away in a cruel accident, or the thankfulness of the children who witness the end of an exemplary and rewarding life in the death of an aged parent. This faith should also inform Christians in their consideration of the current debate over euthanasia and assisted suicide. In approaching death with the hope of the resurrection, the person of faith is willing to rest this radical transition from death to resurrection life in the hands of God. There is no longer any ultimate reason for fearing death, making unseemly for the Christian any kind of desperate scrambling that would seek to avoid it. Recognizing one's mortality and living self-consciously with that reality, accepting and acknowledging the ultimate inevitability of one's own death, goes hand in hand with a belief in resurrection.

These two convictions, that life is a gift from God but that there is a human destiny that transcends this life, are rooted in the God of creation and redemption, respectively. The one conviction roots us thoroughly in this life, which is not to be despised, while the other turns us to an ultimate destiny that brings this life to completion. While both affirm the reality of God, the one belief is this-world centered, stressing the accountability of humans in living out their lives together in the presence of God. The other belief looks beyond this world to a destiny that transcends it, and yet which does not denigrate this world or seek to escape it. Together the two convictions inspire a profound honesty among Christians concerning the world in which they live. That world, on the one hand, is essential to human identity and meaning, the context in which human life and experience occur. It is the gift of the Creator, bringing beauty and enjoyment to human life as well as challenging us to live responsibly toward each other as sojourners along the way. It is a moral universe, bestowing meaning and depth to human relationships and enabling us to find both joy and fulfillment in them. On the other hand, the resurrection faith sees the present order as one that yearns for completion, recognizing a transcendence in which it finds its ultimate consummation. This belief that the world is not our final home provides a liberating perspective, enabling believers to appreciate it but not become enslaved to it, to embrace it but not to be possessed by it. Thus the tension between these beliefs creates a tension within the life of the believer that calls for honesty and balance in relating present experience to future destiny. Under extreme circumstances this balance can be difficult to maintain; Paul himself expresses the tension in his struggle to come to terms with his imprisonment in Philippi: "My desire is to depart and be with Christ, for that is far better" (Phil. 1:23).[5]

A third significant belief among Christians that has a bearing on euthanasia and suicide relates to Christian anthropology. In the language of Reinhold Niebuhr, human beings live at the juncture of nature and spirit, and the challenge is to maintain the tension-laden *unity* of this twofold character of human nature if we are to do justice to its unique character.[6] A besetting problem in the history of the church's anthropology has been the tendency toward a dualistic view of humanity in which the spirit dimension or soul is conceptually separated from the body, becoming the distinctive *humanum*, which defines human existence in contrast to the physical, embodied nature of our existence. Philosophical analysis has helped us recognize the impact of language in creating this kind of dualism in which two concepts—body and soul—are defined as polar opposites. As a noun (defined as a word that denotes a person, place, or thing) the word *soul* is construed as an *entity* within the body, a spiritual substance independent of one's physical being. This is an effect of language, which leads us to *reify* or make a "thing" out of the soul as a way to account for particular dimensions of human experience. An interesting example of this phenomenon is seen in the early modern philosopher, René Descartes (1588–1650), a mind-body dualist himself, who sought to account for their interaction by placing the soul in the pineal gland located in the brain.

Thus our capacities for self-awareness and self-transcendence, our cognitive and affective life, the quest for meaning and the presence of faith and religious experience—all have been ascribed to the soul that inhabits the human body. Within the context of organized religion and in the popular mind, the soul has been identified particularly with human immortality. As the spiritual essence of the human being, the soul is not subject to the ravages of time, physical deterioration, and death, and thus it becomes the basis for human claims to immortality. While this notion of the soul has been a venerable part of Christian theology, it has been contested in recent generations by Protestant theologians in particular, who recognize the concept of an eternal soul as belonging to the Greek intellectual tradition rather than to the Bible. Life after death in the New Testament clearly rests in the sovereignty of God who has raised Jesus from the dead, making resurrection the distinctive claim of Christian faith rather than immortality of the soul.

A more cogent understanding of anthropology for today that is faithful to the Christian tradition would understand the soul as a metaphorical expression, affirming the spiritual as well as bodily character of human existence. This is a view that can affirm our existence as a unity in tension rather than describing it in dualistic terms. We are not spiritual selves who also happen to "have" bodies, but rather are bodies that reveal the spiritual characteristics of intellect, will, and purpose. One might speak of a "spirit-filled" body, or an "ensouled" body, acknowledging the language of Paul, who does not hesitate to bring the Spirit of God into connection with the human body (1 Cor. 6:19).[7] This holistic view resists the temptation either to separate the human being into physical and spiritual "parts," or to reduce the human being to either a physical or spiritual essence, as in naturalism or idealism.

The implications of these anthropological reflections for euthanasia and suicide are twofold: on the one hand, they deter any tendency to define life in a body-centered, vitalistic manner that leads to an inordinate concern to keep the body "alive" at all costs, without regard to those spiritual dimensions of existence that we recognize in the expression *quality of life*. This is to separate body and spirit in a way that absolutizes physical existence and sees the prolongation of that existence as the ultimate goal of medical care, regardless of its quality for the body-self of the patient.

On the other hand, the implications of a holistic understanding of human existence would also avoid the opposite extreme of defining human life exclusively or even primarily in terms of a spiritual self or soul, resulting in the denigration of the body. In the context of death and dying, this view becomes obsessed with quality-of-life considerations that invite a premature termination of a less-than-acceptable existence. In the Christian context, to understand life primarily in spiritual terms tempts one to flee the body too quickly in favor of a perfect existence beyond death. Each of these extremes loses the necessary tension that must be maintained in affirming the unity of the body-self, resulting in medical treatment that fails to maintain a proper balance between keeping a body alive at all costs and tending to the quality of the patient's life. A holistic view of the body-self would stress the obligation to maintain an appropriate balance between these dimensions of existence in caring for the dying patient. Just where the line is to be drawn in maintaining that responsible balance in any given case becomes a matter of moral judgment in light of these considerations.

Medical Technology and the "Sanctity of Life"

In the practice of medicine itself, a number of historical developments have converged to create the kind of ethical problems we are facing in the euthanasia and assisted-suicide controversy. One significant development in contemporary health care has been the emphasis on patient autonomy. This development has been a two-edged sword, encouraging the taking of more responsibility for one's health but also encouraging a philosophical stance that would claim sovereignty over life and death in a way that denies Christian belief. Within the context of the physician-patient relationship, this claim of autonomy has involved a gradual and consistent move away from the traditional, paternalistic belief that "doctor knows best," and that all decisions relating to one's health care should be left to the physician.[8] While the physician obviously brings to the care of the patient a professional competence that can only be appreciated and respected, the point is made that the patient is a person, not just a physical specimen on which the physician "works." As persons, patients are now expected to enter into decision making that affects their future well-being and that of their families. Paternalism has become a favorite whipping boy in much of contemporary medicine, with corresponding changes being made in the instruction of medical students, including much more attention to the importance of informed consent on the part of the patient.

Another highly significant development in health care has been the evolution in medical technology. These changes have been dramatic, signaled by the advent in recent decades of kidney dialysis and artificial respirators and the use of intensive care units, organ transplantation, prenatal surgery, the contraception pill and medically safe abortions, and genetic manipulation. This increasingly sophisticated technology has had a tremendous impact in improving medical care, saving lives that in earlier times would have been lost. Thus medical technology has been a notable blessing, pushing back the boundary line of death and giving new hope to countless numbers of people. At the same time, however, a paradox has emerged. In the care of the terminally ill, the technology involved has had a two-sided effect, not only bestowing life but also in many instances simply prolonging death. The use of technology is subject to human decision, and often the best intentions have resulted not in the restoration of health but the continued maintenance of the patient in a prolonged process of dying. Thus the humanizing impact of modern medicine has brought with it a shadow side that has contributed to the current controversy over euthanasia and assisted suicide. This controversy is accentuated by the movement toward patient autonomy, which has encouraged public protest in the face of medical care that appears to dehumanize the dying patient. Euthanasia societies, together with much public sentiment, have voiced the conviction that people have a right to die "with dignity" rather than suffer the indignity of artificial maintenance by machines that prevent a merciful release of life.

One ought not overlook another dimension of the impact of technology on health care: the transformation of physicians and their relationship to their patients. In a previous era the physician journeyed to the home of the patient, spending time with patient and family as a friend and counselor as well as physician. Technology has fathered machinery that now compels patients to come to the hospital or clinic, where physicians can practice their healing art more efficiently in terms of speed and the number of patients seen. The *personal* dimension of medicine has suffered from these developments, contributing to a certain alienation of the patient and a diminution of respect toward the physician. While there is obviously much reason to be grateful for the vastly improved capacities of health care due to technological progress, it has not occurred without considerable cost. The embittered words of novelist Reynolds Price, speaking from his experience as a patient struggling with catastrophic illness, mirrors too accurately the experience of many patients: "Maybe we have the right to demand that [the physician] display a warning on the office door or the starched lab coat, like those on other dangerous bets— *Expert technician. Expect no more. The quality of your life and death are your concern.*"[9] Any antipathies stirred by this situation are bound to be accentuated where the patient is dying and has to cope with the machinery that stands between her and the medical practitioner.

There is also an unfortunate irony here in the fact that concerns characteristically voiced by the Christian community over the "sanctity of life" have actually played a role in contributing to the dehumanizing impact of technology and public agitation concerning euthanasia. As Daniel Callahan observes:

The power of medicine to extend life under poor circumstances is now widely and increasingly feared. The combined power of a quasi-religious tradition of respect for individual life and a secular tradition of relentless medical progress, creates a bias toward aggressive, often unremitting treatment that seems unstoppable.[10]

The insistence on the sanctity of life has been an affirmation of the inviolability of the individual, a precious truth for Christian faith, and a cornerstone for a democratic society. In this context of care of the dying, however, human sanctity has been reduced to vitalism, or the maintaining of physical life with no attention to the quality of that life. This is an understandable happenstance when people are in life-and-death circumstances, for attention is then riveted on maintaining the basic physiological processes essential to existence. While human life depends on a functioning body, however, human existence is far more than bodily functions. In too many instances, intense efforts to care for human life have resulted in maintaining a biological shell of what was once a human existence, a development that is certainly incongruous with concerns about the sanctity of life. This situation is prompting Christians to reassess the appropriate implications of this conviction for those persons whose thread to life is irreversibly dependent upon the machinery of the intensive care unit.

It is also worth considering the full impact on contemporary medicine of the church's dualistic tendencies in understanding human life—the body/soul dichotomy referred to above. One consequence for the church's role in society has been its implicit, if not explicit, acknowledgment of a limited sphere of concern it brings to society, and therefore a limited realm of influence that it appropriately exercises. That concern has been defined by so-called spiritual realities that stand apart from and in contrast to the material interests of the secular world. The church has become identified with the realm of the soul that finds meaning outside the secular realm, often understood as the realm beyond death in a life to come. The secular world has been left to the practitioners of politics, economics, science, and technology, while the church has withdrawn to its spiritual world in which it can claim its own autonomy, limited as it may be. Thus the idea that the church may have something important to say concerning medical and bioethical issues on the basis of its theological and anthropological convictions is too easily discounted by relegating the church and its theology to another realm of meaning, irrelevant to the moral issues we face.

The impact of this separation of Christian and secular worlds can be seen in the contemporary context of dying, dominated as it is by the instruments and ethos of science and technology. While bringing considerable blessing to society, that ethos has also created intense moral dilemmas in the often obsessive attempt to prolong life at all costs. We have noted how the Christian emphasis on the sanctity of life has made its contribution to this phenomenon, but the actual situation we face is much more the result of two converging factors: the natural desire to save and continue life, and the availability of highly sophisticated, life-preserving tools of medical technology. Together these two elements have led to unusual sovereignty on the part of medical practice over the patient's moment of death, with decisions to use life-sustaining machinery postponing that moment indefinitely. Thus death becomes subject to human decision in a way not experienced before; that moment is literally placed in the hands of the caregivers who must decide whether to continue or to withdraw treatment—whether to maintain life or terminate it. This has to be an agonizing experience, for it concentrates the prospect of life or death in one crucial decision. The desires of the patient, made known through an advance directive, will often compete with the conflicted feelings of the family or with the perspective and ethos of the caregiver. This new sovereignty over the process of dying is a reality—uncomfortable as it is—that technology has created for us, and it constitutes yet another factor that is relevant to the debate over euthanasia, which we want to examine now before turning to assisted suicide.

Euthanasia and "Allowing to Die"

Historically, *euthanasia* (from the Greek, meaning a "good death") has been understood as "mercy killing," or the compassionate hastening of a person's death by overt action in order to save that person from great pain and suffering. With the development of technology that maintains life artificially, it has been necessary to make a distinction between this overt taking of life (as, for example, intentionally raising the amount of morphine being given as a painkiller until it becomes lethal) and the act of withholding or withdrawing treatment, which results in the patient's death. The former has been denoted "active" euthanasia and the latter "passive" euthanasia, in an effort to distinguish between an act of commission and an act of omission. Both acts are clearly responsible for the patient's death, but is there a moral distinction to be made between them? This question has occasioned a lively debate. On the one side are those who argue that there is no moral difference between active and passive euthanasia because the end or purpose of the action is the same in both instances—both intend and seek to bring about the death of the patient. The issue is seen simply as a question of means between the two, or *how* the action is accomplished, while the substance of the matter that determines its ethical character is really the goal or purpose of the means being taken. Therefore, according to this argument, since the end is the same, there is no difference between the two actions from an ethical point of view.[11]

Those who claim that there is a significant moral difference between active and passive euthanasia argue that the latter is based on the recognition that the patient's disease has taken its course and that further treatment is simply impeding the dying process. Withholding or withdrawing treatment is not appropriately seen as *causing* the death of the patient but as *allowing* the patient to die. One is recognizing that there is no longer any hope for the patient's regaining health and that further treatment has become an imposition rather than a life-serving act. I believe this argument is sound; it recognizes that the critical moral issue is whether the caregiver is obligated any longer to sustain life in the case of this particular patient. If, on the basis of compassion and careful judgment and under precautions that prevent arbitrary or irresponsible actions, it is determined that the patient is irreversibly removed from the human community, then the decision to allow the patient to die becomes theologically and morally justifiable. The term *euthanasia* should not be used to describe this kind of decision, because it confuses the moral issue between killing and allowing to die. Given the available medical technology and improved medical care, allowing the patient to die is a decision that is increasingly defining the conclusion of people's lives. If confidence in the medical profession is to be maintained, discontinuing useless or futile treatment in the future will have to be recognized as both a moral and legal imperative.

Often those who stand in the way of allowing a person to die are not physicians but the family or one member of the family who refuses to "let go." Whether with a Christian family or otherwise, this can occur because of complicated relationships that have never been resolved between the dying person and the family member. As far as the theological and ethical issues are concerned, however, Christians who live in the resurrection faith will not let death inspire the kind of mortal fear that leads one to absolutize the value of life without concern for its quality. Life is to be embraced, but not in a way that denies either death's inevitability or the presence of a gracious God in both life and death. The new sovereignty over death and dying bestowed by medical technology is forcing Christians to reflect anew on the fact that it is not within humanity's power to overcome death; the marvelous advances of medicine in pushing back the boundaries of death and providing a more productive and healthy life span are indeed laudable but ought not encourage the notion that mortality itself can and ought to be removed. In an increasingly secularized society, the temptation is strong to understand the malleability of human nature in ways that allow for a significant redefinition of life's boundaries, promising at least a significantly prolonged life span, if not immortality itself. In contrast to this attitude, Christians have reason to be more concerned about efforts to improve the humane quality of life than simply to increase the quantity of its years.[12]

The current definition of death in terms of "brain death" (a flat electroencephalogram) has also contributed to the setting we are describing. It means that the realm of consciousness and cognition in the brain— the neocortex or "upper brain"—can be totally removed and the patient still regarded as alive because the brain stem, or "lower brain," is still functioning. Thus the heart and lungs can be maintained and the patient can be fed intravenously or by a nasogastric tube so that biological life continues; but in terms of personal awareness and presence, the patient is irreversibly removed. Where the patient has been healthy but has sustained, for example, an injury to the head, destroying the upper brain, it may not be a state of terminal illness but a "persistent vegetative state" that offers no real hope for recovery. In this state of removal and isolation, technology bestows a kind of life that is little else than a "living death," stirring revulsion and adding fuel to the arguments of pro-euthanasia groups. As a society we need to seriously consider redefining death in terms of the permanent cessation of consciousness, or neocortical death.[13]

The euthanasia debate inevitably raises the issue of the quality of life as long as people agree that there are certain conditions under which a person should be allowed to die. The decisive factor in that decision is not the degree of suffering experienced by the patient, or the extent to which one can anticipate any future for the patient. The essential criterion, rather, is whether the patient is still aware of others and capable of any kind of relationship. In any given instance, this may not be easy to determine, and in such cases the decision would obviously involve extended deliberation. Nonetheless, if careful and informed judgment determines that the patient has passed over that line and that her condition is irreversible, then for all meaningful purposes she is dead and ought not be "maintained" as a physical organism and nothing more. What we are speaking of here are people who are in a permanent vegetative state, of which there are many thousands located throughout the country. In passing beyond the reach of human relationship they are no longer within the realm of the human, for it is only in relationship that humans receive their personal identity. People in this state will understandably remain precious to their loved ones, who are able to hold them in their memory as ones with whom they had once shared their lives. Their bodily presence must occasion respect and care, but not with the intention of maintaining them indefinitely in this state of living death. Their "appointed time" has now clearly arrived, and to release them to their mortal destiny now becomes our responsibility. This kind of decision is often excruciatingly difficult, but it is a decision that increasing numbers of families are having to make. An appropriate ritual for such occasions is called for, in which Christians acknowledge the departure of the loved one and now remove the last artificial barrier preventing release.

The point must also be clearly made that no matter how hopeless the prospect of a return to health, anyone who remains in relationship with another person remains firmly within our concern and responsibility as a fellow human being. Allowing to die does not mean a diminishment of concern for those who are severely disabled but still are able to relate to another. The quality of that relationship may be minimal, but wherever there is the self-awareness that allows for personal relationships, care and compassion are obligated. In these situations the distinction between care and cure must be clearly maintained, with the understanding that the apparent hopelessness of any cure does not remove the obligation to care for and bring whatever measure of happiness we can to a person who shares our humanity.

The spirit ethics described in chapter 5 brings to this subject a biblical perspective that I believe supports the stance described above. Its strong emphasis on community and the importance of human relationships recognizes the fact that human identity is dependent on our relationships with others. Our capacity for relationships is integral to our personhood, or what we might call the spirit dimension of our humanity. One who is irreversibly removed from human relationships is also denied his own personhood, for self-awareness and awareness of others are interrelated and necessary to each other. The highly descriptive term *vegetative state* denotes the unfortunate creature who has lost this capacity for personal and interpersonal awareness, which is to lose one's personal identity. The insistence on the unity of physical and spiritual dimensions of our humanity would also discourage the notion that regardless of one's physical state, there is "somewhere" a soul that continues to live and identify such a person. A holistic understanding takes seriously one's bodily state as an expression of one's personal or spiritual state. For a spirit ethics, allowing an individual to die when responsible medical judgment recognizes that he has moved irreversibly beyond the capacity for personal relationships, becomes a theological and ethical imperative. Because he is no longer "with us," it is an unacceptable intrusion to maintain his body indefinitely in what has become a tragic semblance of life.

Can euthanasia in its classic sense—an overt act of mercy killing—ever be conceived as a justified, ethical act? Can it be an act of Christian freedom in which one loves the patient, believing that her welfare under the present circumstances is now best served by death? Can it be a responsible act before God and the human community? These questions are more pressing and difficult today than ever before in light of the circumstances we have described concerning a longer human life span and the impact of death-delaying technology. Certainly there are many instances, marked by intense pain and disorientation, where the instinct of compassion could conceivably move one to deliberately hasten the patient's death. That course of action is at least understandable, but it is not a morally responsible act. Killing a patient is never an acceptable, ethical answer to the challenges posed by disease and other disasters, and expecting physicians to officially adopt the practice of euthanasia would be a major threat to their integrity as healing professionals. A better alternative is to develop more effective ways to practice palliative care among physicians, who in this country have been notable for their caution in the use of painkilling drugs. A reorientation within the medical profession on this subject, now under way, is necessary and long overdue. It is a reorientation in which physicians recognize the limitations of the zealous attempt to save life in every instance, and to substitute an emphasis on quality care for those who are dying. The distinction between *preventing* death and *cooperating* with death in light of its inevitability is one that the physician must learn.

Though obviously vulnerable to misuse, the principle in Roman Catholic moral theology called "double effect" can be appropriately applied to situations in which euthanasia becomes an issue. This principle maintains that if the caregiver's intention is to alleviate pain through an increased dosage of painkiller, but the secondary effect is to hasten the death of the patient, the caregiver is not culpable for the patient's death. This would be a case of *risking* death rather than *willing* it, which is a legitimate distinction. There is clearly a delicate line to be drawn here, but the essential issue is the need of combining respect for human life with compassion for the individual patient, which at times can create an agonizing dilemma for the caregiver. There is never a simple rule that resolves the matter, but always the challenge to act with integrity and goodwill in seeking a responsible solution.

There are those Christian thinkers who believe their theological and ethical traditions should allow for a greater freedom and therefore a greater responsibility to make decisions concerning the time and manner of one's death. Hans Küng argues as follows:

> So as a Christian and a theologian I feel encouraged...to argue publicly for a middle way which is responsible in both theological and Christian terms: between an anti-religious libertinism without responsibility ("unlimited right to voluntary death") and a reactionary rigorism without compassion ("even the intolerable is to be borne in submission to God as given by God"). And I do this because as a Christian and a theologian I am convinced that the all-merciful God, who has given men and women freedom and responsibility for their lives, has also left to dying people the responsibility for making a conscientious decision about the manner and time of their deaths....Why should this last phase of life in particular be exempted from responsibility?[14]

Küng makes clear that his discussion is within the context of terminal illness; he is not talking about justifying suicide at any point in one's life, but of taking responsibility for a "dignified" death in the face of great pain and other destructive and demoralizing circumstances. He is moved to take this position by the same factors that have moved us to encourage a greater openness to allowing death to occur. In emphasizing the sovereign responsibility of the patient to decide that his life should be actively terminated, however, Küng crosses a line which I think better not to do. In those cases where one might justify euthanasia because of extreme suffering, the emphasis should be on the compassionate care of the patient, doing everything in our power to enable him to rest peacefully, even if it hastens his death.

A further, complicating factor in this phenomenon is the introduction of legal maneuvering by parties who have an interest in the patient. In many instances the condition of the patient and the nature of the prognosis involve ambiguities that challenge the most astute and knowledgeable physician. There are always possibilities for mistaken judgments, a situation that is simply inherent to medical care. This element of uncertainty and sometimes confusion over the status of the dying patient, and the consequent care that is called for, is now often exploited by use of the courts. Physicians are being sued for decisions that in retrospect have been recognized as medically inappropriate or even harmful, or for decisions that have not coincided with the wishes of the family. This situation has encouraged overly aggressive medical care in order to protect the physician from claims of carelessness or insufficient attention to the needs of the patient. Thus the practice of "defensive medicine" has become commonplace, often resulting in overzealous attempts to maintain life and the further dehumanizing of the patient. While the introduction of managed care is a factor in moderating the practices of overprescribing drugs and overtreating patients, these problems are still significant issues in the care of the dying.

FROM EUTHANASIA TO ASSISTED SUICIDE

The point needs to be made more clearly that there is a significant moral distinction to be made between euthanasia and suicide. The context for euthanasia is either terminal illness and the imminence of death, or a radically altered state of being into which one has entered, such as a permanent vegetative state. Suicide, on the other hand, is a possibility that includes no reference to time in terms of an anticipated death; it can be the resort of a young person as well as an older person, both of whom having decided that the future is not worth waiting for. What the notion of assisted suicide has done is to close the distance between euthanasia and suicide by injecting the element of time. In other words, six months or a year, for example, is stipulated as the limit for one's anticipated life span in order for assisted suicide to be legal. It is still not the challenge of a devastating present, as in the case of euthanasia, but the anticipation of a possibly devastating not-too-distant future. Thus suicide and assisted suicide, as calculated attempts to avoid an anticipated evil, are more obvious examples of the human attempt to exercise sovereignty over life and death than is euthanasia. On these grounds alone suicide poses a more problematic moral and theological issue than does euthanasia.

At the same time, assisted suicide has become a critical social issue for many of the same reasons that euthanasia has. The prospect of being kept "alive" indefinitely instead of being allowed to die is certainly one prominent reason for the agitation surrounding assisted suicide. Given the instinct of self-preservation, people are not normally going to seek ways to terminate their lives. Thus the fact that suicide has become a public issue should certainly constitute a wake-up call for the medical profession. It has been argued that our society, reflecting a high degree of affluence and self-indulgence, simply wants the pain and inconvenience of dying removed or at least minimized as much as possible, and for this reason it has adopted uncritically the "death with dignity" slogan. While there is undoubtedly some truth to this contention, it is inadequate to account for the euthanasia movement. More immediately pertinent to that movement are the legitimate concerns discussed above concerning the impact of technology in prolonging unnecessarily the dying process.

It is important that Christians be sensitive to the attitudinal changes in Western society concerning suicide. These changing attitudes have been apparent within the church itself. In light of the fact that there is no direct prohibition of suicide to be found in Scripture, Christian thinking has been influenced primarily by the writings of prominent theologians. Going back at least to Augustine (354–430), the church has traditionally rendered a harsh judgment on those who willfully take their lives. Augustine maintained that suicide is self-murder and therefore deserves the same passionate condemnation that we reserve for murder. Indeed, since suicide did not allow for the possibility of repentance, it was even worse than murder, guaranteeing an eternal state of condemnation.[15] The Fifth Commandment ("Thou shalt not kill") makes no distinction that would limit the prohibition to the killing of others, and therefore, argued Augustine, it should be understood as prohibiting self-murder as much as murdering one's neighbor. These judgments, echoed in much of the tradition into the modern era, have come under considerable reexamination and revision in recent generations. While most Christians would still judge suicide as contrary to the will of God, the seriousness of their judgment has moderated significantly. This is dramatically seen in Christian funeral rites, where the custom to deny a Christian burial to those who have taken their lives is generally no longer observed. We tend now to see suicide as a case of victimization more than anything else, where an unfortunate individual has been overwhelmed by his life circumstances and has been incapable of coping. While the specific circumstances will possibly occasion varying degrees of censure, sorrow and compassion rather than judgment and exclusion have become the dominant response.

In the current discussion, the act of suicide has become significantly different. While there may well be an undercurrent of despair, assisted suicide involves a rational, deliberate act in which a premature death is chosen as the lesser of two evils. It reveals an assumption that runs counter to Christian faith: life is not a gift from God but my own possession, to be disposed of as I see fit. This assumption brings with it the idea that I have a right to die under the circumstances I choose. The language of rights, as in a "right to die," reflects this thinking of human sovereignty, encouraged by the technology that puts us in a position of having to decide about allowing an individual to die. The appropriate Christian response involves walking a delicate line. On the one hand we agree with "right to die" advocates that current circumstances in the care of many terminally ill people require a more aggressive control of the dying process. But this control is morally and theologically acceptable only within carefully prescribed limitations, where the choice is to *allow* death on grounds of compassion for one who has passed beyond the reach of human relationships. This does not justify the further claim that we have the right to choose whenever we would die on grounds of human autonomy.

There are a number of substantive ethical reasons for rejecting the legalization of assisted suicide. I have already mentioned the challenge it would raise to the integrity of the physician, who is committed to the care of the patient. The life-serving character of the medical profession would be compromised by the image of physicians providing the means or committing the act that leads to death. It is no surprise that the American Medical Association and its state affiliates have been prominent in their opposition to legislation that would legalize assisted suicide. A more widespread impact would have to be the effect that such legislation would have on the elderly and particularly the disabled. Those whose lives are perceived to be on the boundary line of "worthwhile" or "livable" existence would likely find themselves (in their own minds at least, if not in conversation with others) defending their right to continued life and to the likely significant public expense that it entailed. While the freedom of the individual to decide on life or death is lifted up as a reason for assisted suicide, the consequences would likely be a constriction of the freedom of those who chose to live against highly adverse circumstances.[16] Another, larger consideration would be the impact on the public ethos of a policy that advocates death as an answer to one's life-circumstances. To make death an option in meeting life's difficulties should be regarded as moral failure as well as a failure of imagination and ingenuity, rather than an acceptable solution to those difficulties. In this situation of terminal illness, assisted suicide also represents a failure in human compassion in the way we minister to the needs of the dying. Too often the dying person is overwhelmed with a sense of being utterly isolated and forsaken because the needed support system is lacking.

In the Middle Ages, when life was much more vulnerable to sickness and death than it is today, the exhortation *memento mori* (remember that you will die) was a not uncommon reminder appearing in monasteries and homes of believers. In a society in which people devote much energy to ignoring if not denying their mortality, Christians bring a significant witness when they address death with a spirit of realism and of hope. This attitude of faith speaks a particularly powerful message at the deathbed of the Christian where Scripture is read and prayers offered for the dying person in a spirit of hope and anticipation. Death is life's severest reminder that we are not autonomous beings who are in control, but mortal beings who have no alternative but to submit to the inevitable.

That final confrontation need not inspire fear and panic and attempts to avoid it, but can be met with one's family and fellow believers with language of praise and thanksgiving. This faith carries the imperative to minister to the dying, surrounding them with care and the necessary means to ease the burden of pain in one's closing hours. This finally is the most important response that Christians can bring to the controversy concerning euthanasia and assisted suicide.

7

HOMOSEXUALITY

There is scarcely a subject more volatile and disruptive of the life of the church today than homosexuality. The reason for its prominence among those social issues currently demanding the church's attention is fairly obvious: there have been some profound changes in recent generations in our understanding of homosexuality, with new insights and perspectives emerging in response to questions about its nature, its causes, its relation to heterosexuality, and appropriate moral judgments to be made of it. The church has not been unaffected by these developments, with reactions among Christians ranging the full gamut from a vociferous repudiation of any suggestion that the church's tradition should be changed or reassessed, to a cautious willingness to listen further, to a conviction that it is well past time for the church to change its historic stance on this issue. How should the church respond to this situation? There is a twofold task the church faces: it needs to educate itself concerning the developments going on in the public understanding of homosexuality and to consider the moral implications of those developments; and it needs to understand the significance of the changes taking place within the life of the church itself, in which Christian gays and lesbians are now visible as never before.

The Current Scene Concerning Homosexuality

As has been noted several times in these pages, the character of social ethics is inherently dynamic. One contributing factor to this situation is the continuing development of society's knowledge. As noted in chapter 4, ethical judgments are critically dependent in part on empirical evidence, or "the facts of the matter" as they are responsibly determined. These "facts" themselves are subject to change. They may be relatively hard scientific data that compel wide assent on the part of thinking people and clearly define a particular social issue. An example of this would be the effects of tobacco use, which scientific investigation has now established as clearly deleterious to one's health. This fact has obvious implications for the morality of its use, and yet there will always be some who persist in denying what appears quite obvious to most people. The facts in relation to many other moral issues are often not as clear, as for example in the debate over capital punishment in which the actual impact of the death penalty in deterring crime becomes a debatable question. The reality is that very few facts can be divorced from interpretation. It is characteristic of controversial moral issues that agreement is difficult to establish even over the data that define them—what is fact to one person in defining and understanding the issue may not be accepted as fact by the other. Nonetheless, sound ethical judgment does require accurate understanding of the subject at issue; the more clearly one grasps its nature, the more likely a sound moral judgment will be made. Ignorance will skew any moral judgment.

These observations have particular import for the evaluation of homosexuality because the last half-century has seen the first sustained and meaningful efforts to gain a better comprehension of it. These efforts have proceeded in spite of many obstacles, including the massively condemnatory attitudes that have been directed toward gay people[1] and that have discouraged serious research concerning their condition. Any responsible attempt to treat this subject today, however, cannot ignore the new insights that have served to substantially reconstitute the homosexual issue. This does not mean that every question has been answered, for the immensely complicated nature of human sexuality does not lend itself to clear and obvious scientific answers. Here again, given the deeply contested character of this issue, we can expect that any findings will themselves be subject to attack and that contrary data will be proposed. While our purposes here do not allow for extended treatment of these scientific developments, we must acknowledge them and ask how they should affect the church's historic stance on this subject.

The most significant development in recent generations concerning homosexuality has been a shift in focus from the homosexual act to the homosexual person, with particular interest in what causes homosexuality. Definitions of homosexuality have shifted from exclusive reference to same-sex erotic behavior to the nature or orientation of the homosexual person, who is defined as possessing a stable erotic drive directed toward persons of the same sex. Research on this condition has led to the language of "sexual orientation," which reflects the experience of gay persons. At some time during the course of their growing up, usually at a fairly early age, they begin to *discover* that their sexual desire is oriented toward those of the same sex. On the basis of thousands of interviews in a variety of settings, this conclusion seems to fit the vast majority of gay persons.[2] Thus the commonly used term *sexual preference,* is seen to convey the false impression that a personal choice is involved in the determination of one's sexual orientation. The evidence would certainly indicate that this is no more the case with gay persons than with heterosexual persons.

There remains the question as to *how* the homosexual orientation has occurred. The dominant answer in the psychotherapeutic community has been that of Freud, who maintained that psychological factors involving disturbed relations with parents have led to a distorted psychosexual development. With the greater visibility of well-adjusted gays in our society whose upbringing in the home does not fit this hypothesis (that of a possessive mother and a distant father), the idea of accounting for all gay persons in terms of this psychopathology is not as convincing as it once was. In recent decades researchers have investigated hormonal activity as a possible decisive factor, but for many the results have been less than convincing. Hormonal changes can affect the intensity of the sexual drive, but it is not clear that they can affect its direction. The most notable research in recent years has focused on the human brain and genetic factors. One study of the brain claimed to have identified a region of the hypothalamus that varies in size among males depending on their sexual orientation.[3] A team at the National Cancer Institute in 1993 claimed to have identified a region of the X-chromosome that is associated with some forms of male homosexuality.[4] Another noteworthy experiment has compared the incidence of homosexuality in the case of identical twins ("monozygotic"), fraternal twins ("dizygotic"), and genetically unrelated adopted brothers.[5] If there is a genetic dimension to homosexuality, then where it is present we would expect a higher rate of occurrence in both twins who share the same genome than in the other two cases. This in fact is what the study found, with a gay-gay concordance rate of 52 percent with the identical twins, and 22 percent and 11 percent, respectively, with the other two. Yet for many these results remain less than decisive because similar experiments conducted by others have failed to replicate them.[6]

Most scientists are inclined to believe that no one biological answer is persuasive in addressing homosexual orientation. Many will acknowledge the possibility of a genetic predisposition and are likely to believe that the condition is amenable to biological exploration. But the common belief seems to be that there are likely a number of factors, both biological and psychosocial, that have contributed to a homosexual orientation in any given case, with probably differing weights to be assigned each factor from one case to another. Of course, many gays would dispute any attempt to find a biological answer to the question of etiology because they regard homosexuality as a social construction rather than a biological matter. They argue that any attempt to locate a "gay gene" would result in a deterministic explanation for one's sexuality, an explanation that I would have to agree is both reductionist and inadequate in accounting for something as complex as one's sexuality. There is, however, a significant difference between recognizing the biological rootedness of one's sexuality and concluding that we are biologically "determined." Given the state of our knowledge today, which would encourage the notion of a genetic predisposition in understanding homosexuality, what implications does it have for a moral evaluation of the subject?

One implication that follows from what we have learned about sexual orientation is that we can hardly place people under moral judgment for having *discovered* something about themselves. We cannot hold people morally culpable for something they did not choose or for which they are not responsible. At the same time, the recognition of a genetic factor does not insure unanimity on whether gays are innocent or responsible concerning their behavior. Some would argue that there are biological predispositions to all of what they would call sinful behavior, but the responsibility is still ours to refrain from engaging in it. They are inclined to regard homosexuality along the lines of an addiction or a habit one can deny with sufficient discipline or will power (such as an alcoholic condition). I believe a much more persuasive and authentic understanding of one's sexuality would make it an integral part of one's self-identity as a person. It is not a piece of baggage that can be dispensed with at will; it is an immediate and intimate dimension of *who* one is, and that needs to be granted before we can talk about responsible sexual conduct. Thus our recognition of sexual orientation should enable us to see the larger issue of one's sexuality as an expression of personal identity, and to place sexual activity within that context in order to understand it and to arrive at appropriate moral judgments.

Many churches have been in conversation with these new perspectives and have now entered a state of transition concerning homosexuality, tentatively making their way to a more definite reassessment. Given the personal, intimate character of our sexuality, the highly taboo nature of homosexuality, and the possible societal changes implicit in any reassessment of the subject, it is a considerable challenge for the church to engage in the kind of conversation and deliberation the subject requires. Jeffrey Siker's observation is quite apt:

> Participating in constructive discussions means that people must be willing to risk something of themselves, for we are not talking here primarily about some objective "issue" out there, but about real people: about ourselves, about gay and lesbian people among us, about sons and daughters, mothers and fathers, brothers and sisters. This is by definition an intensely personal conversation, for we are talking with and about actual people, about matters of personal identity and self-understanding, about our relationships with one another.[7]

The process is also highly unsettling because long-held ideas about homosexuality are being challenged, and moral judgments that over the centuries have become sacrosanct are being rejected. Nor is there any guarantee as to the eventual outcome of this critical new direction; it can only be pursued in a spirit of prayer that asks for the guidance and mercy of God. It is obviously not a time for dogmatic assertions, for the uncomfortable reality of having to rely on empirical investigation is that the data often remain ambiguous, subject to continuing interpretation and dispute. Nonetheless, for increasing numbers of Christians and their churches, the evidence is sufficient to constitute one among several reasons to seek a change in the church's thinking and attitudes concerning gay people.

While these developments concerning homosexuality are particularly unsettling to many, they should also serve as a reminder that moral positions within church and society have never been entirely static. Christians have changed their minds many times in the course of history concerning many very important moral issues. While planting the seeds for its eventual repudiation, the attitude of Paul toward slavery, for example, could hardly serve as a model for us today. The fact that the status of women in society has profoundly changed over the years has also resulted in radical changes in the morality of gender relationships. The command in Genesis 1:28 to "be fruitful and multiply, and fill the earth," no longer carries the imperative today that it has in the past, given a world now threatened by overpopulation and widespread pollution. One could further mention significant shifts in the moral judgments Christians have made concerning war and peace, political and economic arrangements, and many more commonplace virtues and vices.[8] Many a theological as well as moral "truth" over the centuries has been discarded or abandoned as it lost authority in the face of changing times. The notion of a deposit of eternal truths "once for all delivered to the saints" is entirely inappropriate in regard to our moral tradition, for in this realm we are dealing with our response to the Gospel, not the Gospel itself. The changing character of our moral convictions needs to be recognized and appreciated as a background to addressing the subject of homosexuality.

We are in fact at a genuine learning moment as a church, and it can be a time of significant growth and maturation. Anytime the church addresses a serious, divisive issue, it poses an opportunity to better understand our tradition as well as the world in which we live. I believe the comment of the British ethicist Ian McDonald expresses an important truth that applies directly to our situation: "In Christian ethics there must always be a return to the heart of the tradition precisely at the point where one is engaging with the most contextual of modern problems. It is thus that one begins to hear what the Spirit is saying to the churches."[9] One can read this statement in two different directions—both forward from the tradition to the issue, which will bring a clarifying word and help us address our situation, and backward from the issue to the tradition, which will help us clarify the tradition as we review and reunderstand it. I believe our principal responsibility today regarding the subject of homosexuality is to carry out the latter task without losing those insights of the tradition concerning sexuality that continue to inform and guide us.

Another highly significant factor in the homosexuality controversy relates to the church's own life as a believing community. Now, for the first time, churches are facing the issue of homosexuality with fellow Christians who are professed gays and lesbians. The gay person is not simply "the other," one who is kept at a safe distance as a kind of leper whom it is easy to reject. Now we know the gay person as one of us, a fellow member of the household of faith. This is a radical change, for until recently Christian gays and lesbians have been the most invisible people on earth, particularly in the church, finding it impossible to be themselves in an atmosphere of moral and theological rejection. Whether living as singles or in partnership, Christian homosexual persons have emerged as fellow believers, witnesses to God's grace, and co-workers in the kingdom, fundamentally changing the nature of this debate. Their presence provides yet another element in the experience of the contemporary Christian community that has a bearing on our moral and theological response to this issue.

It may be argued that this distinctively ecclesial dimension to the homosexuality issue does not resolve the theological and moral questions concerning it. Many Christians would contend that the fact that gays and lesbians are members of the household of faith is irrelevant to the fact that the church historically has understood Scripture to render a severe judgment on them. It is precisely here that the issue lies for the church. A spirit ethics is willing to listen more seriously to the contemporary experience of the church as it grapples with difficult moral issues. It assumes that God is at work in the world, and that changes marked by greater understanding, and by the recovery of a people once repudiated and lost to the church, bear the signs of God's presence. The church is being challenged to recognize that its own experience in the present moment, in which a once alienated people are being restored, is a powerful reality that cannot be denied by laws out of the past that have consigned these very people to perpetual judgment. On this issue the tension between the church's present life and experience and its received moral tradition going back to the Bible itself, is probably as intense as any conflict it has experienced.

Given these realities, it is understandable that at this point the church remains seriously divided over how to interpret the significance of what is happening. It needs more time to digest the meaning of the changes going on in its own midst as well as in society. Some scholars have suggested that the events narrated in Acts 10–11, in which the young church is moved by the Spirit to recognize that the gospel of Jesus Christ is intended not just for the Jew but for the Gentile as well, could well serve as an analogy for what is happening today.[10] The critical question for the early church was whether it was "big enough" to embrace the alien Gentiles without first requiring them to become Jews. A similar question for the contemporary church is whether it is "big enough" to include homosexual Christians and minister to them as the homosexual persons they are rather than requiring them first to become heterosexuals (or at least expecting them to *act* like heterosexuals!). The larger society is not going to provide us with any direction on this issue; it is one for the church itself to address and resolve.

THE AUTHORITY OF SCRIPTURE AND HOMOSEXUALITY

Unlike the euthanasia and assisted suicide topics, where the Bible is essentially silent as far as any explicit message is concerned, there are several biblical references to activities we today would describe as homosexual.[11] Within our limits here we cannot begin adequately to address each of these passages. Given their considerable weight in shaping the church's position on homosexuality, it is appropriate to note some of the reservations now being expressed about the way they have been interpreted.

1. Turning first to the Old Testament, of the several passages that are cited, two are taken from the Holiness Code in Leviticus ("You must not lie with a man as with a woman..."). To cite these passages as Scripture for the Christian raises serious problems. Most scholars would say that the Hebrew Holiness Code is a body of requirements that has its own integrity within the life of the Hebrew people, and ought not be applied as Scripture to the life of the Christian community, whose relation to the law of Israel has been radically changed. In any event, any reference to the Holiness Code, given its character, has to betray a principle of selection that implicitly constitutes the justification for applying these and not other particular passages to our situation today.

2. There is a variety of interpretation of the Sodom and Gomorrah story, with conclusions concerning what is condemned ranging from inhospitality (which is the context in which Jesus refers to Sodom in Matt. 10:15), to homosexual activity, to gang rape. There is sufficient ambiguity here to question the usual, assumed meaning of the text.

3. The New Testament does not give much attention to the subject of homosexuality, with just three passages normally cited and all from letters written by or ascribed to Paul. It does not appear to be a critical moral issue for Jesus or for the New Testament community generally, but admittedly there is limited value in any argument on grounds of silence.

4. One of the problems we encounter in going back to the Bible is that *homosexuality* is a word first coined in the modern era, which means there is no word directly addressing this subject in the New Testament. There are problems of meaning and interpretation in connection with the two Greek terms that are used to describe what is presumably homosexual activity *(malakoi* and *arsenokoitai),* but it is likely that they relate back to the language of the Holiness Code in its prohibition of sleeping "with a man as with a woman."

5. There is the question whether the subject being addressed by Paul in the important Romans passage is actually the issue that the tradition has assumed. An increasing number of New Testament scholars have challenged the assumption that Paul is arguing on behalf of a heterosexual viewpoint in opposition to homosexual practice. On the basis of Greek sources contemporary to Paul, a case can be made that the Greek words *para phusin* ("contrary to nature") do not refer to sexual orientation—an assumption we moderns quite naturally make—but to the struggle with erotic passion. Those passions can get out of hand with the development of insatiable desires that are expressed indiscriminately

and irresponsibly, whether in heterosexual or homosexual activity.[12] Even if we were to assume the traditional view that Paul is condemning heterosexual persons who on grounds of lust are giving up their normal erotic activity in favor of homosexual acts, Paul's language would highlight the changes that have occurred in the modern era through scientific investigations of homosexuality. With our understanding of the homosexual orientation, which results in erotic desires for persons of the same sex, homosexual activity is not the "perverted" activity of heterosexual persons, but the quite natural activity of homosexual persons. This insight has led the biblical scholar Robin Scroggs to conclude that "Biblical judgments against homosexuality are not relevant to today's debate."[13]

There is no question that the Bible and Christian tradition have been overwhelmingly understood as conveying a negative judgment of homosexual activity, and while this judgment is increasingly contested on several grounds, it remains difficult to argue that Scripture in fact does not deliver a negative judgment on this subject. Beyond this issue, there is still the question as to what weight Scripture should bear in addressing this particular matter, given what the church has learned and is experiencing today. In the dialogue between the church and its Scripture, there is considerable dissonance experienced by the church in reading, for example, the argument of Paul in Romans 1. Paul includes those engaged in homosexual acts (or at least this is what we have assumed he means) among the people whom God in his wrath has "given up" to evil passions and the worship of idols. How can we relate such people to the homosexual persons we know who are "in Christ" and share with us the baptismal covenant, the sacramental meal, the hearing of the Word? Is the apostle saying that Christians who are gay are living examples of God's wrath by the very fact that they have discovered they are gay? If we take this passage in Romans 1 at face value, do we have any alternative but to excommunicate them forthwith, particularly if they are sexually active and living in partnerships? Or are we to suffer their presence in silence as long as they fulfill our expectations to remain in isolation from each other?

The conclusion to which I believe we are driven is that particular passages of Scripture relating to the homosexual world are not going to settle this issue for the contemporary church. As noted earlier, a church vitally involved with the issues facing its people does not turn to Scripture without engaging it in dialogue, recognizing that our experience today as Christians in the world gives the shape and form to the questions we ask of Scripture and therefore also to the kinds of answers we discern. Though we would earnestly wish for a clear and definitive word from Scripture, the nature of the issue is such that we are thrown back on our powers of discernment as people of faith, informed and shaped by the Gospel and by the values and vision conveyed by the biblical message as a whole.

This involves an understanding of scriptural authority that is not bound in literal fashion to the text. Our discussion of reader response criticism in chapter 3 recognized the inevitably contextual nature of our approach to Scripture, which in turn brings a greater openness to what we may find there and an appropriate caution about thinking that we can simply replicate every historical judgment we find in Scripture. Instead, the church brings its contemporary experience into conjunction with Scripture, and the possibility of new interpretations and new insights emerge from that conjunction. This is not an attempt to get out from under the Bible's authority, but rather an attempt to responsibly interpret that authority in light of our changing experience and understanding of homosexuality. The church is facing new realities and is traveling over fresh ground in regard to this subject. We must honestly face the prospect of revising long-held beliefs—which we have identified with Scripture itself—that no longer hold true in light of our experience today. We must resist the temptation to find security by returning to old and familiar teachings that can no longer serve the church and are actually now proving to be highly destructive to significant numbers of people in the household of faith.

The Impact of the Tradition

Reassessing biblical authority in regard to homosexuality, we confront the fact that perhaps even more weight is exercised by extrabiblical sources on this particular topic. There is the considerable weight of the church's tradition, dominated by natural law teaching and related conceptual formulations such as the Lutheran "orders of creation" teaching. The concept of natural law has exerted profound impact on understandings of human sexuality. It has dominated Roman Catholic teaching, which defines the purpose of all genital activity as procreation. With this understanding, it is clear that homosexuality must be repudiated. Cardinal Joseph Ratzinger states the Catholic position as follows: "Homosexual activity is not a complementary union, able to transmit life; and so it thwarts the call to a life of that form of self-giving which the Gospel says is the essence of Christian living. This does not mean that homosexual persons are not often generous and giving of themselves; but when they engage in homosexual activity they confirm within themselves a disordered sexual inclination which is essentially self-indulgent."[14] This statement *assumes* (rather than being able to demonstrate) that only heterosexual activity, in contrast to homosexual, has the capacity to express sexually the personal gifts of genuine love or the giving of self to another person. It is a purely theoretical argument that shows no interest in investigating the homosexual unions of innumerable Christians whose lives together have demonstrated those characteristics of commitment that we surely identify with genuine love. Or what of the heroic expression of love on the part of gay persons in ministering to their partners and others suffering from the ravages of AIDS?

As a Christian community, we need to move away from the kind of rational, universal thinking about human sexuality that coerces everyone into the same mold, often with great human cost. It is encouraging that some Catholic scholars today are softening the character of natural law teaching; they maintain the importance of the biological and heterosexual paradigm but are willing to modify the implications they draw from it. For example, Lisa Sowle Cahill wants to maintain the "normative" character of heterosexual relations but also acknowledges that the experience of gay Christians belongs in the church's conversation concerning sexuality and that a heterosexual model or ideal "does not necessarily exclude variant realizations" under particular circumstances: "…the heterosexual ideal or paradigm need not entail a prohibition of those genital acts through which homosexual couples express and strengthen a committed relationship."[15]

One of the unfortunate aspects of natural law thinking is its "plumbing" character, in which sexuality is understood primarily in terms of genital activity. Its treatment of homosexual persons is consequently in danger of turning them into "sex machines," or losing sight of their humanity. Indeed, the whole discussion of sexuality, from whatever point of view, is in danger of this fallacy of losing sight of the person who is much more than his or her genital activity. Any excessively physicalist approach to homosexuality becomes a discussion of *what* the person is rather than *who* the person is. This results in a form of caricature that prevents us from seeing the real person in any sense of wholeness, including the psychological need of companionship that is met by a permanent relationship with another person. The church has too often been obsessed with the genital aspects of homosexuality, failing to recognize in gay partnerships the more important, personal dimensions of this kind of continuing, committed relationship.[16]

Many in our society regard the cause of homosexual persons as but one more case of a group of malcontents claiming discrimination and oppression in order to push their own set of "rights" at the expense of the long-suffering majority. Often this attitude is supported by fears of what might happen to society if the gay community assumes more power and status. There are also genuine apprehensions within the church that contribute to an adamant stance in opposition to any change in the church's position. Many fear the possible consequences for both church and society of any appearance that the church may be willing to give up a long-held position on this matter. This latter point is illustrated by the comment of the noted German theologian Wolfhart Pannenberg, who warns, "Those who would press the Church to change the norm of her teaching in this question [of homosexuality] must understand that they press the Church toward schism."[17] There is a genuine justice issue here that involves both church and society. Justice can be understood primarily as a means of preserving and sustaining the existing social order, but a justice informed by Christian love—what Paul Tillich calls a "transforming" or "creative" justice—seeks to realize a more humane social order. If we are to move in that direction, we will have to revise natural-law thinking within the church, not in the sense of rejecting all structures and boundaries important to responsible sexual behavior, but by bringing a more contextual and empirical character to its expression and becoming more modest about the implications we would draw from it.

SEEKING A VIABLE STANCE

As we have noted, the historical impact of natural-law teaching in the realm of sexuality has been the establishment of heterosexuality as the exclusive norm for everyone's sexual behavior, with the consequence that any variant sexual behavior is regarded as evil.[18] There is no room here for any recognition of the fact that a minority of the population discover they do not fit into the heterosexual category. Two opposite poles are created by this kind of thinking, the one being God-intended, the other being the result of the fallen human condition, or original sin. Thus an either/or is created on a universal scale, with those at the wrong pole finding themselves doubly cursed, because not only their human condition as sinners but their sexual condition warrants the judgment of God. In order to be "saved," it is not enough that they believe in Jesus Christ; they must also transform themselves from homosexual to heterosexual persons. It is understandable that those churches that deny the status of homosexuality as a genuine orientation must also believe that if one *really* believes in Christ, one's homosexuality will be overcome. Needless to say, this contention has been the cause of much tragedy and intense anguish among gay Christians raised in those churches.

One possible response to the argument of natural law, which makes heterosexuality morally exclusive, is to counter with the contention that homosexuality is just as good as its opposite. Thus "straight is good" is counteracted with "gay is good." This kind of argument is beside the point in the sense that neither assertion can be made without reference to the critical factor of one's sexual orientation. In other words, a more contextual understanding is required. I would recognize the foundational character of heterosexuality and its normative status among the vast majority of the population. But for those who discover their homosexual orientation, the norm for them becomes homosexual behavior. This is the "contextual" character of this approach, which recognizes the decisive importance of each person's sexual orientation and relates one's proper behavior to one's orientation. This viewpoint recognizes the profound personal and existential truth that people must be able to affirm who they are in their sexual relationships, acting with integrity as sexual beings. To impose heterosexual behavior on a homosexual person is a denial of who that person is; to deny the possibility of a homosexual person living in partnership with another person is also to deny who that person is.

Whatever goes into the making of one's sexual orientation, it does not constitute one's destiny before God. The God of the gospel speaks to one's heart, not to one's sexual orientation. Whether one is hetero- or homosexual, what one *does* with one's sexuality is the issue. What is good or bad, right or wrong, is a moral judgment applied to one's personal character or to one's behavior, not to one's sexual orientation, which is a given—a part of one's humanity. Sexuality is not a matter of either orientation being equally good, so take your pick. That way of stating the issue remains on the abstract, universal level; it is also irrelevant, because a genuine choice between them is not open to us.[19] My point rather is that we should be concerned that a person can be himself or herself and relate to others as a sexual being in a way that enables oneself and one's loved one to flourish and to be renewed as sexual beings. Because heterosexuality is by far the dominant orientation and enables the continuation of the race, it understandably serves as the usual reference point in talking about sexuality. The standards and expectations we place before our children as they grow up, relate to others, marry, and have children understandably reflect the expectations of the heterosexual world. But we ought not lay those expectations on the homosexual person.[20]

What this means then is that homosexuality is neither a "perversion" nor a "deviancy" for the homosexual person. The critical moral question for persons of both heterosexual and homosexual orientations is "What is responsible sexual behavior for me?" Here I believe that the moral expectations we bring to the sexual union of a man and woman—that they live together in a spirit of commitment and fidelity—poses a trustworthy ideal for all persons living in sexual intimacy, regardless of their orientation. This argument assumes that homosexual relationships can provide the context in which people can flourish as human beings.[21] It assumes that genuine, covenantal relationships can be realized in same-sex unions. There is too much evidence at this point to argue on grounds of a theological anthropology—as does Cardinal Ratzinger, for example—that gay relationships are inherently abortive of human flourishing and personal growth, or incapable of expressing genuine love and affection. On the contrary, sexual intimacy among gay and lesbian couples is a normal part of the companionship they find in each other and contributes to the mutual love that characterizes their relationship. All of society should be concerned to establish those structures that enable and encourage loving, stable partnerships in the gay community.

It is important to recognize that I am not arguing that any sexually intimate relationship is acceptable as long as the persons involved truly love each other and find no harm being caused to either party. I believe that social responsibility is defined by the boundaries established by society, and that any heterosexual couple who live their life together is obligated to legalize that relationship as husband and wife. Similar, if not the same structures, I would argue, should apply to homosexual couples who enter into a common life.[22] These structures would convey the same legal obligations and the same legal benefits applied to heterosexual couples. By giving legal sanction to gay and lesbian couples, the state would encourage and society would expect the same kind of commitments expected of husband and wife, which in turn would give much greater stability to the homosexual community and encourage their integration into society in a way that would benefit all of us. The research of social scientists is now beginning to corroborate the positive impact of stable partnerships in the gay community.

> One study found that even male homosexuals were happier when they were "close-coupled," i.e., living in a "quasi marriage." Such men did less cruising, spent more time at home, maintained higher levels of affection for their partner, had higher levels of sexual activity but fewer sexual problems, and less regretted their homosexuality, than did the typical homosexual male respondent. The researchers characterize them as enjoying "superior adjustment."[23]

OBJECTIONS AND ALTERNATIVE APPROACHES

One obvious objection to the stance we have taken relates to Scripture. How can one who takes the Bible seriously depart from what appears to be a clear and unequivocal witness on this topic? While taking Scripture seriously, we have spelled out in chapter 4 the conditions by which we understand its proper authority. The question cannot be resolved by treating the Bible like a sacred text that does not allow for critical engagement with the believing community. The basic issue becomes the proper balancing of the biblical witness with the experience of the church, and here Christians will differ. One of the more persuasive advocates of the traditional biblical interpretation concerning homosexuality, Richard Hays, acknowledges that the most serious challenge to that position would come from the experience of the church, and he is willing to leave open the possibility that "after sustained and agonizing scrutiny by a consensus of the faithful," it could be acceptable to "contradict" the witness of Scripture.[24] My own reading of the experience of the faithful leads me to recommend that the change in the traditional interpretation begin now, while it is conceivable that his own perspective may lead to a change later. At least the principle of critical engagement with the text on the part of the church always leaves open this possibility.

Another kind of objection is made by those who argue that gays and lesbians—or at least gays—are not capable of the kind of enduring commitment that society expects of the heterosexual couple, and therefore the church would be naive to recommend their acceptance as full participants in church and society. This contention not only overlooks the many exemplary unions common to the homosexual world,[25] but it also fails to recognize that we have not yet had a society in which homosexuals have been given the status and responsibilities that would encourage permanency in their relationships. They have been forced into a world of desperation and hopelessness, which has encouraged the traits opposite to those we would want to cultivate and support. It is at the very least premature to make such judgments of the homosexual community. Among Christian gays and lesbians, permanency and commitment are clearly lifted up as ideals for their unions. The larger question here is the capacity of gay Christians to live sanctified lives of faith, hope, and love, a question whose answer will become more obvious to more people as the level of acceptance of gay persons is raised. I am well aware that many people, also within the church, are scandalized by these assertions. They are convinced that gay people comprise a degenerate subculture whose "lifestyle" is promiscuous and pornographic, obsessed with exploitative sexual practices that are far removed from the sanctified life. This characterization should be exposed as the vicious lie that it is. Within both the homosexual and heterosexual communities there is a subculture of this sort, but for neither group does it accurately describe the lives of the vast majority.

The point is also made that procreation and children do not inherently belong to a homosexual relationship, depriving it of an important dimension of the responsibility of heterosexual couples in raising children and nurturing future citizens of society. The implication is that homosexual partnerships lack those features that encourage permanency in the face of pressures that threaten their commitment. This argument may have carried more weight a few generations ago, but now the attitude toward having children has changed among heterosexual couples, with childless marriages becoming fairly commonplace. This does not cancel out the responsibility of the couple to live faithfully with each other and participate fully in the life of their community. Children, while bringing rich blessing to a marriage, do not constitute its justification nor its essential ingredient. Obviously, "generativity" is important to the future of the race, but it is not a requirement or necessarily even an expectation that one could lay on every married couple. Given the seriousness of the overpopulation problem, it is conceivable that an increasing number of couples will choose to make their contribution to the future generation by adoption rather than procreation. One can see the desire of homosexual couples to adopt children and give them parental nurture as being an encouraging sign of their commitment to family and to the larger society. In light of the formidable obstacles, many gay and lesbian couples should inspire us with their desire to identify with the goals of society and to make their contribution to the common good. As Christians we have had ample opportunity to see this occur among those gays and lesbians who are part of the body of Christ.

Another objection often heard from family-centered organizations among the Religious Right is that any support given to the homosexual community constitutes an assault on the traditional family. It reflects an exclusivist viewpoint that sees any kind of variant sexual expression, no matter how responsibly conducted, as an offense and threat to the heterosexual world. On the contrary, to support homosexual unions by giving them legal recognition should be helpful to the whole society, because it would encourage stability and responsibility in the homosexual community. It should also mitigate the homophobia that has been so depressingly heavy in our society, because it would encourage a change in attitudes as gays and lesbians are removed from second-class citizenship and become increasingly integrated into the society. On the assumption that any kind of prejudice is a debilitating social evil, this could only be seen as a positive development. Any move toward a more just society benefits all of us.

My sense concerning this objection is that it is not only based on heterosexual exclusivism but is also rooted in ignorance and fear. People seem to believe that if homosexual persons are invited into society as full participants, the young in particular may be enticed into believing that they might give homosexual life a try. What we know about sexual orientation discourages this kind of thinking. It may occur on the margins as part of growing up and self-discovery for some young people, but visions of youths flocking into a homosexual lifestyle are absurd. The more likely development is that increasingly our society will take a "live and let live" attitude, recognizing the differences in sexual orientation and acknowledging the importance of integrity and responsibility in everyone's sexual life. This kind of development would obviously depend on greater knowledge and understanding than is now generally the case in our society, but one would hope that the church could be a significant force in encouraging that kind of understanding as well as upholding the ideals of integrity and responsibility for all people in their sexual life.

I am quite aware of the difficulties raised by these ideas. People respond to issues of sexuality at the visceral level, which often blocks the likelihood of their hearing any reasons based on logical thinking; their "guts" are telling them something different, and it carries more weight than cognitive arguments. One's emotions on an issue of this kind are not irrelevant or unimportant, and any fears they generate must be sympathetically heard and addressed. For example, there is genuine fear that a more accepting view of homosexuality would lead to crumbling social structures, to lust and concupiscence running amok, to uncontrollable sexual urges being fed and encouraged by loosening moral standards. I believe the church above all should sympathetically but emphatically challenge this instinctive kind of response that reflects more ungrounded fear and ignorance than a responsible grasp of the issues involved.[26] We need more confidence in the experience of the church today and also more confidence in society. Homosexuality must be seen first as an issue of justice and humaneness; we should be more concerned to address people's humanity than their sexuality, and to understand their sexuality as much more than genital activity. If we press toward this goal in our thinking and attitudes, the better lights of our nature may yet enable us to realize a more just society in regard to this troubled realm of human relationships.

Stephen L. Carter's point concerning tolerance and respect, noted in chapter 2, bears particular importance in regard to our discussion here. Carter argues that in a divided, pluralist society such as our own, even tolerance is not sufficient; we need to cultivate respect for each other and be willing to find common ground that will help us to deal with people we have perceived in the past as adversaries.[27] It is conceivable that the church, on the basis of its common life, which includes gays and lesbians, will come to a stance that is more understanding and respectful than what is found generally in the society. At this point the church should be a model in its openness to the homosexual person and in its willingness to challenge dominant attitudes that denigrate and in many ways literally destroy these people.[28]

Many Christians and churches have drawn the line between homosexual behavior and Christian faith in an absolute manner, judging the behavior, if not always the orientation, of homosexual persons as totally incompatible with the teaching of the church. In light of what they understand from the Bible and tradition, they believe that the church would be mortally wounded if it did not repudiate and exclude from its fellowship anyone who engaged in such behavior. For them, homosexuality has become one—perhaps the primary one—of several moral issues in contemporary society that pose the most serious threat to the church's identity. One might say that it has become a *status confessionis* issue for them, which is highly significant because it makes moral practice rather than theological confession fundamental to defining the church. In this case, to be a Christian is to reject the homosexual person.

Should homosexuality be the defining issue in determining the identity and integrity of the church? Should racism be the defining issue, or poverty, or homophobia? Or do such ideas involve us in an ill-advised and ultimately self-destructive quest for moral purity within the church? My comments at the outset would indicate the fallacy in trying to absolutize any kind of moral response in the church, for it would identify that response with the gospel of Jesus Christ itself and condemn all those who fail to measure up to the standard we have chosen. It is not that morality is unimportant—there is no question that racism and sexism in the church, for example, compromise its integrity and undermine its witness to the world. More important to the church's identity, however, is its recognition that we are all sinners before God and are absolutely dependent on God's grace. This means that we dare not absolutize any one moral standard as a way of determining who is an acceptable Christian or who qualifies for church membership. The temptation toward exclusivism of any kind can come from the ideological left as well as the right, but in either case the church should hold to a theological and moral compass that insists on both justice in society and an inclusive, grace-oriented church.

Other voices in the church maintain it is essential that we continue to draw the line between homosexual behavior and an acceptable Christian morality, but that we do it in a spirit of acceptance of the gay person. Whether believing that homosexual behavior is inherently evil or that its acceptance would threaten the destruction of the church, people holding this view insist that the traditional stance should be maintained. A distinction is made, however, between an ethical judgment and pastoral care. We can judge the behavior, but there is an obligation to act pastorally in regard to the homosexual person. This bifurcation of gay persons from their acts appeals to many Christians (often expressed in the statement "Love the sinner but hate the sin"); the problem is that it totally ignores the existential realities of the gay person's life. If acts follow from nature, then to condemn the act but affirm the person is a self-contradiction, saying something like, "I accept you, but not really *you*." Not surprisingly, this position leads to inconsistencies of various kinds, including the willingness to "look the other way" if the pastor is aware of homosexual partners in his or her congregation.[29]

One can certainly understand this approach as an effort to avoid the fallout that would occur from taking a clear stance on this issue, whether for or against. The problem is the crisis it generates in regard to the integrity of the church, not unlike the difficulty experienced by the armed forces in their "don't ask, don't tell" approach. It is dependent on the willingness of people to maintain a fabric of dishonesty, and for that reason it is obviously no long-term solution—and perhaps not a short-term solution, either. To attempt to justify a distinction between the church's public teaching and its actual practice would certainly be regarded by the Christian gay person as unacceptable hypocrisy. While acknowledging this fact, it is also a reality of our human predicament that often and inevitably we find ourselves in situations of compromise. It may be that in this difficult period we will be forced to live for some time with compromise, dealing with long-held attitudes and traditions that prevent the church from taking a clear stance on behalf of its gay and lesbian members. If this is the situation we face, it is all the more important that we are quite intentional about maintaining a program of education throughout the church so that these attitudes and traditions are gradually changed.

As this discussion reaches its conclusion, its governing assumptions, developed in the beginning chapters of this work, invite our reflection.

We argued that a spirit ethics, which takes seriously the presence of God in the life of the congregation, will be attentive to the Spirit's promptings in the common life of believers. The Scriptures and tradition have shaped the identity of the church, but they continue to be known and digested within the life-experience of God's people who are today themselves a part of the continuing narrative of God's presence in the world. The church is discovering something new about itself as Christian gays and straights come together in worship and service, a fact that must be taken seriously. Luke T. Johnson's observation is pertinent here: "If in fact theology has to do not alone with ideas but with faith in the living God, pastoral or practical theology is the research arm of theology."[30] It is on the practical front, in the concrete experience of the church that new things are happening that cannot be adequately addressed by reciting the moral judgments of the past. At the same time, the people of God are still obviously "on the way" and cannot conclude that they now have arrived at the final word from either their past or their present, on this issue or any other. The direction they ought to take will be found not simply from exploring the wisdom of the past but the wisdom and insights from their present as well, united with the prayer that God will yet lead them into a faithful and responsible future.

8
GENETICS AND THE FUTURE OF HUMANITY

While euthanasia/assisted suicide and homosexuality are topics that have taken on new shape and meaning as a result of developments in scientific research and technology, genetics is a topic in which the impact of those developments has been and continues to be particularly dramatic, bestowing an open-endedness to genetics that is both exciting and disturbing to contemplate. Ascertaining the facts, as has been noted, is a challenge with every social issue, but particularly in genetics the assessment of scientific and technological work and its consequences constitutes a very divisive issue in itself. As with the other two subjects, the developments in this field are challenging the church to rethink the tradition concerning the nature of the human being, and in this case in particular, the biological limits to the future development of humanity. The unsettled terrain concerning the nature of this subject would caution us about being too confident in our moral judgments, and yet the stakes are sufficiently high that we cannot afford to sit back in silence and simply wait to see what happens. The apparent *direction* in which genetic research and experimentation are taking society has become a major issue for scientists, philosophers, ethicists, and theologians of all persuasions. While exciting new developments are unfolding, they have a history that warrants our attention.

THE QUESTION OF EUGENICS

One of the ironies in the history of medicine is that the more successful the medical establishment has become in treating and curing illness and disease, the more damage has been done to the health of the human gene pool. Where people suffering from any number of diseases in past generations have died without leaving progeny, modern medicine has enabled them to live longer and to have children, and thus spread their genetic inheritance to future generations. This has led certain people schooled in the natural sciences to argue the necessity of genetic testing and screening and the forming of public policies that would ultimately improve rather than pollute the gene pool. Among the first activities reflecting these kinds of concerns, however, ideological as well as medical reasons played a prominent role—specifically ideas of race and culture. The British biologist Sir Francis Galton, who coined the term eugenics in 1883, defined it as "the study of the agencies under social control which may improve or impair the racial qualities of future generations physically or mentally."[1] Galton, a cousin of Charles Darwin, wanted to ensure that "the more suitable races" would prevail over "the less suitable races," a mode of thinking that led to tragic consequences in the story of Nazi Germany. Given this background, any talk about improving the population's genetic health has occasioned suspicion and often serious reservations.[2]

Darwin himself also harbored eugenic concerns. In his *The Descent of Man*, he refers to all the heroic attempts to check the "elimination" of people who would otherwise succumb to disease, noting the consequence that weak members of society now continue to "propagate their kind." Nonetheless, he offers the hope that "the weak in body and mind" might refrain from marriage so that society might avoid "the undoubtedly bad effects" that would come from the proliferation of their offspring.[3] A prominent representative of these ideas in twentieth-century United States was Hermann J. Muller, professor of zoology at Indiana University and author of *Studies in Genetics* (1962). Echoing Darwin's observation, Muller noted that society now comes to the aid of those who, "for whatever reason, environmental or genetic, are physically, mentally, or morally weaker than average," leading him to the conclusion that "genetically based ability and reproductive rate are today negatively correlated."[4] The consequences, he thought, were bound to be disastrous.

> This is an ironical situation. Cultural evolution has at long last given rise to science and its technologies. It has thereby endowed itself with powers that—according to the manner in which they are used—could either wreck the human enterprise or carry it upward to unprecedented heights of being and of doing. To steer his course under these circumstances man will need his greatest collective wisdom, humanity, will to cooperate, and self-control. Moreover, he cannot muster these faculties in sufficient measure collectively unless he also possesses them

in considerable measure individually. Yet in this very epoch cultural evolution has undermined the process of genetic selection in man, a process whose active continuance is necessary for the mere maintenance of man's faculties at their present none-too-adequate level. What we need instead, at this juncture, is a means of *enhancing* genetic selection.[5]

The concrete solution proposed by Muller as a way to enhance genetic selection was to establish "germ-cell banks" (in Muller's time this meant sperm banks, but he looked forward to the possibility of egg storage as well) that would keep in deep freeze the germ cells of outstanding people. He anticipated a development in the mores of society so that people voluntarily would take advantage of this opportunity: "Practically all peoples venerate creativity, wisdom, brotherliness, loving-kindness, perceptivity, expressivity, joy of life, fortitude, vigor, longevity. If presented with the opportunity to have their children approach nearer to such goals than they could do themselves, they will not turn down this golden chance, and the next generation, thus benefitted, will be able to choose better than they did."[6] Whether this optimism of Muller is warranted is certainly debatable, but the larger question is whether he and Darwin are correct in their assumption that society is destined for a genetic apocalypse if the present trend is continued. Assuming that they are, the consequences have been framed in a memorable way by the notable biologist and member of the Eastern Orthodox Church, Theodosius Dobzhansky: "We are then faced with a dilemma—if we enable the weak and the deformed to live and to propagate their kind, we face the prospect of a genetic twilight; but if we let them die or suffer when we can save them, we face the certainty of a moral twilight. How to escape this dilemma?"[7]

There are many voices that would dispute or at least significantly modify the Darwinian assumption. Even the officers of the American Eugenics Society, while reaffirming their long-range goal of improving genetic potentialities, nevertheless conclude on the basis of a six-year study that "neither present scientific knowledge, current genetic trends, nor social value justify coercive measures as applied to human reproduction."[8] Marc Lappé, Associate for the Biological Sciences at the Institute of Society, Ethics, and the Life Sciences, argues that even identifying the "unfortunately" genetically endowed person becomes increasingly problematic when we recognize that every individual bears a small but statistically significant number of deleterious genes. The more accurate assessment, he maintains, is that a genetic burden is what the *family* is laden with rather than the population as a whole. The only way that imposing procreative sanctions on behalf of the gene pool could ever be justified, argues Lappé, would be the demonstration of a clear and present danger of genetic deterioration in the population as a whole, a demonstration that has never been achieved.[9]

Unlike the church's stance in regard to euthanasia and suicide, or homosexuality, there is no extensive history of Christian perspective on the issue of genetics and the human future. There are no clearly defined positions buttressed by appeal to Scripture that have shaped the mind of the church on this matter. One obvious reason for this is its relatively recent arrival on the historical scene. The dynamics of history have once again created a new issue that demands the church's attention. In this case it is difficult to identify specific passages from Scripture—as has been done, for example, with homosexuality—in an attempt to deliver a definitive and conclusive word on the subject. The one incident from Scripture that is cited is the story of Jacob and Laban in Genesis 30–31, where Jacob engages in selective breeding of goats in order to strengthen his flock and weaken the flock of Laban. Apart from the intrigue, one might see the story as an expression of appropriate human authority over the animal world, where "genetic manipulation" occurs for human purposes. The ancient Hebrews saw no theological or ethical problems in this manifestation of sovereignty over one's property. Because the subject thus provides little occasion to cite verses from the Bible as a way of addressing it, the church can profitably turn to larger theological and ethical perspectives that are rooted in its Scripture and tradition to gain some orientation in addressing the many ethical questions being raised.

Before I leave the subject of eugenics, some questions need to be raised about matters of fact concerning the human gene pool as well as matters of judgment concerning the seriousness of its impact on the future of society. Should the church see genetic health as an important factor in maintaining the common good of society, and assume the obligation to do what it can to educate people about the importance of maintaining a healthy gene pool? While many Christians believe that efforts to control the human genetic future are an acceptable expression of our stewardship of creation, questions quite naturally arise about the appropriate limits of that control. What purposes and goals should guide us, and what are the full ramifications of "enhancing" the human prospect through genetic manipulation? Among concerns being expressed is the constant danger of associating genetic health with notions of genetic superiority and inferiority, leading to discriminatory policies that are inherently destructive to a healthy, inclusive society. Another is that we may be embarking on a new and totally unrealistic path of "biological salvation," directed by the scientific establishment. These are issues I want to address in this chapter, but first some additional information relating to the world of genetics needs to be considered. The development of new genetic programs has redefined the nature of eugenics as it finds expression today.

GENETIC TESTING AND SCREENING

The beginnings of medical genetics go back to the Austrian monk Gregor Mendel (1822–84), whose work with pea plants established the basic principles of genetics. Centering his work on the inheritance breeding of colors, he concluded that traits of color were inherited in units that were later to be called genes. This groundwork provided the basis for understanding the transmission of genetic disease. In 1953 the discovery of deoxyribonucleic acid (DNA) as the chemical that encodes genetic information ushered in the molecular genetic revolution. Some twenty years later the era of genetic engineering had begun with the capacity to isolate, purify, and characterize genetic elements and introduce them into foreign cells. These procedures, called recombinant DNA technologies, allow for gene therapy through the transfer of a normal gene carried by a vector (a self-replicating element, such as a virus) into a cell where it replaces or corrects the function of a defective gene. In genetic diseases identified with a particular gene, as in Huntington's disease, the possibility of gene therapy is promising and yet to date has not been achieved.

The means by which genetic programs gain information is through testing individuals to determine whether they possess one or more abnormalities in their genetic code. The need for complete accuracy is obviously essential when testing the presence or absence of a genetic disease, but unfortunately this is not always achievable. One formidable problem is that detecting genetic mutations (changes that may or may not signal a defective gene) can be quite difficult when a large number of mutations are possible. The test may be falsely negative if other mutations are present in addition to the one specifically being pursued. In order to reach larger numbers of the population, genetic screening is also conducted in regard to specific diseases. Particularly where a specific segment of the population is vulnerable to a certain genetic disease, screening programs have been profitably employed. Examples would be screening for Tay-Sachs disease among Ashkenazi Jews (East European descent) and for sickle-cell disease among African Americans. Mandatory screening on human populations is rare, depending on whether there is a clear benefit to the person involved. An example would be the

screening of newborns for phenylketonuria (PKU), which can be suc-
cessfully treated through diet if detected soon enough.

As currently practiced, genetic testing is likely to occur at four different stages in human life: prenatal period, neonatal period, premarital
counseling or in connection with a reproductive decision, or where one's
family history would indicate a significant risk of developing a genetic
disease. Technological achievements such as ultrasonography and
fetoscopy have enhanced the capacity to do research and testing in utero,
making prenatal testing more common and effective. Pregnant women
are now able to use reasonably accurate and less costly testing for some
two hundred diseases, but possibilities of therapy are still limited. Decisions concerning genetic testing may be made in consultation with one's
family physician, but in recent years the genetic counselor has assumed
professional status and is usually involved in testing decisions. The work
of the counselor is highly sensitive, with professional guidelines stressing
the need to maintain absolute neutrality in regard to the options laid
before the client. The possibility, or even advisability, of being completely
neutral is challenged by critics, but nonetheless there can be a meaningful effort on the part of the counselor to respect the autonomy of the
client and to refrain from pressing one's own sentiments. According to
genetic counselor Elizabeth Thomson, counselors are intent on helping
people to comprehend the medical facts, to understand the genetic contribution to a particular disorder, to help families understand their
reproductive risks and options, to help them make the best choices in
light of their own values and beliefs, and to help people who have genetic
disorders to make the best possible adjustment to their situation.[10]

The increasing prominence of genetic testing and screening has
inspired considerable debate over the ethical issues they raise. LeRoy
Walters identifies four issues central to those debates at the public policy
level:

1. freedom and coercion in genetic testing and
   screening,
2. the confidentiality or disclosure of test results,
3. access to genetic-testing services, and
4. the probable benefits and harms of genetic testing
   and screening programs.[11]

As to the first issue, the widespread screening of the newborn for
genetic defects carries such an obvious benefit that the vast majority of
parents desire it rather than seeing it as coercive. On the other hand,
mandatory testing on a *contingent* basis, where one must be tested if one

applies for insurance, or for a particular job, raises serious problems of discrimination and exclusion based on the testing results. The intent of testing should be to assist people in determining answers about their genetic condition and personal health rather than to give others occasion to discriminate against them. At the same time, it must be recognized that knowledge of one's genetic condition places responsibilities upon oneself. This might take the form of appropriate self-care, or a decision not to have children,[12] or a change in one's expectations of others. For example, for a young man to expect a considerable investment in time and money on the part of his employer to train him for a highly sophisticated and responsible job, knowing that his health will not allow him to work for more than a year or two at the most, raises questions of personal honesty and one's sense of obligation to the employer.

The second issue concerning confidentiality and disclosure raises questions as to who should have access to the information about one's genetic condition. Typically, this relates to family members and to employers and insurers. If one's condition raises serious implications for other family members and one chooses not to inform them, leading to the likelihood of serious harm being done, the duty to maintain confidentiality must be challenged. The value of people's lives takes precedence over the obligation to confidentiality. In the case noted above of a young man and his employer who plans a considerable investment in him, the question is more complicated. One might argue that the employer should recognize that there is risk in every instance of investment in an employee: he or she may leave in a year for another, more attractive position, or may have an accident that is severely disabling. The difference in this case is that one already knows the likely future of the employee, and the moral issue is whether one is justified to ignore it. Employer-employee relations enter into this question so that one might ask whether in the impersonal, corporate world an employee should be made to feel this kind of obligation to one's employer. Yet also here in the "public" realm (which our discussion in chapter 5 recognized as a realm of law rather than gospel), a discriminating sense of obligation is called for; a Christian would not want to be in a position of taking advantage of others for his own selfish reasons. One appropriate response in this case would be that personal integrity requires the divulging of this information, but only if the company's policy acknowledges its responsibility in this kind of situation to continue the young man's employment in his current position.

The third area of access to genetic testing services raises the question of costs for people who may not be in a position to pay them. When the results of an initial test are positive or unclear, there may be subsequent testing and other procedures that are not covered by insurance. Or some insurers may cover the testing but not any additional costs of counseling that turn out to be necessary. The state of California has addressed this kind of access problem by charging a one-time nominal fee that guarantees a person's access to whatever diagnostic tests are necessary. Whether through the government directly or through the insurance industry, this kind of medical service ought not be limited to those who have the means to pay for it.

As to the fourth issue of benefits and harms of genetic testing and screening, the benefits are fairly obvious: greater knowledge that may enable critical treatment for a genetic condition or enable one to avoid transmitting genetic disease to one's offspring. The possible harms, however, are also real: coercive programs that lead to employment or insurance discrimination, as well as testing that is less than accurate. One significant problem that poses harm to potential parents and prenatal life is the fact that our capacity to diagnose genetic disorders in fetal life far exceeds our ability to correct those disorders. In this situation the prospective parents are left with an excruciating dilemma on whether or not to abort. It is understandable under these circumstances that many couples who are strongly opposed to abortion decide to forego prenatal testing. On the other hand, couples for whom prenatal testing has determined that the unborn child has an affliction such as Down syndrome, can benefit by preparing for the arrival of their special-needs child.

While eugenics concerns are always in the background, it is fair to say that most people involved in the work of genetic testing understand its purpose on a much more personal and individual level. Testing and screening are intended to assist individual people who have or may have genetic disorders, and are not motivated by any grand design to improve the human race. They are diagnostic and preventive measures that may lead to therapeutic care, focusing on those diseases resulting from defective genes and bringing helpful information and counsel to those who seek it. If this work makes a contribution to a healthier gene pool, that may be seen as a positive consequence, but it is not the immediate purpose of this activity. While much of the critique that genetic testing and screening receives does not discount its importance for the lives of individual people, it does raise the issue whether eugenics has not reentered the scientific house through the back door. The term *genethics* has recently come into vogue, referring to the social, ethical, and theological implications of the new genetic technologies. The concerns raised by these developments have received renewed impetus in recent years with the inauguration of the vast governmental program called the Human Genome Project. That project is critically important to the subject here, warranting some description and evaluation.

THE HUMAN GENOME PROJECT

The Human Genome Project (HGP), a three-billion-dollar operation, is remarkable in terms of its scope and ambition, involving governmental and scientific collaboration on an international scale in an effort to dramatically expand our knowledge about the purpose and function of genes ("genome" refers to the full complement of genes in an organism). The HGP began officially on October 1, 1990, and was expected to be completed in fifteen years, a goal now shortened to twelve years. The information gained will be stored in databases around the world, contributing to the understanding of many current mysteries surrounding genetic development and disease. Ted Peters provides a more specific description of the project:

> [The HGP] studies DNA with three goals in mind: sequencing, mapping, and diagnosing. The first goal is to learn the sequence of the three billion base pairs or nucleotides that comprise the DNA chains in our forty-six chromosomes. The second is to locate the genes on a DNA map—that is, to locate the estimated 100,000 smaller sequences on the DNA chains that code for proteins and determine what kinds of bodies we have. The third goal is the one that draws public support in the form of government funding for research: the identification of those genes that predispose us to disease. At the beginning of HGP it was estimated that 5,000 or more human diseases are genetically based. Finding those genes and developing therapies to counteract their effects holds immense promise for improving human health and well-being.[13]

Given their present knowledge, scientists are able to focus on particular regions of chromosomes where certain disease-related genes are located in determining their investigation of base pairs, otherwise their sheer number would be overwhelming. With considerably more knowledge of where important genes are located and how they function, scientists will be better able to develop tests for diagnosing large numbers of diseases. They should also be better equipped to develop methods for gene therapy, but the initial results will have the greatest impact on the effectiveness of genetic testing and screening. Since but a small fraction of human genes are known at the present time, and a yet smaller number understood, the prospects of the HGP are obviously exciting to contemplate.

Whatever the end result of the HGP, its goals essentially have been those of genetic programs that have already been in place, namely, to reduce the incidence of congenital diseases and to improve the health of those who inherit them. This will continue to be done through genetic counseling and testing, prenatal diagnosis, prenatal therapy (though recognizing that this is still in the experimental stage), and neonatal testing, screening, and therapy. Success in these programs, however, should be dramatically increased through the knowledge that is gained, given the fact that virtually every disease has a genetic component. For example, over 4,000 single-gene diseases are known, but at the present time only two hundred can be prenatally diagnosed. Since single-gene diseases provide the best prospects for gene therapy, the knowledge to be gained in their diagnosis is highly promising. Admittedly, there are many more complex diseases, like diabetes, for example, in which many genes may be involved. Further complicating the scene is the fact that environmental factors play a role in most diseases, and these factors are not always easy to determine. Now, however, the enhanced possibilities of understanding the genetic component should contribute to a better comprehension of the environmental factors as well.

Given this disease-focused goal of the project, the director of the National Center for Human Genome Research and professing Christian, Francis S. Collins, is moved to say that Jesus' own healing ministry "is the theological justification for the Human Genome Project....This initiative is a natural extension of our commitment to heal the sick."[14] While Collins's statement is genuine and understandable, it also is a painful reminder that the therapeutic potential of the HGP is far from being realized. The fact is that we are gaining voluminous information about the human genome without corresponding progress in the capacity to heal those with genetic diseases. This raises serious ethical issues for parents who are told that the embryonic life being carried by the mother suffers from a severe genetic condition, with no possibility of being cured. Such information, of course, can be debilitating at any stage of one's life, as in the case of the twenty-year-old woman who is told she has Huntington's disease. While appropriate counseling can assist the individual and other family members in coping with it, there remains a distressing gap between the information being gained and our capacity to use it therapeutically. There is real danger here of people believing that the HGP will prove to be an immediate panacea for all genetic disorders, which clearly will not be the case in the foreseeable future.

There are also economic incentives to proceed with new tests, contributing further to the diagnostic-therapeutic gap. The prospect of considerable earnings encourages the creation of new tests, with little or no attention to the long- or short-range impact they will have on the lives of those who are tested. "Without some independent body that will advise doctors of the exact nature of the information that a new test can yield, and of the extent to which test information can improve patients' lives, there is real danger that people will be swept into tests that they do not understand and given information that will prove harmful to them."[15] It is not a matter of trying to stop the flow of information as much as being discriminating in its use. This means that the medical profession will have to make a concentrated and sustained effort to keep informed on the fast-breaking developments in this area, and more attention will have to be given to developing and making more accessible the services of genetic counselors. In this as well as many other areas of scientific and technological development, the economic and commercial engine threatens to drive the whole operation, turning health care into a commodity whose primary function is to serve the interests of those who are profiting from it.

Another serious reservation prompted by the creation of the HGP relates to its cost as a government project in comparison with other commitments to the common good. Philip Kitcher addresses this issue:

> There are far more children whose lives are smashed in their early years through social causes than who suffer from the ravages of defective proteins. So the critics confront the HGP with a serious question: why is public money expended on trying to prevent the birth of children with rare combinations of alleles [genetic mutations], while social programs that could benefit many more go wanting?...[T]he worry is that the ultimate rationale for the project is cast in terms of improvements to the quality of human lives, and it is inconsistent for a society that tolerates large social causes of reduced quality of life to offer any such rationale. The best case against the HGP would demand that it be accompanied by an equally serious commitment to attacking social problems that lower the quality of human lives.[16]

Kitcher recognizes that pragmatically one might respond that we had best do what we can with the funding available and not be held hostage "to grander social ventures with uncertain prospects," but he believes the uncertainty of such ventures is something to which the HGP itself is not immune, given the human factor in all such massive endeavors. There are clearly basic issues of political and moral philosophy involved in this kind of argument, and Kitcher suggests the HGP might serve as the occasion to profitably reexamine the assumptions involved.

Another development that has drawn concern from a number of Christian commentators is the increasing prominence of genetic testing and screening, particularly of the pregnant woman. This testing is based on the assumption that the potential parents want a genetically healthy child, which involves an implicit standard of being free from "serious" genetic disorders. If the parents are told that their baby will suffer from a genetic defect, then their offspring falls under a negative judgment, being seen as subnormal or less than desirable. The judgment can take the form of a choice for aborting the fetus, particularly since the possibility of genetic therapy in the womb is severely limited. This difficult situation raises a number of critical questions: what is the character of parental commitment to life in the womb? Is it morally acceptable that it be conditional, depending on how "healthy" the potential child will be? How "serious" must the defect be in order to abort? Are we increasingly developing a mentality that treats new life as a commodity in a consumer culture, with the expectation that anything desirable should be as close to perfection as possible? "What seems to be happening is that an urge to alleviate suffering is gradually being transformed into a demand that abnormality be eliminated.... [A]s genetic tests become routine, [the genetic counselor's] practice will become a quest for perfection rather than an effort to eliminate genetic disease."[17]

While the cheapening of life in a consumer culture is a legitimate and important concern, the above questions raised by genetic testing also lift up the troubling issue of abortion. Christians appear hopelessly divided over whether there is a morally significant difference between life in the womb and life after birth—or between life in the early and later stages of pregnancy. One's convictions on this matter will either allow or prohibit the possibility of there being a "window" for making a life or death decision during pregnancy. One approach among those who feel strongly about assaults on the sacred value of human life is to draw the line at conception, arguing that full legal rights should belong to prenatal life from the very beginning. Others will contend that while abortion is never desirable, absolutizing fetal life has never been a consistently Christian point of view. The realities of life, they believe, may at times result in an abortion decision as the lesser of two evils. Willingness to make that decision usually assumes that morally and theologically the relationship of potential parents to the prenatal child is of a different nature than what it is following birth—or even following "quickening," when the woman becomes aware of new life within her and a relationship begins. Nonetheless, Christians who keep open the abortion option as a sometime tragic necessity may still agree that to the extent that prenatal testing fosters an attitude that jeopardizes acceptance of the child, its routine use should be resisted. They would insist that absolutizing prenatal life from the point of conception is not the only way—nor the most effective way—of challenging the destructive mentality of convenience and consumerism.

Implicit in the above discussion is the question whether there is such a thing as human life that is "not worth living." Genetic testing is confronting an increasing number of couples with that question; in our discussion of euthanasia and assisted suicide (chapter 6) the same issue arose under the expression "quality of life," an issue accentuated once again by the impact of technology but at the opposite end of the life span. An immediate problem in genetic testing is the margin of error that may be present, as well as the fact that the severity of the disability in the experience of the child may be difficult to predict. These realities in themselves would inspire extreme caution about terminating a pregnancy. Assuming that the technical information is clear beyond any reasonable doubt, Christians will still differ on this decision on the basis of their understanding of the nature of fetal life and the relation it establishes with the potential parents. Those who take an absolutist position, identifying prenatal life from conception as warranting the full protection of the law, would reject any attempt to terminate a genetically disabled fetus regardless of its stage of development. Because the fetus is a human person in this view, it could not be aborted any more than a disabled child or adult could be killed. "[T]here is no inherent moral difference between abortion for reasons of genetic deformity and executing adults who are genetically handicapped."[18]

Christians who are not willing to take this kind of absolutist position are challenged to make several distinctions that hold ethical significance. One relates to the stage of pregnancy when the discovery is made that the fetus is genetically disabled. If it is beyond the first trimester, that fact may determine the decision whether to abort. Another, more fundamental distinction relates to the seriousness or severity of the genetic disorder. It may range from anencephaly (no cerebral cortex or cognitive capacity, with death occurring in a matter of days or weeks), trisomy 13 (extreme retardation, small head, and other physical deformities), and infantile spinal muscular atrophy (death likely occurring within six months), to mild cases of Down syndrome (although retarded, the child can live happily in families or communities), spina bifida (hydrocephaly, which can be corrected at birth; paralysis of the legs; usually normal mental capacity), and cystic fibrosis (lung infections, usually death by mid-twenties). Considering the possibility of abortion in view of these disorders involves a decision about quality of life, which may be informed by such factors as brevity of life, the physical and psychological burden for the child, and the hardship that the child's care would impose on the family.[19]

Attempting to arrive at some helpful guidelines on this kind of decision making, John C. Fletcher proposes a definition of what would constitute a "serious" genetic or congenital disorder:

> By "serious genetic disease" I mean a disease in which the child struggles for all or the majority of its life simply to survive the disease without adequate therapy, and that the child's chances for human growth and communication would be completely or to a great degree submerged or overwhelmed by the disease.[20]

While it is impossible to know with absolute certainty whether a given child will be "overwhelmed" by a particular disease, the clearly devastating character of some genetic disorders is sufficient to justify an abortion decision in the minds of many Christians. It becomes a simple matter of compassion in which one would not will on another a birth that one would not accept for oneself. Indeed, to decide for abortion in the case of a severe genetic disorder, which would involve a very early death, can be seen as exercising the role of nature in the absence of the miscarriage that would ordinarily occur in cases of that kind. I recognize in these types of decisions the dangers of misuse of power and control to which all human decisions are subject, but that reality should not prevent us from making the hard but compassionate decisions that life at times requires of us. This is a far different kind of decision from one motivated by a desire for convenience or a desire to avoid parental responsibility.

There are many other ethical issues raised by genetic testing and the Human Genome Project in particular that we cannot address here.[21] Apart from other political and economic issues, including questions of universal access to genetic services, there are concerns about reproductive technology that are related to genetics. Fertilization techniques, including in vitro fertilization and artificial insemination by husband and by donor, the use of germ cell banks, and "womb service" or the use of surrogates, raise issues concerning embryonic life and the proper limits of manipulation in procreation. The significant progress in recent years in the technology of cloning is now raising serious questions about the possibility of cloning human beings. While these subjects certainly invite attention, this concluding section must be limited to some underlying questions of a theological as well as ethical nature that arise from genetic programs, raising issues of human identity and human destiny.

In particular, the focus will be on what is often referred to as genetic intervention or gene transfer (or, in a more grandiose vein, "genetic engineering") and its implications for the human future.

GENETICS, HUMAN IDENTITY, AND THE HUMAN FUTURE

There is an underlying philosophical assumption encouraged by genetic programs—and given particular impetus by the HGP as it affects the outlook of society—that warrants the attention of Christians. It relates to what many would call the "geneticization" of society, which encourages the idea that human identity is fundamentally a matter of one's genetic constitution, making physical-chemical categories definitive in describing and understanding humans. It is an interpretive framework that can be called "genetic reductionism," or the effort to explain everything concerning human life and experience in a way that reduces humans ultimately to their genes.[22] It reflects the fact that the quest for new knowledge concerning human life is never free of assumptions that create the framework of meaning in which new knowledge is assimilated. As Arthur Caplan observes:

> Another reason for special ethical attention [to HGP] is that expanding knowledge of human genetics is likely to cause a conceptual revolution in our understanding of human nature and in human self-perception. Concepts such as normality, unnaturalness, disability, personal responsibility, equal opportunity, paternity, parentage, race, ethnicity, instinct, and family are closely tied to beliefs and opinions about the biological constitution of human beings....New knowledge resulting from mapping the genome has the potential to force shifts in our metaphysical and ethical self-understanding.[23]

These "shifts" of which Caplan speaks are capable of seriously diminishing the full richness of human identity and experience, denying the depth and breadth of the human spirit. A "gene-dominated" understanding of human nature, undoubtedly encouraged by the HGP, will fail to recognize the role of "nurture" as well as "nature" in human identity as well as in matters of health and disease. Any kind of reductionism in understanding humanity leads to a tunnel vision, which is comfortable but inadequate. From a Christian point of view, to understand human reality solely from a genetic standpoint represents but one more abortive attempt on the part of a scientific worldview to understand humanity exclusively on its own terms, a "totalizing" effort of which postmodern thinking has been particularly critical.

Not only from scientific thinking but also from the side of Christian theology there are some challenging ideas that need to be addressed in the area of genetics and humanity. One can identify two clearly opposed views in theology on the subject of humanity and its relation to the natural environment, each bearing contrary ethical implications. The one view sees nature as "good," reflecting the design and purpose of God as witnessed to by the Genesis creation story ("and God saw that it was good"). An implication drawn from this conviction is that due respect is to be given to "the way things are"; there are structures to life that are not to be tampered with on behalf of human purposes, no matter how noble, for those purposes are inescapably mixed with ambition and self-serving that can reap harmful, if not destructive, results. Where there are expressions of human disability as in genetic disease, they not only are important reminders of our brokenness, but present us with the opportunity of serving disabled people in a spirit of compassion. Their anomalies are not good in any *absolute* sense, but the Christian believes that *ultimately* they will prove to be good, because God works to achieve his purposes also through them.[24] While this view does not necessarily lead to complete passivity in the face of pain and disability, it does emphasize a spirit of acceptance and a willingness to shape oneself to live with difficult realities rather than to change them. The notion of "stewardship" or responsibility for God's creation runs strong in this perspective, though that term does not have to connote complete resignation in regard to things as they are.

An opposing view is expressed in the notion of human beings as "co-creators" with God.[25] While recognizing human creatureliness, this view at the same time would emphasize the destiny of human beings to work with their Creator in fashioning a better world. Because they are created in God's image, humans have the creative capacity to bring about change in the structures of life, which ought not be seen as absolute barriers for human imagination and creativity. This view would agree that God's creation is good, but the reality is that it now manifests its fallen character as well, not only in human sin but in every expression of human disease and sickness. These negative features of human life are not to be "lived with," but are to be challenged by the human vision, using the gifts with which God has endowed us. The advances of science and technology are not to be regarded with suspicion but welcomed as God's gifts, fashioned through human hands and promising a more humane world in which to live. Recombinant DNA technology is but one more example of humanity's capacity to push back the boundaries imposed by a fallen world and promises yet more humanizing achievements that to this point have not even been imagined. The future is a standing invitation to bring change and new direction to the human story.

One might be tempted to read each of these views as simply an ideological expression, the one conservative and the other liberal. Yet each of them reflects important elements in the Christian tradition, and consequently each of them needs the other to prevent a one-sided perspective that suffers from a lack of balance. The first view understands the importance of structures and the capacity of human beings to be motivated by a spirit of hubris that fails to recognize human limitations. Given the human condition, curbing our use of technology may well be an act of wisdom rather than cowardice or timidity. On the other hand, the second view lifts up and celebrates the distinctively human capacity to give shape and form to the future. Assuming that humans can act with sufficient wisdom in fulfilling that mission, to shirk responsibility would be renouncing their destiny. This view sees the issue as ultimately a matter of confidence in God and being willing to act on that confidence on behalf of a more humane world. Not only pride but apathy are root sins that characterize the human condition, and not to press at human boundaries would be to succumb to apathy and lack of faith.

These opposing perspectives come to expression quite explicitly in regard to that form of genetic intervention that is called germline therapy. Until now there has been a tendency to draw a definitive line between somatic and germline therapy. The former involves genetic manipulation of a person's body cells apart from gametes or germline cells, with the consequences limited to the body of that person. The latter, or germline therapy, involves genetic manipulation of reproductive cells (eggs of females and sperm of males) that consequently exercises an impact on the bodies and lives of succeeding generations. The line between them has served to sanction a responsible use of somatic therapy but to reject germline therapy altogether. A principal argument for this position is that there are too many unknowns in working with germline cells, and given the extensive, irreversible nature of the consequences, wisdom would dictate that we refrain from engaging in this kind of experimentation. Among Christian ethicists, the cautious stance of Paul Ramsey has cast a long shadow on the consideration of this subject: "When concern for the species replaces care for the primary patient, and means are adopted that are deep invasions of the parameters of human parenthood as it came to us from the Creator, will we not be launched on a sea of uncertainty where lack of wisdom may introduce mistakes that are uncontrollable and irreversible?"[26] These "mistakes" may include the possibility of harmful pathogens being created for which there is no immunity and which could be highly destructive. There is also concern about the costs involved, which are seen as excessive in view of the limited number of people who would profit from such therapy. Some also see germline therapy as likely to open a Pandora's box by encouraging attitudes in support of all kinds of efforts at enhancing the human genetic condition.

Those who affirm humanity as co-creator with God in fashioning the human future are aware of the dangers of germline therapy, but they see the potential for good as outweighing the force of these negative judgments, particularly as we gain more knowledge of the process. Any good coming from genetic therapy would be multiplied indefinitely when involving germline cells. Many arguments tend to make it a question of vision and courage versus a failure of heart and nerve. In both negative and positive stances, however, the issue most often tends to be argued not so much on grounds of principle that would make germline therapy intrinsically wrong or intrinsically right, regardless of context or circumstances. Rather, the arguments tend to be based on a judgment of the present state of genetic science and technology, allowing for the possibility of changing perspective. To this situation Christian views of anthropology and history also come into play, with those opposed emphasizing the sinfulness of the human condition and those in favor emphasizing human potential implicit in the teaching of the *imago dei*. The latter stance is exemplified in the writings of theologian Ted Peters:

> The theological concept of anthropology with which we have been working emphasizes human creativity placed in the service of visionary beneficence, and I think that even germline modification should be considered one possible means oriented toward a beneficent end. I have been arguing that if we understand God's creative activity as giving the world a future, and if we understand the human being as a created cocreator, then ethics begins with envisioning a better future. This suggests we should at minimum keep the door open to improving the genetic lot and, in an extremely modest way, influencing our evolutionary future.[27]

There is one more line of division drawn between what is regarded as morally acceptable and unacceptable in genetic engineering, and that relates to both somatic and germline therapy. It is the line between therapy and enhancement, between correcting a defective gene and "improving" one's genetic material to achieve a desirable social goal.[28] An example would be the difference between genetic intervention to correct a disorder like Huntington's disease or cystic fibrosis, and an intervention to increase one's stature, or to add a few decades to one's life, or to enhance one's intellectual capacities. Much of the discontent that people feel about genetic intervention relates to these latter possibilities, often seen as elements of a "slippery slope" to which genetic engineering is likely to lead. While making the distinction between therapy and enhancement is ethically responsible, it is clear that the line between the two is not always clear. One factor that makes the line fuzzier is the use of gene transfer for the purpose of preventing disease rather than curing it. Would this be therapy or enhancement? As one moves from diseases like cancer that are obviously "there" to the realm of mental illnesses, the line also becomes more obscure. Is the improvement of one's capacity for voluntary recall therapy or enhancement?

Whatever the difficulties in determining these distinctions, they do convey a valid concern about possibilities of misusing genetic interventions. Given the comprehensive, identity-forming character of our genetic endowment, the problem involves our humanity and the concern that these developments not assault our understanding of what it means to be human. Eric Juengst has posed the issue as one of fairness, stating the alternatives as enhancement versus achievement: Are we to enable people to succeed in society through genetic intervention, giving them an edge against others who depend on their own natural efforts at self-improvement? Looking at the issue in this way, it becomes a matter of social values and the morality of giving advantages to a few that are not available to others. It could be seen as a civil rights issue because the use of gene manipulation to enhance one's place in society would not be available to those unable to afford it.[29] Another valid concern is to draw lines that prevent the use of genetic manipulation from becoming the servant of every whim and fancy found in consumer culture. The attempt to forge standards that reflect values of fairness and authenticity would hardly guarantee the absence of hard cases that are difficult to decide—no rule does—but at least it would provide helpful direction in the deliberation that would be required. Appropriate professional guidelines and federal regulations would be needed to keep the scientific community in line with the standards that are adopted.

Assessing these arguments from a spirit-ethics point of view, I have stressed the importance of moral deliberation in which judgment and discernment are exercised. This is often a process of weighing and balancing, which in this case involves consideration of the human potential for both good and evil. In a dramatic way, genetic intervention poses possibilities of humane achievement and much good, extending to countless numbers in future generations. At the same time, it poses possibilities of catastrophe, not just because of the human capacity for evil but because of such negative factors as ignorance and false self-confidence. At these kinds of critical junctures in the human story, Christian faith brings a spirit of hope and confidence in what humanity, by God's providence, can achieve, but at the same time a confidence tempered by realism that is fully aware of human fallibility. Relating this to the genetic prospect, the Christian community has reason to cautiously support those efforts that would enable a responsible technology to eliminate future genetic disorders that till now have burdened the human race. The critical issue is whether we know sufficiently the full implications of what we would be doing. As long as scientific and medical questions have not been fully answered concerning physical harm that could be inflicted on living and future persons, attempts at germline therapy would be ethically indefensible. To absolutely close the door now, however, on grounds of principle, would, I believe, betray a lack of confidence that would be unbecoming for the faith community. Christians should be particularly alert, however, to the many ethical issues raised by germline therapy, including also factors of cost and accessibility.

This orientation of confidence tempered by realism leads one to question the tendency of some Christians to give considerable theological weight to genetic engineering, associating it with the redemptive work of God. Ronald Cole-Turner refers to genetic engineering as "redemptive technology," arguing that our knowledge of God's redemptive purpose provides direction for the transformation of nature; it enables us to identify technology as "an increasingly efficient and productive mode of divine activity."[30] When a theologian unites the concept of redemption with genetic engineering in this way, technology as an expression of human achievement and ingenuity is inappropriately united as a partner in God's redemptive action in Jesus Christ. This compromises the integrity of the biblical story, to say nothing of the church's understanding of divine grace and the new life in Christ. In order to avoid serious confusion concerning the church's message, the potential and promise of genetics should be understood within the realm of creation rather than redemption. The language of redemption also gives rise to inflated notions of a *Homo futurus* that "genetic modification" can supposedly produce, including the generation of such theological virtues as faith, hope, and love in the persona of future humans.[31] I believe these kinds of ideas would equate a genetic utopia with the kingdom of God, attributing more power and autonomy to humans than they are able either to exercise or to handle. The church must be alert to the implications of any expression of "biological salvation," which inevitably replaces the good news of the gospel with a new law of genetic improvement.

The overall impact of the Human Genome Project may well support the concerns of those who caution against the dangers of geneticizing public consciousness. That process leads to exaggerated notions about the role of one's genes in the creation of individual identity and a consequent inflation of expectations from the possibility of achieving a healthier gene pool. This kind of thinking can easily result in increased discrimination against those whose lives are marked by genetic disorders. One philosophical expression of geneticizing or "genocentric" thinking today is evident in such writers as geneticists Francis Crick and James D. Watson and sociobiologist Edward O. Wilson, who advocate a thoroughgoing biological determinism. The reductionism inherent in these views seriously limits the nature and horizons of the human being. The spirit dimension of human life, while rooted in a biological organism, cannot be limited by the ideas of those who are ruled by a narrowly scientistic or empiricist frame of mind. Human consciousness, including our moral experience, resists all efforts at explanation and description that are limited to molecular biology.

An opposite set of issues is posed by apologists of religion who would accuse the scientific establishment of attempting to usurp the place of God as Creator. A notable example of this was the effort of Jeremy Rifkin of the Foundation on Economic Trends to persuade church leaders in 1995 to repudiate the patenting of human and animal life forms ("We believe that humans and animals are creations of God, not humans, and as such should not be patented as human inventions"). Many scientists and theologians were skeptical of this kind of protest, arguing that it was basically ill-informed. While recognizing the worthy intentions of those who would resist activity that appears to exceed appropriate human limits, they believed that greater understanding of all the dimensions of the scientific enterprise involved in this issue would likely have changed the minds of many of these church leaders.[32] The patenting issue poses a good example of the exceedingly difficult and complicated nature of the ethical problems posed by the HGP. On the one hand, if human genes are in the public domain, the incentive to develop practical therapies would be significantly curtailed. On the other hand, the injection of marketplace competition has stimulated the entrance of venture capitalists into the realm of gene therapy, causing some second thoughts about the wisdom of gene patenting. While the die has been cast on this matter, further deliberation will be necessary in the forging of future public policy.

Concluding Reflections

Throughout these pages I have recognized the ongoing dialogue and deliberation within the church as the essential ingredient in appropriating the ethical content of Scripture and bringing to bear its authority. It is dialogue rooted in the conviction that the Spirit of God is at work in the life of the church, which in itself is no guarantee of the church arriving at the most responsible decisions or reaching unanimity on contested ethical issues, but which does beckon us onward in confidence to continue the dialogue. At the basic level of our identity as the body of Christ, we hear and appropriate the good news of Jesus Christ and claim him as Savior and Lord. What this means for the moral life is then worked out among ourselves and in the daily encounter with others at both individual and corporate levels of life. The future-directed nature of faith keeps the vision of the kingdom of God before us, a constant reminder of the unfinished character of our lives and the open-ended nature of the moral ideals and aspirations by which we live. The motifs of freedom, agapeic love, and responsibility, shaped and informed by the Christian message and appropriated through the existential experience of repentance and forgiveness, have provided in these pages the framework for our orientation toward the world and its moral issues that compel our attention.

Within this context of the believing community the authority of Scripture for the moral life takes on the character of a living witness, expressing the identity of the community as followers of Jesus Christ who are called to faithful obedience. The nature of that obedience is described in a variety of ways, as I have noted, whether in the language of agapeic love, the fruit of the Spirit, or with other ideals and admonitions appropriate to life "in Christ." But absolutely essential to any discussion of scriptural authority for the moral life is the ongoing engagement of the church with the moral environment of society and the issues that this raises for the church. This engagement is shaped and informed by the scriptural witness but, at the same time, it forms and influences the way the church understands and appropriates that witness. It is a process that creates and necessitates dialogue that both calls us back to our roots and engages us with the issues of society. This process constitutes a hermeneutical circle in which both scriptural heritage and contemporary experience interpret each other, bringing about a creative situation in which the church can speak with a fresh and powerful word to society.

In bringing together Scripture and the moral life, we have emphasized the nurturing and formative role of Scripture as part of the church's teaching tradition. The Bible's importance to the Christian community makes necessary a process of interpretation that reflects the faithful commitment, as well as other peculiar characteristics, of the particular Christian community that is doing the interpreting. Also, as rich in depth and variety as the ethical content of Scripture is, there are many possibilities for gleaning the kinds of direction and support that one is seeking in addressing any particular topic. This means that the role of Scripture for the moral life becomes the church's responsibility as it interprets and applies the biblical message in ways that authentically express the church's identity. This involves wisdom and discernment as essential features of the life of the church as it attempts to bring love, justice, and responsible action to bear on the issues of the day.

In our consideration of each of the three social issues discussed in these closing chapters—euthanasia and assisted suicide, homosexuality, and genetics—the truths and insights of Scripture and tradition were brought into conversation with those issues as they are currently experienced. The discussion has included continuing reference to underlying theological convictions as a means of guiding the ethical imperatives, ideals, and virtues at which I have arrived. In some instances, I have been clearly guided by the dominant tradition (on suicide), while on others I have taken issue with it (on homosexuality). My attention to the context has been demonstrated in seeking out the factual material that gives the particular shape and form to the subject being addressed, and which can even lead us to take issue with the prevailing judgments of the tradition. Of course, given space limitations, much has been left unsaid in each chapter in terms of relevant theological material as well as insights from other sources that often have been assumed rather than explicated. Entering into my conclusions has been a long history of conversation and discussion in a variety of congregational and other settings within the church where I have profited from the insights and perspective of many members of the household of faith. If I have learned one thing about Christian ethics, it is that we are not alone on our journey but can profit from a host of witnesses who have gone before us and who walk beside us.

An important point in each of the three issues we've addressed is the fact that each can be the occasion for significant assaults on the humanity and personhood of certain individuals. Given the Christian orientation, this is a point that cannot be left unchallenged. Euthanasia and assisted suicide are being advocated as public policy options that people have a "right" to exercise in the name of individual autonomy, but the end result threatens a cheapening of the lives of those who are disabled and who are made to feel that they must justify their existence. Gays and lesbians are also denied their humanity when they are defined and then judged on the basis of their sexuality. Heterosexism does not allow the recognition of homosexual persons as genuine human beings, whose sexual orientation is an integral part of their humanity, but at the same time whose lives and personhood cannot be restricted to their sexuality. Finally, genetic programs, while carrying great potential as a means of preventing or at least modifying the devastating impact of genetic disease, are also subject to misuse in becoming the occasion for discrimination against those who suffer a genetic disorder. More widespread use of genetic testing and screening may also encourage a definition of humanity that is increasingly impatient with physical and mental disabilities, even of the mildest kind.

The concern with exclusion in which some people are discriminated against for not measuring up to a community standard has been reflected in our treatment of each of these social issues. That concern is clearly rooted in several important Christian convictions to which we have referred throughout this work. One of these convictions is that humans are created in God's image and therefore have an inherent value that other humans—either individually or corporately—cannot withdraw or ignore without coming under judgment. The other conviction is the explicitly Christ-centered unity that Christians experience and celebrate, expressed strikingly by Paul in Galatians 3:28—"You are all one in Christ Jesus." The Christian community itself can sometimes convey the aura of exclusiveness to the outsider, but in doing so loses its authentic character. The essence of Christian community is its capacity to reach out and embrace the stranger. This means that hospitality is an essential feature of genuine Christian community, for it expresses to the outsider the Christian experience of the gospel, which has claimed sinners and brought them into community. The capacity of the church to be a leaven in society, living out the spirit of love and seeking justice in the human community, is directly dependent on its faith and its commitment to him who is the supreme example of love, the Lord of the church.

NOTES

INTRODUCTION

1. James Barr, *The Bible in the Modern World* (New York: Harper & Row, 1973), 113.

2. See Jeffrey S. Siker, *Scripture and Ethics: Twentieth-Century Portraits* (New York: Oxford University Press, 1997), chaps. 8–9.

3. Robin Gill, *Christian Ethics in Secular Worlds* (Edinburgh: T. & T. Clark, 1991), 17.

4. See Ronald H. Preston, *Confusions in Christian Social Ethics* (Grand Rapids: Eerdmans, 1994), 114f.

5. It should be noted that Jeffrey S. Siker as a biblical theologian has made an invaluable contribution to furthering the conversation between Christian ethicists and biblical scholars with his recent book (see above, note 2).

1. POSTMODERNISM AND CHRISTIAN ETHICS

1. One can refer to postmodernism as a philosophical outlook identified with the works of a small group of thinkers, such as Jacques Derrida, Jean-Francois Lyotard, Jean Baudrillard, and Michel Foucault in France and Richard Rorty in the United States. One can also refer to it as a Western cultural phenomenon in which some of the ideas of these and other related thinkers appear to be affirmed in many instances of cultural attitudes and beliefs. It is in this latter, more general sense that my remarks are made here. Much postmodern thinking is excessively obscure, and the reader will find help in any number of descriptive and evaluative works. Among Christian appraisals, see Stanley Grenz, *A Primer on Postmodernism* (Grand Rapids: Eerdmans, 1996); Brian D. Ingraffia, *Postmodern Theory and Biblical Theology* (Cambridge: Cambridge University Press, 1995); Paul Lakeland, *Postmodernity: Christian Identity in a Fragmented Age* (Minneapolis: Fortress Press, 1997); Roger Lundin, *The Culture of Interpretation: Christian Faith and the Postmodern World* (Grand Rapids: Eerdmans, 1993); and J. Richard Middleton and Brian J. Walsh, *Truth Is Stranger Than It Used to Be: Biblical Faith in a Postmodern Age* (Downers Grove, Ill.: InterVarsity Press, 1995).

2. See Robin Gill, *Moral Leadership in a Postmodern Age* (Edinburgh: T. & T. Clark, 1997), 17–19.

3. Diogenes Allen, "Christian Values in a Post-Christian Context," in Frederic B. Burnham, ed., *Postmodern Theology: Christian Faith in a Pluralist World* (San Francisco: Harper & Row, 1989), 23.

4. See Philip Goodchild, "Christian Ethics in the Postmodern Condition," in *Studies in Christian Ethics*, vol. 8, no. 1 (Edinburgh: T. & T. Clark, 1995), 20–32. Goodchild observes: "The consequences of any religious appeal to an absolute

that transcends death are extremely shocking: any destruction is permitted in the name of such an absolute. This factor has frequently been present in religious wars—and it exemplifies how any theological approach to ethics can be perilous" (28).

5. Merold Westphal has done the Christian community a significant service in pointing out this truth. See *Suspicion and Faith: The Religious Uses of Modern Atheism* (Grand Rapids: Eerdmans, 1993).

6. Zygmunt Bauman, *Postmodern Ethics* (Cambridge, Mass.: Blackwell, 1993), 10.

7. Martha Nussbaum, "Virtue Revived," *Times Literary Supplement*, July 3, 1992, 9–11. Quoted in Gertrude Himmelfarb, *The De-Moralization of Society* (New York: Random House/Vintage Books, 1994), 250–51. For a helpful discussion of the implications of this turn to particularity, see Gene Outka, "The Particularist Turn in Theological and Philosophical Ethics," in Lisa Sowle Cahill and James F. Childress, eds., *Christian Ethics: Problems and Prospects* (Cleveland: Pilgrim Press, 1996), 93–118.

8. Alister McGrath, "Christian Ethics," in Robert Morgan, ed., *The Religion of the Incarnation* (Bristol, England: Bristol Classical Press, 1989), 200.

9. For an insightful treatment of the nature of trust as a basis for life in community, see Knud E. Løgstrup, *The Ethical Demand*, rev. ed. (Notre Dame, Ind.: University of Notre Dame Press, 1997).

10. William C. Spohn, *What Are They Saying about Scripture and Ethics?* rev. ed. (New York: Paulist Press, 1995), 98–102. Spohn elaborates further on his Jesus-centered ethics in *Go and Do Likewise: Jesus and Ethics* (New York: Continuum, 1998).

11. While working on this chapter, I was forcefully reminded of this fact by the TV series *Inspired by Bach*, featuring cellist Yo-Yo Ma playing the Bach cello suites accompanied by a variety of other art forms. One segment of this series united the Fifth Suite with an interpretive Kabuki dance, creating a stunning example of aesthetic beauty transcending two disparate cultures—in this case those of an eighteenth-century German composer and a twentieth-century Japanese dancer. Each part of the suite evoked a sublime response in the dancer to such universal themes as hope, mourning, denial, prayer, dream, and reconciliation.

12. Bernard Adeney, from his own extensive experience in living among other cultures, makes this observation: "Goodness has two outstanding characteristics. One is that beyond all the significant differences in cultural expressions of goodness lie qualities of character or virtue that shine with clarity across cultures. The other is that all virtues and vices are made real in cultural forms. They cannot be perceived in the abstract. You do not have to live in another culture long to recognize goodness and evil in the people you meet....some qualities of character stand out." I would agree with Adeney's observation that most apparent among these character qualities are those that Paul lists among the "fruit of the Spirit" in Galatians 5, virtues that "transcend culture. They are seen in people from every race, religion and cultural group." See his *Strange Virtues: Ethics in a Multicultural World* (Downers Grove, Ill.: InterVarsity Press, 1995), 25.

13. Gregory Baum, *Essays in Critical Theology* (Kansas City, Mo.: Sheed and Ward, 1994), 19.

14. Ibid., 23–26.

15. John T. Noonan Jr., "Development in Moral Doctrine," *Theological Studies*, 54 (1993), 662–77.

16. Alasdair MacIntyre is a Thomistic theologian whose work reveals significant motifs from postmodern thought, exercising a profound influence on Christian ethicists well beyond his own tradition. See his *After Virtue* (Notre Dame, Ind.: University of Notre Dame Press, 1981) and *Whose Justice? Which Rationality?* (Notre Dame, Ind.: University of Notre Dame Press, 1988). For a discussion of Roman Catholic moral theology in regard to moral truth and historical change, see David Hollenbach, S.J., "Tradition, Historicity, and Truth in Theological Ethics," *Christian Ethics*, 60–75.

17. See Outka, "Particularist Turn," 104–106.

18. This point is well expressed by H. Richard Niebuhr, whose sensitivity to the historicality of human existence anticipates much of the Christian response to postmodernism: "It is not evident that the man who is forced to confess that his view of things is conditioned by the standpoint he occupies must doubt the reality of what he sees. It is not apparent that one who knows that his concepts are not universal must also doubt that they are concepts of the universal, or that one who understands how all his experience is historically mediated must believe that nothing is mediated through history." See *The Meaning of Revelation* (New York: Macmillan, 1962), 18–19.

2. The Church in a Pluralist Society

1. We should recognize here the several meanings that come into play with the word *church*. In most cases our discussion treats the church as a theological concept, defined by Christian faith as the "body of Christ" and, thus, an object of faith. It is the church in its theological self-awareness, and in this use it functions as an abstraction and ideal that empirical churches seek to embody. While expressed in the singular, this concept embraces the many church groups that identify the church in the world. In this chapter we often are addressing the church as many and diverse institutions in society—as "churches"—that are subject to the influences of the culture. Depending on the context, we may be referring to individual congregations or to denominations. At other points, we may be referring to the church in terms of its traditions or teachings, which express the church's unity as well as its diversity. When the empirical church is the focus, the plural form is generally used; when the church in its theological character as the community of faith is referred to, the singular form is used.

2. Stephen L. Carter, *The Culture of Disbelief* (New York: Basic Books, 1993), 93.

3. Ian S. Markham, *Plurality and Christian Ethics* (Cambridge: Cambridge University Press, 1994), 193.

4. George A. Lindbeck, "The Church's Mission to a Postmodern Culture," in Frederic B. Burnham, ed., *Postmodern Theology: Christian Faith in a Pluralist World* (San Francisco: HarperCollins, 1989), 37–55.

5. Robert N. Bellah, "Christian Faithfulness in a Pluralist World," in *Postmodern Theology*, 89.

6. Peter Berger has written perceptively about these developments, noting the emergence of more vigorous attempts on the part of some churches to claim absolute truth at the very time that a relativist spirit characterizes our culture. He argues the genuine Protestant alternative of "faith alone" to every effort to claim

"certain knowledge," or religious security, whether through an infallible church, an inerrant Scripture, or a "born again" religious experience. See his article, "Protestantism and the Quest for Certainty," *The Christian Century* (August 26–September 2, 1998), 782–85, 79–96.

7. Ronald F. Thiemann, *Religion in Public Life: A Dilemma for Democracy* (Washington, D.C.: Georgetown University Press, 1996), 162. For a more extensive treatment of Thiemann's nonfoundationalist position, see his *Revelation and Theology: The Gospel as Narrated Promise* (Notre Dame: University of Notre Dame Press, 1985).

8. Edward F. Tivnan, *The Moral Imagination: Confronting the Ethical Issues of Our Day* (New York: Simon & Schuster, 1995), 245–47.

9. Herbert McCabe, "New Thinking on Natural Law," *Herder Correspondence* 4 (1967), 347–52. Quoted in George M. Regan, C.M., *New Trends in Moral Theology* (New York: Newman Press, 1971), 141. Thomas Aquinas himself noted the greater possibility of error as one moves from quite general natural law principles to specific applications. See *Summa Theologiae*, I–II, Q. 94, a. 4.

10. One can argue that postmodern skepticism is quite understandable as a reaction to overinflated truth claims rooted in the Enlightenment confidence in reason. Claims of indubitable certainty on the one hand and absolute skepticism on the other are both misleading and inadequate, each feeding on the other. See Lesslie Newbigin, *Proper Confidence* (Grand Rapids: Eerdmans, 1995), chap. 3; and Ronald F. Thiemann, *Constructing a Public Theology* (Louisville: Westminster/John Knox, 1991), 48–51.

11. Reinhold Niebuhr is particularly astute in addressing this subject, recognizing a place for universal claims that would challenge postmodern thinking, but also acknowledging that such claims can indeed give support to postmodern suspicion of universal judgments. The judgments of reason "can be alternately the instrument by which the self-as-subject condemns the partial and prejudiced actions of the sinful self, and the vehicle of the sinful self by which it seeks to give the sanctity of a false universality to its particular needs and partial insights" (*The Nature and Destiny of Man*, vol. 1, (New York: Charles Scribner's Sons, 1951), 284–85). Niebuhr is suspicious of the ideological content of definitions of moral concepts such as justice, claiming that "it is not possible to state a universally valid concept of justice from any particular sociological locus in history" ("Christian Faith and Natural Law," *Theology*, vol. 40,(February 1940), 88).

12. Jeffrey Stout, *Ethics after Babel* (Boston: Beacon Press, 1988), 3. Stout argues for an ethics that displays an appropriate modesty and humility in light of its contextual character, but that need not succumb to moral skepticism or relativism. See also his chapter, "On Having a Morality in Common," in Gene Outka and John P. Reedy, eds., *Prospects for a Common Morality* (Princeton, N.J.: Princeton University Press, 1993), 215–32.

13. Stanley Hauerwas has been a particularly forceful advocate of this point, posing the believing community with its narrative tradition as the source of Christian ethics in a postmodern world. See his *A Community of Character: Toward a Constructive Christian Social Ethic* (Notre Dame: University of Notre Dame Press, 1981).

14. Ibid., 61. Paul Ricoeur makes this point with particular eloquence: "But tradition...even understood as the transmission of a *depositum,* remains a dead tra-

dition if it is not the continual interpretation of this deposit: our 'heritage' is not a sealed package we pass from hand to hand, without ever opening, but rather a treasure from which we draw by the handful and which by this very act is replenished." See his *The Conflict of Interpretations: Essays in Hermeneutics* (Evanston, Ill.: Northwestern University Press, 1974), 27.

15. Thomas W. Ogletree, *The Use of the Bible in Christian Ethics* (Philadelphia: Fortress Press, 1983), 176.

16. See Jeffrey Stout's article, "Tradition in Ethics," *Westminster Dictionary of Christian Ethics*, ed. James F. Childress and John Macquarrie (Louisville: Westminster/John Knox, 1986), 629–31.

17. The term is David Tracy's; quoted in *Constructing a Public Theology*, 23.

18. This point is well made by Stephen L. Carter in *The Culture of Disbelief*, 68–74.

19. Stanley Hauerwas, *After Christendom?* (Nashville: Abingdon Press, 1991), 45–50. See also his *A Community of Character*, chap. 4.

20. See Baum, *Essays*, chap. 4.

21. Ronald F. Thiemann argues that the church as well as every group in a democratic society must recognize the validity of liberty, equality, and mutual respect as values that govern participation in the public realm. They may not always be understood in the way that the church believes they should, but they are necessary to public dialogue, and their reigning interpretations are variously subject to support as well as critique. See his *Religion in Public Life: A Dilemma for Democracy*, 156–58.

22. It is less than convincing for Hauerwas to say that his argument "does not mean that we must give up working for justice in the societies of modernity" (*After Christendom?* 68) when in effect he is clearly saying that we sacrifice our integrity when we do so. A further indication of the sectarian character of his approach to church and society is his espousal of pacifism, a viewpoint that abdicates concern with the state as a moral agent in favor of addressing the individual Christian's relation to war. I appreciate the need of churches assuming a more countercultural stance, but not at the expense of yielding their responsibility to address the state as a center of political and economic power.

23. Max Stackhouse, "Theo-cons and Neo-cons on Theology and Law," *The Christian Century* (August 27–September 3, 1997), 760.

24. Lisa Sowle Cahill, *Sex, Gender, and Christian Ethics* (New York: Cambridge University Press, 1996), 69.

25. One sees a similar, reinforcing position among neoconservative writers in recent decades, such as sociologist of religion, Peter Berger (*The Social Construction of Reality* with Thomas Luckmann [1966], *The Homeless Mind* [1973]). Berger is impressed with the permanency of economic and political megastructures and the futility of any attempt on the part of the church to change them. He consequently sees mainline churches as having made a major mistake in emphasizing social and economic justice and encouraging political involvement in order to change society for the better. See Baum, *Essays*, 85–87.

While the expectation that the church will "transform" society is a pretentious notion, promising more than anyone can deliver, the church as a community identified with the God of Scripture has every reason to maintain a confident spirit about the possibilities of change. Its sense of imperative about challenging injustice and contributing to a more humane society is rooted in its convictions as the people of God. As often noted, the primary issue in such activity is not how "successful" the church will be, but how faithful.

26. See Douglas F. Ottati, "God and Ourselves: The Witness of H. Richard Niebuhr," *The Christian Century* (April 2, 1997), 346–49.

27. Max L. Stackhouse, *Public Theology and Political Economy: Christian Stewardship in Modern Society* (Grand Rapids: Eerdmans, 1987), xii

3. Determining "What the Bible Says"

1. Our discussion here of biblical scholarship makes no attempt to describe its richness in terms of the variety of methodologies that have evolved, such as source, form, redaction, and social-science criticism. Our purpose is to describe the critical approach in generic terms for the purpose of contrasting it to postmodern approaches to the text. *Historical criticism* is a general term used for critical biblical scholarship's attempt to recover the events and meanings presented by the biblical material.

2. The attempt of fundamentalists to bring scientific precision to their treatment of Scripture is discussed by George Marsden, *Fundamentalism and American Culture: The Shaping of Twentieth-Century Evangelicalism* (New York: Oxford University Press, 1980).

3. The observation of biblical theologian James D. Smart is pertinent to this subject: "Much of the difficulty that surrounds this problem of authority has arisen from the attempt of churchmen to make God's authority visible, tangible, and incontestable in a way that it never was for prophets or apostles or for Jesus himself. The authority of God's word everywhere in Scripture is invisible, intangible, and contestable." *The Strange Silence of the Bible in the Church: A Study in Hermeneutics* (Philadelphia: Westminster, 1970), 98.

4. See Walter Wink, *The Bible in Human Transformation* (Philadelphia: Fortress Press, 1973).

5. *Ibid.*, 62.

6. See Roy A. Harrisville and Walter Sundberg, *The Bible in Modern Culture* (Grand Rapids: Eerdmans, 1995), chap. 12. Harrisville and Sundberg identify an "Augustinian tradition" in biblical criticism (exemplified by such giants as Rudolf Bultmann and Ernst Kasemänn) that has resisted the Enlightenment hegemony in historical criticism by recognizing the indispensable role of faith. Peter Stuhlmacher argues this point in his "hermeneutics of consent," in which scholars take the text seriously by giving up their own attempt to control the text's meaning, remaining open to, or "hearing," the message of transcendence that is being communicated there. See his *Historical Criticism and Theological Interpretation of Scripture*, trans. Roy A. Harrisville (Minneapolis: Fortress Press, 1977), 83–91.

7. Robin Scroggs, "Beyond Criticism to Encounter: The Bible in the Postcritical Age," in *The Text and the Times: New Testament Essays for Today* (Minneapolis: Fortress Press, 1993), 262–63.

8. Daniel Patte, *Ethics of Biblical Interpretation: A Reevaluation* (Louisville: Westminster/John Knox, 1995), 90–91. Among Christian ethicists, Stanley Hauerwas makes a similar point, arguing that the approaches of both fundamentalism and historical criticism are governed by rational assumptions that ignore the neces-

sary context of a believing community for appropriating and understanding the
text. See his *Unleashing the Scriptures: Freeing the Bible from Captivity to America*
(Nashville: Abingdon Press, 1993), chap. 3.

9. As with historical critical research, here again it is beyond the scope of this
work to spell out the many dimensions of literary theory. For a helpful overview
of various critical approaches in contemporary literary theory, from deconstruc-
tion to feminist criticism, see Steven Lynn, *Texts and Contexts: Writing About Literature with Critical Theory*, 2d ed. (New York: Longman, 1998). My reference to
reader response criticism is intended as a general term to express the orientation
of postmodern hermeneutical thinking, which locates the source of meaning not
in the author and text but in the "fusion of horizons" (Hans-Georg Gadamer)
created by the meeting of reader and text, leaving room for continuing reinter-
pretation and the emergence of new meanings with every subsequent reading of
the text. The interest is not in returning to a pristine "original meaning" but in
the creation of new meaning in a new situation.

10. See Robert M. Grant and David Tracy, *A Short History of the Interpretation of
the Bible*, 2d ed. (Minneapolis: Fortress Press, 1984), chap. 16.

11. Roger Lundin, Anthony C. Thiselton, and Clarence Walhout, *The Responsibility of Hermeneutics* (Grand Rapids: Eerdmans, 1985), 94.

12. Lesslie Newbigin, *Proper Confidence* (Grand Rapids: Eerdmans, 1995), 104.

13. Edgar V. McKnight, *Post-Modern Use of the Bible* (Nashville: Abingdon Press,
1988), 108.

14. Lundin, Thiselton, and Walhout, *Responsibility of Hermeneutics*, 80.

15. Darrell Jodock, *The Church's Bible: Its Contemporary Authority* (Minneapolis:
Fortress Press, 1989), 129–43.

16. Carl E. Braaten and Robert W. Jenson, eds., *Reclaiming the Bible for the
Church* (Grand Rapids: Eerdmans, 1995), x.

17. This viewpoint expresses my disagreement with Stanley Hauerwas, whose
appropriate emphasis on the believing community as the necessary context for
understanding Scripture becomes a kind of absolute alternative to the rational-
ism he sees in both historical criticism and fundamentalism. One can define biblical criticism in terms of a set of assumptions that place it in absolute antithesis
to Christian faith, but this hardly does justice to the positive use of critical biblical scholarship on the part of many scholars whose work is motivated by faith.

18. H. Richard Niebuhr, *The Meaning of Revelation* (New York: Macmillan,
1962), chap. 2.

19. Bruce C. Birch and Larry L. Rasmussen, *Bible and Ethics in the Christian Life*,
rev. ed. (Minneapolis: Augsburg, 1989), 150. For a more general discussion of the
ways in which the Bible has been understood within the life of the church, see
David H. Kelsey, *The Uses of Scripture in Recent Theology* (Philadelphia: Fortress
Press, 1975).

20. This view of inspiration makes its contribution to the changing perspective
on the historical controversy between Roman Catholicism and Protestantism
regarding the relation of Scripture to the church's tradition. Reformation
churches are more ready today to acknowledge the inadequacy of the old "Scripture vs. Tradition" argument, recognizing instead the necessary dialectic involved
in the church's relation to its Scripture. The church with its tradition both interprets and is interpreted by Scripture; it both shapes the understanding of Scripture and recognizes its own self-understanding as shaped by that Scripture.

Biblical authority, therefore, is no simple, linear matter; the Bible holds the church accountable at the same time as it "submits" to the interpretation of the church in the exercise of that authority.

21. Birch and Rasmussen, *Bible and Ethics*, 150.

22. Brevard S. Childs, *Biblical Theology in Crisis* (Philadelphia: Westminster, 1970), 99.

23. Walter Brueggemann, *Interpretation and Obedience: From Faithful Reading to Faithful Living* (Minneapolis: Augsburg Fortress, 1991), 125.

24. Childs, *Biblical Theology*, 126.

25. Just how definitive the role of the church is in shaping the individual's moral life will, of course, depend on a number of factors, but the point is that if the Christian message nurtures a distinctive moral character and outlook on life, it does so through the formative impact of the Christian community upon the families that constitute it.

4. The Ethical Content and Authority of the Bible

1. There are some notable differences among Christian communions in their understanding of the moral implications of the Christian message, and this is understandable. In some cases a given community claiming the name of Christ may adopt practices that are actually destructive in their impact (as in some cultic groups), in which case they lose their identity and integrity as a Christian community.

2. John Hales, *Golden Remains* (1659), 4. Quoted in Christopher Hill, *The English Bible and the Seventeenth-Century Revolution* (New York: Allen Lane, the Penguin Press, 1993), 43.

3. See Willard M. Swartley, *Slavery, Sabbath, War, and Women* (Scottdale, Pa.: Herald Press, 1983), chap. 1.

4. For a popular account of the misuse of Scripture in the support of a variety of causes, see Jim Hill and Rand Cheadle, *The Bible Tells Me So: Uses and Abuses of Holy Scripture* (New York: Anchor Books/Doubleday, 1996). The publication of this kind of book would indicate the growing public awareness of this problem and the undoubtedly increased skepticism that greets any reference to the Bible within the context of social issues. The emergence of the Religious Right, with its heavy reliance on Scripture, has certainly encouraged this skepticism.

5. See Donald Juel, "The Authority of the Scriptures: An Assessment of a Conversation," *Currents in Theology and Mission* vol. 23, no. 3 (June 1996), 192–99.

6. The terms we use here are found in Richard B. Hays, *The Moral Vision of the New Testament* (San Francisco: HarperCollins, 1996), 3–7. Hays adds a fourth and culminating term, the *pragmatic* task of actually embodying or putting into practice the ethics of Scripture. Dimensions of that task will concern us in chapter 5 where I discuss a "Spirit ethics."

7. For other ways in which the ethical material of Scripture has been ordered and described, see C. Freeman Sleeper, *The Bible and the Moral Life* (Louisville: Westminster/John Knox, 1992); James M. Gustafson, *Theology and Christian Ethics* (Philadelphia: Pilgrim Press, 1974), chap. 6; and Hays, *Moral Vision*, 208–9.

8. The distinctive view of Karl Barth on this subject warrants comment. Barth understands biblical ethics in terms of the "command" of God, giving that term a much broader scope than it receives here as he discusses the distinctive com-

mands of each person of the Trinity. His concern is to distinguish commands from principles and ideals that, as we noted in chapter 1, stand at a greater distance from the realm of decision making than do commands and consequently require more reflection and judgment in applying them to the concrete situation. Embedded as they are in narrative accounts, God's commands, says Barth, are sufficiently clear and specific as to make unnecessary any human interpretation. See his *Church Dogmatics* II/2, trans. G. Bromiley, et al. (Edinburgh: T. & T. Clark, 1957), 661–71.

Barth is concerned that any reliance on human reason in arriving at the proper interpretation of God's commands is to open the door to all kinds of self-serving conclusions, far removed from the moral intention of those commands. He is clearly correct in citing the danger, but he is far from convincing in his argument that interpretation is foreclosed by the specificity of God's commands. The very fact that the church is divided over many issues of interpretation concerning the will of God would indicate that the "precision" and "specificity" that Barth avows are hardly apparent. The dangers he seeks to avoid are inherent to the genuine engagement of God's Word with human beings; to seek to avoid the risk of interpretation is questionable on both theological and ethical grounds.

9. Allen Verhey, *The Great Reversal: Ethics and the New Testament* (Grand Rapids: Eerdmans, 1984), 40–43.

10. Thus some would emphasize, for example, the spirit of reciprocity and mutuality Paul introduces in the admittedly hierarchical relationship he presents between husband and wife. See ibid., 67.

11. At the turn of the last century, Johannes Weiss and Albert Schweitzer interpreted this eschatological dimension in Jesus' teaching in quite radical terms, with particularly Schweitzer giving such an ascetic and extreme character to Jesus' ethics that in effect his teaching was removed from any meaningful connection with our own times. It was an "interim ethics," intended for the short period between Jesus and the soon-to-occur eschaton. There is ample reason to reject Schweitzer's interpretation, understanding it in the context of his own desire to challenge the liberal theology of the nineteenth century that had "domesticated" Jesus' teaching with its idealist philosophy and notions of evolutionary development. At the same time, the achievement of both Weiss and Schweitzer in lifting up the eschatological context for Jesus' teaching remains a permanent contribution. See J. I. H. McDonald, *Biblical Interpretation and Christian Ethics*, New Studies in Christian Ethics, ed. Robin Gill (Cambridge: Cambridge University Press, 1993), chap. 3.

12. Trutz Rendtorff, *Ethics*, vol. 1, trans. Keith Crim (Philadelphia: Fortress Press, 1986), 22.

13. The importance of recognizing the context of the biblical text is a reminder of the indispensability of critical historical work. One of many examples would be the controversial statement on the part of the apostle Paul that "women should keep silence in the churches" (1 Cor. 14:34). In light of other statements made by Paul that stand in contradiction to it (for example, the reference to women praying in church in 1 Cor. 11:13), it is quite likely that this remark reflects his earlier discussion in chapters 12–14 about charismatic excesses in the Corinthian church. Recognizing this helps us to avoid making a universal rule out of a passage of this kind, failing to see that its meaning is governed by the

context in which it appears. See Richard N. Longenecker, *New Testament Social Ethics for Today* (Grand Rapids: Eerdmans, 1984, reprinted by Regent College Bookstore, Vancouver, B.C., 1995), 86. For other possible understandings of this passage, see Hays, *Moral Vision*, 54–55.

14. Hays, *Moral Vision*, 193–205.

15. Ibid., 202.

16. See Thomas W. Ogletree, *The Use of the Bible in Christian Ethics* (Philadelphia: Fortress Press, 1983), 152–53.

17. Jack T. Sanders, *Ethics in the New Testament: Change and Development* (Philadelphia: Fortress Press, 1975), 130.

18. Wayne A. Meeks, *The Origins of Christian Morality: The First Two Centuries* (New Haven: Yale University Press, 1993), 216. One of the theses emerging from this impressive study is that Christian ethics must be "polyphonic." Unity in teaching and practice could not be coerced at the beginnings of the Christian movement, nor can it be today. In the midst of diversity we can only trust in the church's "common sense," derived from its memory and tradition as well as from its current experience, to maintain a responsible course (217).

19. Robin Scroggs, "The Bible as Foundational Document," *Interpretation*, vol. 49, no. 1 (January 1995), 19. See the discussion in Walter Brueggemann, "Biblical Authority in the Post-Critical Period" (under "Scriptural Authority"), *Anchor Bible Dictionary*, vol. 5, ed. David Noel Freedman (New York: Doubleday, 1992), 1049–56.

20. Luke T. Johnson, *Scripture and Discernment: Decision Making in the Church* (Nashville: Abingdon Press, 1996), 40–44.

21. Ibid., 42.

22. Constitution, Bylaws, and Continuing Resolutions of the Evangelical Lutheran Church in America, 2.03.

23. Johnson, *Scripture and Discernment*, 43.

24. What has come to be called "situation ethics" recognizes this moral ambiguity and has appropriately challenged every expression of legalism in the church. At the same time, however, a thoroughgoing situationism fails to appreciate the importance of law in establishing a moral framework or "ground rules" for society (or for any community). Rules designed to protect the community necessarily carry the weight of moral imperatives, making it always a serious matter when circumstances challenge the application of such rules.

25. Thomas G. Long sees the authority of Scripture functioning within the pattern of conversation that goes on in a congregation: "Scripture is an important, authoritative, and normative voice—a 'loud' voice, so to speak—but in congregational context it exerts its power conversationally and not unilaterally." See his chapter "Living with the Bible," in Choon-Leong Seow, ed., *Homosexuality and Christian Community* (Louisville: Westminster/John Knox, 1996), 64–73.

26. Hays, *Moral Vision*, 310.

27. David Kelsey observes that "part of what it means to call a text or set of texts 'scripture' is that its use in certain ways in the common life of the Christian community is essential to establishing and preserving the community's identity." See his *The Uses of Scripture in Recent Theology* (Philadelphia: Fortress Press, 1975), 89.

5. SPIRIT ETHICS AND A RESPONSIBLE CHURCH

1. See Richard B. Hays, *The Moral Vision of the New Testament* (San Francisco: HarperCollins, 1996), 120–25.

2. Hans Conzelmann, *A Commentary on the First Epistle to the Corinthians*, Hermeneia Series (Philadelphia: Fortress Press, 1975), 209. See James D. G. Dunn, "The Spirit and the Body of Christ" in *The Christ and the Spirit: Pneumatology*, Collected Essays, vol. 2 (Grand Rapids, Eerdmans, 1998), 343–57.

3. We cannot begin to address here the richness of meaning in New Testament references to the Spirit. In Luke and Acts we see more emphasis on prophetic and charismatic utterance in connection with the Spirit, while in Paul the connection of the Spirit with salvation is paramount. At the same time, Paul exalts the spiritual gift of prophecy because of its potential for edifying the church (1 Cor. 14:1-6). The same kind of argument, I believe, applies to his connecting the Spirit with the moral life. Love builds up the body of Christ in that it "bears all things, believes all things, hopes all things, endures all things" (1 Cor. 13:7).

4. This is a theme that recurs in Stephen E. Fowl and L. Gregory Jones, *Reading in Communion: Scripture and Ethics in Christian Life* (Grand Rapids: Eerdmans, 1991).

5. John Howard Yoder, *The Priestly Kingdom: Social Ethics as Gospel* (Notre Dame, Ind.: University of Notre Dame Press, 1984), 35.

6. My position here reflects a Lutheran understanding of the centrality of justification in the Christian life, but which at the same time would avoid any hint of dualism that divorces forgiveness from the moral life. The current renaissance in Luther studies among Finnish scholars has stressed the importance in Luther of the *unio cum Christo*, or the indwelling of Christ in the believer as inherent to the justification of the sinner. This point is made in contrast to the heavy emphasis on the forensic understanding of justification in the Formula of Concord and in much of the Lutheran tradition. While this Finnish contribution is significant and helpful, I am not enthused with its suggestion that this indwelling of Christ, or participation in the life of Christ, introduces the orthodox doctrine of *theosis*, or "divination" of the believer. This kind of language invites an ontological understanding that endangers the recognition that the believer never *arrives* at completion but is always in process. For an introduction to Finnish Luther scholarship, see Carl E. Braaten and Robert W. Jenson, eds., *Union with Christ: The New Finnish Interpretation of Luther* (Grand Rapids: Eerdmans, 1998).

Whether one speaks in Christological language or the language of the Spirit, the new life in Christ clearly aims at conforming one's life to that of Jesus. The historical contentions between Lutheran and Reformed traditions in understanding sanctification revolve more around what we can and ought to expect in the realm of *visible evidences* of faith in the moral life, which for Lutherans raises the specter of legalism.

7. Bernard T. Adeney, *Strange Virtues: Ethics in a Multicultural World* (Downers Grove, Ill.: InterVarsity Press, 1995), 41.

8. Thomas Ogletree presents an excellent discussion of moral theories in chapter 2 of *The Use of the Bible in Christian Ethics* (Philadelphia: Fortress Press, 1983).

9. Gilbert Meilaender argues in *Faith and Faithfulness: Basic Themes in Christian Ethics* (Notre Dame, Ind.: University of Notre Dame Press, 1991), chapter 5, that

teleological or consequential theory is unacceptable to Christian ethics because its focus on future consequences and achieving the "greatest good" is an expression of hubris; it denies our limitations in place and time, encouraging a lack of trust in God in its attempt to engineer a future outcome. The reservations I have expressed would recognize the point of Meilaender's argument, especially in regard to the grand scale inherent to utilitarianism ("the greatest good for the greatest number"), but it strikes me as excessive and contrary to Christian experience to reject every expression of teleological thinking. Christians quite naturally can place their moral intentions and purposes in the hands of God with an appropriate spirit of humility, asking for the best possible outcome. It is quite possible for the futurist orientation of Christian faith itself, for that matter, to generate forms of hubris (as in overconfident predictions about when and how God will be acting in the future), but that does not refute the necessity of that orientation.

10. Ogletree, *Use of the Bible*, 32.

11. The emphasis on responsibility in our discussion of the Christian life certainly reflects the impact of H. Richard Niebuhr. See his *The Responsible Self: An Essay in Christian Moral Philosophy* (New York: Harper and Row, 1963). Niebuhr argues that responsibility expresses an *alternative* ethical theory to deontological and teleological thinking, replacing images of the human being as *citizen* (deontology) and *maker* (teleology) with the image of *responder*, which recognizes the conviction of faith that we are creatures who live out our lives in response to the activity and presence of God in the world. While this clearly has the advantage of incorporating a faith perspective into ethical theory, I would argue that the other theories remain useful in describing important dimensions of moral experience. Nonetheless, the joining of the two themes of responsibility and character (with descriptive language informed by faith) is particularly helpful in expressing the *stance* of the Christian as a moral decision maker, without denying appropriate expression of the other theories in the dynamics of one's decision making. By *stance* I am referring to a viewpoint that expresses one's faith in terms of theological and anthropological convictions and the meaning of history. It is the intellectual side of a life-orientation described in terms of being "in Christ" and whose future is ordered by the eschaton of God.

12. The most influential Christian ethicist representing the peace churches is John Howard Yoder, whose classic work, *The Politics of Jesus* (Grand Rapids: Eerdmans, 1972, rev. 1994), offers an eloquent challenge to the social ethics of mainline churches. See also his *The Priestly Kingdom* and *The Royal Priesthood: Essays Ecclesiological and Ecumenical*, ed. Michael G. Cartwright (Grand Rapids: Eerdmans, 1994).

13. A helpful sourcebook on the historical roots of two-realm teaching, going back to biblical sources and to subsequent developments beyond Luther, is Karl H. Hertz, ed., *Two Kingdoms and One World: A Sourcebook in Christian Social Ethics* (Minneapolis: Augsburg, 1976).

14. The Lutheran theologian Christian Luthardt (1823–1902) is a notable example of this viewpoint: "The gospel has absolutely nothing to do with outward existence but only with eternal life....Christianity wants to change man's heart, not his external situation." The Lutheran jurist Rudolf Sohm (1841–1917) expresses the same sentiment when he says that concerns of public life "should

remain untouched by the proclamation of the gospel, completely untouched." Quoted in Robert Benne et al., "'Two Kingdoms' as Social Doctrine," *Dialog*, vol. 23, no. 3 (Summer 1984), 210. In quotes of this kind, one sees clearly the danger of two-realm thinking: in making the case that the gospel cannot govern a world based on law, there must follow an immediate "however," which too often did not appear. The tendency of the German church in the post–World War I years to isolate itself from the world of politics, a development now richly documented, crippled its response to the rise of a fascist Nazi government.

15. Here is where the tension in the two-realm teaching comes to clear expression. While drawing the line is necessary, it cannot create a dualism that hermetically divides the two realms. It does not mean that Christians cannot bring their theological and ethical convictions to bear in the realm of their work or vocation; the point rather is that law instead of gospel governs one's relationships in carrying out one's responsibilities in the public world. As governing motifs, one can and must speak of realms of law and gospel (or whatever terminology one wants to use), but the Christian will recognize that the quality of life in the public realm can be enhanced by a spirit of respect and concern for others that people can bring to those relations that constitute the political and economic life of a society. Redemptive actions can occur in surprising places, even where the expectations properly call for judgment under the rule of law.

16. A major difficulty for Lutherans has been the limitations inherent to the concept of law in describing the public realm. There is, furthermore, the negative image associated with Luther's particular understanding of law, which fails to convey the positive, enabling character of law in its structuring of human relationships. Stewart W. Herman argues that Lutherans need to recognize this "contract" character of law beyond its "criminal" or judgmental use associated with Luther. See his "Luther, Law, and Covenants: Cooperative Self-Obligation in the Reconstruction of Lutheran Social Ethics," *Journal of Religious Ethics*, vol. 25, no. 2 (Fall 1997), 257–75.

17. From a public symposium, "The Democratic Soul," *Religion and Values in Public Life* (The Center for the Study of Values in Public Life at Harvard Divinity School), vol. 6, no. 1 (Fall 1997), 2.

18. Wolfgang Schrage, *The Ethics of the New Testament*, trans. David E. Green (Edinburgh: T. & T. Clark, 1988), 19.

19. See Dunn, "Spirit Kingdom," 136–141.

20. Schrage, *Ethics of the New Testament*, 21.

21. Paul Tillich spells out the rich meaning of the kingdom of God in its relation to the Spirit ("Spiritual Presence") and eternal life, noting both its inner-historical and transhistorical meaning in that the kingdom both participates in and transcends history, giving it ultimate significance in terms of a final consummation. See *Systematic Theology*, vol. 3 (Chicago: University of Chicago Press, 1963), 356–61.

22. Richard N. Longenecker, *New Testament Social Ethics for Today* (Grand Rapids: Eerdmans, 1984; reprinted by Regent College, 1995), 94.

6. EUTHANASIA AND ASSISTED SUICIDE

1. Walker Percy, *The Thanatos Syndrome* (New York: Farrar, Straus and Giroux, 1987).

2. Vigen Guroian, *Life's Living toward Dying* (Grand Rapids: Eerdmans, 1996), xxvii.

3. See Jack Kevorkian, *Prescription Medicide: The Goodness of Planned Death* (Buffalo, N.Y.: Prometheus Books, 1991).

4. In Guroian's book, rich in insight as it is and certainly helpful to the Christian community, the one weakness, to this reader, is its failure to appreciate the impact of technology in creating the problems surrounding death and dying. The "thanatos syndrome" does not address the justified concerns that many, both Christian and non-Christian, bring to this contemporary phenomenon in which people are treated in intrusive ways that do no more than prolong the process of dying. While "death with dignity" can parade as a banner for a number of questionable assumptions concerning human autonomy, it still flags a critical ethical problem in terminal care that needs to be addressed.

5. In ministering to children who were "dangerously ill" in nineteenth-century England, the Anglican Church's book of prayers could be accused of losing a proper balance in these words prescribed for the use of the minister: "And now tell me, my child, when you thus think of the joys of the next world, and the miseries of this, whether you would not willingly change this present life for that happy one which is to come; and whether it will not be better for you, if God so require it, to hasten immediately to the presence of God, rather than by staying longer in this life to expose yourself to the danger of losing all these great delights, by falling into sin." *Offices for the Clergy in Praying with, Directing, and Comforting Sick, Infirm and Afflicted (Visitatio Infirmorum)*, 3d ed. (London: Joseph Masters, 1854), 395. Quoted in Morten Kelsey, *Healing and Christianity* (Minneapolis: Augsburg Fortress, 1995), 77, n. 16.

6. Reinhold Niebuhr, *The Nature and Destiny of Man*, vol. 1 (New York: Charles Scribner's Sons, 1964), 12–18.

7. The startling reference of the apostle Paul to the human body as "a temple of the Holy Spirit within you" (1 Cor. 6:19) occurs within the context of a discussion of Christian freedom as well as of ecclesiology, but it warrants mention also in regard to Christian anthropology. Faith in the presence of God in our midst is faith in the Holy Spirit, but Paul particularizes that presence by uniting the Spirit with each of our *bodies*. There is no dichotomy of the physical and the spiritual here; Paul is saying that the Spirit of God lays claim to our bodies and brings with that claim an imperative to live responsibly, or "in the Spirit." To think of the Holy Spirit is also to think of our bodies in response to God's presence.

8. See Tom L. Beauchamp and James F. Childress, *Principles of Biomedical Ethics*, 4th ed. (New York: Oxford University Press, 1994), 120–88, 273–91.

9. Reynolds Price, *A Whole New Life: An Illness and a Healing* (New York: Penguin Books, 1995), 146.

10. Daniel Callahan, "Editorial," *Hastings Center Report* (January/February 1989 Supplement), 31. Quoted in Kenneth L. Vaux, *Death Ethics* (Philadelphia: Trinity Press International, 1992), 16.

11. See James Rachels, "Active and Passive Euthanasia," in *The New England Journal of Medicine*, vol. 292, 1975, 78–80. For a more extensive treatment, see his *The End of Life: Euthanasia and Morality* (New York: Oxford University Press, 1986).

12. See Daniel Callahan, *What Kind of Life* (New York: Simon and Schuster,

1991), chap. 9. Callahan quotes Condorcet's history of human progress, published in 1795, which expresses the boundless optimism of the Enlightenment: "Would it be absurd then to suppose that this perfection of the human species might be capable of indefinite progress; that the day will come when death will only be due to extraordinary accidents or to the decay of the vital forces, and that ultimately, the average span between birth and decay will have no assignable value? Certainly man will not become immortal, but will not the interval between the first breath that he draws and the time when in the natural course of events, without disease or accident, he expires, increase indefinitely?" (251).

This confidence inherent to the Enlightenment mind is clearly present today and calls for some healthy Christian realism. The illusion is widespread that every limit to the human condition is subject to removal by human ingenuity and the tools provided by science and technology. This is seen in the inflated expectations people bring to medicine, that it "postpone death, stall or reverse biochemical aging processes, restore youthful anatomical features, and in general eliminate or alter anything that is unwanted." See Gerald P. McKenny, *To Relieve the Human Condition* (Albany: State University of New York Press, 1997), 221–22. McKenny is one among many in a growing chorus of voices that argue the necessity of an appropriate sense of human limitations.

13. See Robert D. Truog and James C. Fackler, "It Is Reasonable to Reject the Diagnosis of Brain Death," *The Journal of Clinical Ethics*, vol. 3, no. 1 (Spring 1992), 80–81.

14. Hans Küng and Walter Jens, *Dying with Dignity: A Plea for Personal Responsibility*, trans. John Bowden (New York: Continuum, 1995), 37–38.

15. Augustine, *The City of God*, trans. Marcus Dods (New York: Modern Library, 1950), Book 1:24, 25, 17. See Robert N. Wennberg, *Terminal Choices: Euthanasia, Suicide, and the Right to Die* (Grand Rapids: Eerdmans, 1989), 53–57.

16. See Allen Verhey, "Choosing Death: The Ethics of Assisted Suicide," *The Christian Century* (July 17–24, 1996), 716–19.

7. Homosexuality

1. For the sake of convenience, we will use the term *gay* to refer to the homosexual population, including both male and female.

2. The first serious research on a significant scale concerning gay persons in this country was initiated by the Institute for Sex Research at Indiana University, under the leadership of Dr. Alfred Kinsey. In the train of that beginning, the National Institute of Mental Health Task Force on Homosexuality was formed, and research continued, resulting in a groundbreaking book by Alan P. Bell and Martin S. Weinberg, *Homosexualities: A Study of Diversity among Men and Women* (New York: Simon and Schuster, 1978). Already in the 1950s a highly influential study was conducted by Dr. Evelyn Hooker in which the notion of homosexuality as a psychopathology was effectively refuted.

3. Simon LeVay, "A Difference in the Hypothalamic Structure between Heterosexual and Homosexual Men," *Science*, vol. 253 (1991), 1034–37.

4. Dean Hamer, et. al., "A Linkage between DNA Markers on the X Chromosome and Male Sexual Orientation," *Science*, vol. 261 (1993), 231–37.

5. J. Michael Bailey and Richard Pillard, "A Genetic Study of Male Sexual Orientation," *Archives of General Psychiatry*, vol. 48 (1991), 1089–96.

6. For a balanced overview of scientific developments in homosexual research and their ethical significance, see Timothy F. Murphy, *Gay Science: The Ethics of Sexual Orientation Research* (Irvington, N.Y.: Columbia University Press, 1997). Several articles on this subject appear in Jeffrey S. Siker, ed., *Homosexuality in the Church: Both Sides of the Debate* (Louisville: Westminster/John Knox, 1994), 93–134.

7. Siker, *Homosexuality in the Church*, xv.

8. One obvious example is the shift in the church's thinking about war caused by the emergence of the nuclear age. The whole notion of justifiable warfare, a staple in the position of most churches, has been fundamentally challenged in a world in which war brings the threat of nuclear holocaust. One effect of the Vietnam War was to force churches to recognize the way in which just-war thinking had led them invariably to sanction their government's decisions to go to war. See Donald W. Shriver, "The Biblical Life in America: Which Past Fits Us for the Future," in David W. Lotz, ed., *Altered Landscapes* (Grand Rapids: Eerdmans, 1989), 348–54.

9. J.I.H. McDonald, *Biblical Interpretation and Christian Ethics* (New York: Cambridge University Press, 1993), 162.

10. See Jeffrey S. Siker, "Homosexual Christians, the Bible, and Gentile Inclusion: Confessions of a Repenting Heterosexist," in *Homosexuality in the Church*, 178–94.

11. The classic biblical texts cited in reference to homosexuality are the following: Genesis 1 and 2 (the creation story); Genesis 19:1-9 (Sodom and Gomorrah); Judges 19 and Ezekiel 16:46-58 (parallel texts to the Genesis 19 story); Leviticus 18:22 and 20:13 (Holiness Code); Romans 1:24-27; 1 Corinthians 6:9; and 1 Timothy 1:10.

12. See Dale Martin, "Heterosexism and the Interpretation of Romans 1:18-32" in *Biblical Interpretation*, vol. 3 (1995), 332–55. David E. Fredrickson, a New Testament theologian at Luther Seminary in St. Paul, Minnesota, in a richly documented unpublished paper titled "Natural and Unnatural Use in Rom. 1:24-27: Paul and the Philosophic Critique of Eros," supports Martin in arguing that Paul's language follows that of Stoic and other moral philosophers of his time who distinguished between types of sexual desire, from ordinary or natural desire (where sexual activity is likened to the satisfaction of hunger through eating) to an inordinate desire, where sexual passion leads to all kinds of excessive, indiscriminate expression. The Romans passage can clearly be understood within this framework rather than the heterosexual/homosexual framework we bring to it. Fredrickson concludes that "Rom. 1:24-27 highlights the problem of passion and its consequences rather than the violation of a divinely instituted norm of male and female intercourse" (12).

13. Robin Scroggs, *The New Testament and Homosexuality* (Philadelphia: Fortress Press, 1983), 127.

14. Cardinal Joseph Ratzinger, "Letter to the Bishops of the Catholic Church on the Pastoral Care of Homosexual Persons (1986)," in Siker, *Homosexuality in the Church*, 42.

15. Lisa Sowle Cahill, "Homosexuality: A Case Study in Moral Argument," in *Homosexuality in the Church*, 72–73. See Cahill's *Sex, Gender, and Christian Ethics* (New York: Cambridge University Press, 1996) and Ted Peters, "Feminist

and Catholic: The Family Ethics of Lisa Sowle Cahill," in *Dialog*, vol. 35, no. 4 (Fall 1996), 269–77.

16. I am reminded of a conversation I had with a recent graduate of our seminary who is gay. He had "come out" and had professed his intent to his synodical committee to remain celibate, which satisfied the regulations of his church. His concern was that the church seemed incapable of recognizing the human need of companionship and personal support that is met by living in partnership with another person. The church's policy of enforced celibacy for its gay pastors is far more than a denial of genital activity; it is a denial of a basic human need for personal companionship that imposes a tremendous burden on any person who does not bring the charism of celibacy to his ministry. The excessively erotic atmosphere today in our understanding of sexuality also has an impact on this matter, encouraging an obsession with genital activity in defining sexual relationships. In other historical periods—notably the nineteenth century—people have been more inclined to assess same-sex relations under the category of friendship rather than emphasizing genital activity, allowing for a more relaxed and balanced attitude on the part of both society and church.

17. Wolfhart Pannenberg, "You Shall Not Lie with a Male: Standards for Churchly Decision-Making on Homosexuality," *Lutheran Forum*, vol. 30, no. 1 (February 1996), 29.

18. This perspective that imposes the norm of heterosexuality on all persons has been characterized as "heterosexism" and challenged as the basic problem in society's refusal to recognize a genuine, multiform expression of sexuality in the human family. See Patricia Beattie Jung and Ralph F. Smith, *Heterosexism: An Ethical Challenge* (Albany: State University of New York Press, 1993).

19. This point also relates to the prospect of same-sex unions. Theologian Max Stackhouse argues that "a sound theological ethic will not advocate the equality of same-sex unions and heterosexual marriages." This way of stating the matter actually blurs the primary ethical issue at stake. That issue is not "equality" but the integrity of the gay community, which requires stability in its sexual practice and common life as much as does the straight community. See his article "Theo-cons and Neo-cons on Theology and Law," *The Christian Century* (August 27–September 3, 1997), 758–61.

20. The term *Gnosticism* has been used to describe the arguments of those who today are challenging the church's tradition concerning homosexuality, but it is not clear to me how it would apply to my argument. Ancient Gnosticism rejected matter and regarded sex of any kind as the worst example of indulgence in the material world, a view that has little to do with the point I am making. It may be that any argument that justifies a responsible homosexual existence is seen as an attempt to spiritualize it, ignoring or denying the physical realities of the homosexual lifestyle and focusing attention on "rights" and a transcendent notion of justice. My argument, on the contrary, takes the physical and psychological realities of gay existence seriously by acknowledging their importance to a responsible moral judgment. It recognizes both the need for and the possibility of gay and lesbian persons living out their sexuality in a morally responsible manner and as an expression of their Christian vocation. I suspect that the charge of Gnosticism is used as a convenient though inappropriate way of discrediting any argument that does not absolutize the norms and structures of heterosexuality.

Notes

21. Some would argue that as soon as one departs from the heterosexual, universal norm, one invites every form of sexual aberration. This does not follow, however, from making one's sexual orientation determinative of appropriate sexual relations when we recognize the goal of personal mutuality and human flourishing that applies to both homosexual and heterosexual relationships. Sexual activity such as incest or pedophilia, for example, substitute the erotic gratification of the adult at the expense of the child for the ideal of two adults whose sexual relationship reflects both loving commitment and responsible activity according to established structures of society. The homosexual community demonstrates an appropriate sense of responsibility when it seeks social structures that would provide legal status and stability for their partnerships.

22. On this subject, see Joseph Monti, *Arguing about Sex: The Rhetoric of Christian Sexual Morality* (Albany: State University of New York Press, 1995), 248–55, and Jung and Smith, 181–86.

23. *Sex, Gender*, 94–95. The reference is to Ball, et. al. *Homosexualities*, 132, 219–20.

24. Richard B. Hays, *The Moral Vision of the New Testament* (San Francisco: HarperCollins, 1996), 399.

25. The social commentator Richard Rodriguez quotes a woman in San Francisco as saying to him, "The only happily married people I know are gay couples," to which he responds, "Maybe that's part of the irony of our time, that people who didn't have that intimacy have been spending more time on it." (From an interview with Virginia I. Postrel and Nick Gillespie in *Reason Magazine*, August/September 1994, 35–41.) Rodriguez, who is himself gay, notes the quest for stability reflected in the movement of gay couples into Victorian homes, "symbols of nineteenth century domestic stability."

26. This is not to deny the overwhelming pervasiveness of eroticism in our society and the need to challenge its corrosive impact on our understanding of human sexuality. The trivializing and banalizing of sex has become a national burden for which we pay in countless ways. My point, however, is that our problems are caused by the mixing of sexuality with consumerism, not by efforts to establish justice and understanding on the part of the majority population toward homosexual persons.

27. Stephen L. Carter, *The Culture of Disbelief* (New York: Basic Books, 1993), 93.

28. Douglas John Hall reflects on the new freedom that mainline churches are assuming in light of their growing "disestablishment" in American society. This freedom is expressed in their willingness to allow society's marginalized people to take their place in the church's community. See his article "A Theological Proposal for the Church's Response to Its Context," *Currents in Theology and Mission* (December 1995), 422.

29. This viewpoint is found, for example, in Robert Benne, *Ordinary Saints* (Minneapolis: Fortress Press, 1988), 151–52. Benne advocates abstinence in the homosexual community but at the same time recognizes that partnerships marked by permanency and commitment are preferable to promiscuity. As a result, the church should "discreetly support" homosexual unions at the same time that it publicly continues to press for abstinence among gay persons.

30. Luke T. Johnson, *Scripture and Discernment: Decision Making in the Church* (Nashville: Abingdon Press, 1996), 51

8. GENETICS AND THE FUTURE OF HUMANITY

1. Quoted in Arthur J. Dyck, "Eugenics in Historical and Ethical Perspective," in John F. Kilner, Rebecca D. Pentz, and Frank E. Young, eds., *Genetic Ethics: Do the Ends Justify the Genes?* (Grand Rapids: Eerdmans, 1997), 25.

2. Unfortunately, even in the United States the history of eugenics reveals a depressing tendency toward the racist and classicist thinking that felt justified in controlling the reproductive capacities of "undesirable" people. During the early decades of the twentieth century, over half of the states established sterilization laws that resulted in some 30,000 people being sterilized by 1939, most of them in prisons and homes for the mentally ill and for many of them against their will. In Germany between 1934 and 1937, an estimated 400,000 sterilizations took place. See ibid., 27.

3. Charles Darwin, *The Descent of Man and Selection in Relation to Sex* (Princeton, N.J.: Princeton University Press, 1981), 501–2. Quoted in Marc Lappé, "Moral Obligations and the Fallacies of 'Genetic Control,'" in Thomas A. Shannon, ed., *Bioethics*, rev. ed. (New York: Paulist Press, 1981), 420–21.

4. Hermann J. Muller, "Genetic Progress by Voluntarily Conducted Germinal Choice," in Paul T. Jersild and Dale A. Johnson, eds., *Moral Issues and Christian Response*, first ed. (New York: Holt, Rinehart and Winston, 1971), 426.

5. Ibid., 427.

6. Ibid., 431.

7. Theodosius Dobzhansky, "Man and Natural Selection," in *American Scientist,* vol. 49 (1961), 285–99. Quoted in "Moral Obligations," in Shannon, *Bioethics,* 421.

8. Quoted in "Moral Obligations," in *Bioethics*, 422.

9. Ibid., 426–27.

10. Elizabeth Thomson, "Genetic Counseling," in Kilner, et. al. *Genetic Ethics,* 147–48.

11. LeRoy Walters, "Reproductive Technologies and Genetics," in Robert M. Veatch, ed., *Medical Ethics*, 2d ed. (Boston: Jones and Bartlett, 1997), 224. My discussion of each of these issues draws largely on material from Walters.

12. It is particularly appropriate for Christians to recommend adoption as a splendid alternative in cases where a couple decides not to have their own children. Opening one's heart and home to a child in need of a family is one of the more powerful witnesses of the capacity of love to reach out and embrace the stranger. One of society's most crying needs is legislation on the part of states that would encourage and facilitate adoption on the part of qualified couples.

13. Ted Peters, *Playing God? Genetic Determinism and Human Freedom* (New York: Routledge, 1997), 3. For an engaging account of the historical background and development of the Human Genome Project, see Tom Wilkie, *Perilous Knowledge: The Human Genome Project and Its Implications* (London and Boston: Faber and Faber, 1993), chap 5.

14. Francis S. Collins, "The Human Genome Project," in Kilner, *Genetic Ethics,* 95.

15. Philip Kitcher, "Who's Afraid of the Human Genome Project?" in *Philosophy of Science Association Journal,* vol. 2 (1994), 318.

16. Ibid., 320.

17. Liz Hepburn, "Genetic Counseling: Parental Autonomy or Acceptance of

Limits?" in Maureen Junker-Kenny and Lisa Sowle Cahill, eds., *The Ethics of Genetic Engineering*, Concilium, 1998/2 (London: SCM Press, and Maryknoll, N.Y.: Orbis Books, 1998), 37–38. Eberhard Schockenhoff makes a similar observation: "The routine use of general screening procedures can lead to a change in the assessment of handicap and illness in the consciousness of the population and a tendency to regard any deviation from 'normality' as an intolerable limitation." See his "First Sheep, Then Human Beings? Theological and Ethical Reflections on the Use of Gene Technology," in Junker-Kenny and Cahill, *Ethics of Genetic Engineering*, 88.

18. Scott B. Rae, "Prenatal Genetic Testing, Abortion, and Beyond," in Kilner, Pentz, and Young, *Genetic Ethics*, 140.

19. See J. Robert Nelson, *On the New Frontiers of Genetics and Religion* (Grand Rapids: Eerdmans, 1994), 38–41.

20. John C. Fletcher, *Coping with Genetic Diseases* (San Francisco: Harper and Row, 1982), 131. Quoted in Nelson, *On the New Frontiers*, 41.

21. Recognizing the importance of the many ethical issues that would be raised by the project, funding was included to establish the Ethical, Legal, and Social Implications (ELSI) program. Approximately 5 percent of the HGP budget is to be spent on ELSI projects.

22. Walter Gilbert, the Nobel laureate in genetics, has predicted that eventually it will be possible to micro-record on a compact disc all the information necessary to a complete and comprehensive description of a human being. "A person will hold up a CD and say, 'This is me.'" Nelson, *On the New Frontiers*, 89. Ted Peters calls this perspective the "gene myth," or a cultural thought form that says, "It's all in the genes!" Its consequence is genetic determinism. See Peters, *Playing God?* xiii and *passim*.

23. Arthur L. Caplan, *If I Were a Rich Man Could I Buy a Pancreas?* (Bloomington: Indiana University Press, 1992), 125.

24. See Michael S. Beates, "God's Sovereignty and Genetic Anomalies," in Kilner, Pentz, and Young, *Genetic Ethics*, 49–59.

25. While I use the term *co-creator* as a shorthand way of describing the vocation of human beings as creative co-workers with God in fashioning a more humane world, the term *created co-creator* has been systematically and influentially developed by theologian Philip Hefner as the core concept of an anthropology that would speak to the worlds of both science and religion. See his *The Human Factor: Evolution, Culture, and Religion* (Minneapolis: Fortress Press, 1993).

26. Paul Ramsey, *Fabricated Man* (New Haven: Yale University Press, 1970), 124. In a 1989 unpublished document, the World Council of Churches strengthened an earlier, negative position taken in 1982 by recommending a "ban" on germline engineering, at least "at the present time." WCC, "Biotechnology: Its Challenges to the Churches and to the World" (Geneva: World Council of Churches, 1989), 2.

27. Peters, *Playing God?* 144. In view of the historic natural-law teaching in the Roman Catholic moral tradition, which has discouraged any kind of "tampering" with human structures, it is remarkable that the Catholic Health Association sees germline intervention as a desirable goal "toward which biomedicine could reasonably devote its efforts." Quoted in Peters, *Playing God?* 146–47.

28. See LeRoy Walters and Julie Gage Palmer, "Enhancement of Genetic Engineering," *The Ethics of Human Gene Therapy* (New York: Oxford University Press, 1997).

29. Eric Juengst, "Gene Therapy for Cancer Prevention," public lecture at the symposium, "Ethical Boundaries in Cancer and Genetics" (St. Jude Children's Research Hospital), Memphis, Tennessee, May 28, 1999.

30. Ronald Cole-Turner, *The New Genesis: Theology and the Genetic Revolution* (Louisville: Westminster/John Knox, 1993), 106. Cole-Turner maintains that the doctrine of creation is inadequate in providing direction for the new technology and, therefore, the language of redemption is required. This ignores the healing resources inherent to created life, as well as the image of wholeness it projects. The greater danger, I believe, is the hubris that lies close to every effort to transform or redeem humanity and create a new order or life. No technology is going to usher in the kingdom.

31. Paul D. Simmons, *Birth and Death: Bioethical Decision-making* (Philadelphia: Westminster, 1983), 240–45. The observation of Hans Jonas concerning the utopian impetus created by technological achievements certainly applies to Christian as well as secular thinkers: "By the kind and size of its snowballing effects, technological power propels us into goals of a type that was formerly the preserve of Utopians. To pit it differently, technological power has turned what used and ought to be tentative, perhaps enlightening plays of speculative reason into competing blueprints for projects, and in choosing between them, we have to choose between extremes of remote effects. . . ." Hans Jonas, *The Imperative of Responsibility: In Search of an Ethics for the Technological Age* (Chicago: University of Chicago Press, 1984), 21.

32. See Peters, *Playing God?* chap. 5.

INDEX OF BIBLICAL PASSAGES

INDEX OF
SUBJECTS AND NAMES

Jesus Christ
  and authority of Scripture, 78
  as "concrete universal," 20–21
  eschatological teaching of, 68–69,
    185 n.11
  and moral responsibility, 20–22
  and spirit ethics, 4, 85–86
Jodock, Darrell, 54–55
Johnson, Luke T., 76–78, 80–81, 148
Jonas, Hans, 197 n.31
Juengst, Eric, 169
Jung, Patricia Beattie, 193 n.18
Justification/Sanctification, 187 n.6

Kelsey, David, 183 n.19, 186 n.27
Kevorkian, Jack, 110
Kierkegaard, Søren, 32–33, 50
Kingdom of God, 69, 73, 90,
  101–04, 172, 189 n.21
Kinsey, Alfred, 191 n.1
Kitcher, Philip, 161
Küng, Hans, 123

Lappé, Marc, 153–54
Law, 17, 65–67, 94
Lessing, Gotthold, 13
Liberation theology, 3
Lindbeck, George, 29–30
Locke, John, 86
Løgstrup, Knud, 178 n.9
Long, Thomas G., 186 n.25
Longenecker, Richard N., 104
Love. *See* agapeic love
Luthardt, Christian, 188 n.14
Luther, Martin, 89, 98–99, 187 n.6,
  189 n.16
Lynn, Steven, 84 n.9
Lyotard, Jean–Francois, 39, 177 n.1

MacIntyre, Alasdair, 24, 179 n.16
McCabe, Herbert, 32
McDonald, J.I.H., 134
McKenny, Gerald P., 190–91 n.12
McKnight, Edgar, 52
Markham, Ian S., 28
Marsden, George, 182 n.2

Martin, Dale, 192 n.12
Meeks, Wayne, 74–75, 186 n.18
Meilaender, Gilbert, 187–88 n.9
Mendel, Gregor, 155
Modernism, 9–10
Morality
  and a common humanity, 22–25
  and contextuality, 24
Muller, Hermann, J., 152–53
Murphy, Timothy F., 192 n.6

Natural law, 138–41
Newman, John Henry, 23–24
Niebuhr, H. Richard, 25, 41, 56, 179
  n.18, 188 n.11
Niebuhr, Reinhold, 13, 113, 180
  n.11
Noonan, John T., Jr., 23
Nussbaum, Martha, 15–16

Ogletree, Thomas W., 36, 95, 187
  n.8
Outka, Gene, 178 n.7

Pannenberg, Wolfhart, 140
Patte, Daniel, 49
Paul
  and death, 111–12
  ethics of, 69, 82
  and homosexuality, 184–5
  and the Spirit, 86–89, 187 n.3
Percy, Walker, 110
Peters, Ted, 159, 168
Pluralism, 27–34
  and the Bible, 29–34
  and the church, 30–34, 41–42
  and relativism, 27–28
Postmodernism, 9–14, 24–25,
  39–42
  and the Bible, 1–3
  Christian appraisals of, 177 n.1
  and feminism, 11–12
  hermeneutics of, 50–55, 183 n.9
  and narrative, 16
Price, Reynolds, 116
Protestantism, 23, 183 n.20